Security, Political Autonomy and Development of Andaman and Nicobar Islands

About the Editors

Dr. Swapan Kumar Biswas did his P.G. & Ph.D. from Calcutta. Presently, he is teaching in P.G. Department of Political Science, Jawaharlal Nehru Rajkeeya Mahavidyalaya, Port Blair in the capacity of Associate Professor. He has published two books on tribal and non-tribal of Andaman. He has attended International Conferences in Ludwig-Maxillion University in Germany & Utara Malaysia University in Malaysia. He has organized a number of seminars sponsored by UGC, ICSSR, ICHR, NIAS in JNRM and presently doing project under UGC on Voting Behaviour of Indian Voters. He has to his credit many articles published in various reputed national & International journals.

Dr. Manis Kumar Raha: An eminent Anthropologist, retired as Joint Director, Anthropological Survey of India. Now, serving as expert in different projects and also attached to different Universities and research Institutions. He has published a large number of books, articles and book review and has a dept contribution to the tribal society of India and Andaman & Nicobar Islands. He was examiners of Ph.D. thesis of different universities and was President, Anthropological & Archaeology section, Indian Science Congress, 1996.

Dr. Palash Chandra Coomar: He has retired as Joint Director of Census Operation, Government of India. Earlier he was in Anthropological Survey of India. He undertook research work among different tribal and non-tribal communities in Bay Islands and different other parts of India. He has published a number of books, articles and presented paper in Ludwig-Maxillion University in Germany. He is also a Ph.D. examiner and examiner of M.A. & M.Sc. Examinations.

Security, Political Autonomy and Development of Andaman and Nicobar Islands

Edited by
Swapan Kumar Biswas
Manis Kumar Raha
Palash Chandra Coomar

CONCEPT PUBLISHING COMPANY PVT. LTD.
NEW DELHI-110059

ISBN-13: 978-93-86682-30-7

First Published 2018

Published and Printed by

Since 1974

Concept Publishing Company Pvt. Ltd.
A/15-16, Commercial Block, Mohan Garden,
New Delhi-110059 (INDIA)
T : 25351460, 25351794, *F* : 091-11-25357109
E : publishing@conceptpub.com *W* : www.conceptpub.com

Cataloging in Publication Data--Courtesy: D.K. Agencies (P) Ltd. <docinfo@dkagencies.com>

National Conference on "Strategic Importance, Political Autonomy and Sustainable Development of A & N Islands" (2011 : New Delhi, India)

Security, political autonomy and development of Andaman and Nicobar Islands / edited by Swapan Kumar Biswas, Manis Kumar Raha, Palash Chandra Coomar.

pages cm

Running title: Security, political autonomy and development of A & N Islands.

Papers presented at a UGC sponsored National Conference on "Strategic Importance, Political Autonomy and Sustainable Development of A & N Islands, held in New Delhi in 2011.

ISBN 9789386682307

1. Sustainable development—India—Andaman and Nicobar Islands—Congresses. 2. National security—India—Andaman and Nicobar Islands—Congresses. 3. Andaman and Nicobar Islands (India)—Politics and government—Congresses. I. Biswas, Swapan Kumar, editor. II. Raha, Manis Kumar, editor. III. Coomar, Palash Chandra, 1956- editor. IV. India. University Grants Commission, sponsoring body. V. Title. VI. Title: Security, political autonomy and development of A & N Islands.

LCC HC437.A77S43 2011 DDC 338.95488 23

DEDICATED

To
All those Freedom Fighters who received inhuman treatment and torture in the hand of colonial rulers in Cellular Jail,
and also to
those who have played important roles in the development of the Andaman and Nicobar Islands of the present day.

Foreword

Mumbai 2008 woke up India to the fact that threats to national security need not be necessarily be land-based. For years, we have to busy fortifying our borders, putting up barbed wires along the international borders with Pakistan and Bangladesh. While this initiative is not trivial or irrelevant, it highlights an important dilemma in security preparedness, which is that often we land up fighting yesterday's battles.

The ability of Pakistan-based militants and terrorists to enter India, specifically Punjab and later Jammu & Kashmir alerted us to the dangers of leaving our land borders unguarded. In the aftermath of Mumbai, the Government of India has focused on upgrading coastal security, primarily by assisting State Governments to strengthen marine police infrastructure, to purchase high-speed boats etc. The navy has gone in for a very comprehensive tracking and monitoring in real-time of all maritime movements as part of maritime domain awareness (MDA).

In fact, this entire beefing of coastal security should have been thought off before. We seemed to forget that our coastline is 7600 km., of which 1900 km. is in the Andaman & Nicobar Islands alone, an attitude that is happily changing. The islands represent a security challenge as well strategic advantages to India, but historically both have not been appreciated in Delhi, a state of affairs that must change. Fortunately, our old mindset that saw development as opposed to security needs is giving way to seeing them as complimentary. And that is the way forward. That is why I am particularly happy that a comprehensive, '*Security, Political Autonomy and Development of Andaman & Nicobar Islands*', edited by Swapan Kumar Biswas,

Manis Kumar Raha and Palash Chandra Coomar is coming out. This is an extremely comprehensive volume bringing together strategic thinkers, historians, political scientists, administrators, development professionals, geographers, demographers and economists on one platform. It is only when the practioners and the thinkers come together that human societies advance. An administrator without a sound grasp of theory is inherently limited in her/his effectiveness, and a theorist without a solid empirical grounding is just a day-dreamer.

It is not often remembered that India's eastern coastline does not run from Sunderbans to Kanya Kumari, but is actually a thousand kilometre to its east. The Andaman & Nicobar Islands stretch 800 km. from north to south. East Island and Landfall Islands in the north are barely 20 kms. from Myanmar's Coco Islands. The southernmost point of Great Nicobar Island is around 140 km. from Banda Aech in Sumatra (Indonesia), and just 30 km. off the main shipping route leading to the Malacca Straits. Around one-third of global trade, one quarter of global oil flows and over two-thirds of China's oil imports passes through these Straits.

There are 572 islands, islets and rocks; census lists 36 inhabited islands but around half of such inhabited islands, there is only a police or forest post. During wind and sea conditions, most of the habitations are on the eastern sides of the islands and large section of North, Middle, South and Little Andamans, and Great Nicobar have absolutely no human presence. Nor are these areas easily accessible from the land side.

The population of the islands which was increasing by almost 50 per cent in each decade, seems to have stabilised at around 4 lakh. The epicentre of the 2004 Tsunami was quite close to Great Nicobar, and the islands particularly the tribal dominated Nicobars suffered excessive losses of lives. Islands like Katchal are almost a third smaller, with large scale subsidence as a result of tectonic shifts. The physical and psychological effect of the tsunami has been devastating for the Nicobarese who have withdrawn from sea faring quite dramatically. In hindsight, the government decision to carry out all the reconstruction, which has led to a quantum jump in the availability of infrastructure, has deprived of the Nicobarese of the opportunity to rebuild their lives and their social capital. The Nicobarese had, in the aftermath of the tsunami, asked for assistance like supply of tools etc. so that they could rebuild their houses, their villages and their common facilities. But the government housed them in temporary accommodation and gave them generous allowances, and carried out the reconstruction work through contractors and labour brought from the Indian mainland. The end-result is much higher quality housing and social infrastructure but low vitality and high dependence.

The population of the Andamans is highly cosmopolitan, with Bengali, Tamil, Telugu and Malayalam spoken widely with Hindi as the *lingua franca*. Health and education indicators are far above the national average. Though there are three general colleges and an engineering college, tens of thousands of school graduates go to mainland India for higher studies. In the absence of employment opportunities, most especially those with professional qualifications do not come back. Instead, there is a flow of manual labourers into the islands since the high per capita income means a shortage of labour.

The islands are home to India's only unified joint services command, with the three services holding the post of Commander-in-Chief by rotation. Port Blair has a relative concentration of defence assets. There is an Air Force Station at Car Nicobar with minimal assets — it had seen huge casualties in the tsunami and is slowly rebuilding its infrastructure. There are air strips at Diglipur (North Andamans) and at Campbell Bay (Great Nicobar Island), which would need upgradation to handle bigger aircrafts. The Navy has declared the latter as a naval air station but that is basically aspirational at present. There is the presence of an army establishment just outside Port Blair.

The biggest challenge facing the Andaman Nicobar Command (ANC) is that being a joint command, it is nobody's responsibility. Leaving the Coast Guard asides for a moment, none of three services see it as integral to their planning. Hence, there is reluctance to transfer assets — ships, aircrafts, battalions, artillery — to the ANC. The ANC is the responsibility of the Integrated Headquarters, but which is still in an incipient stage. The net result is that though the ANC prepared acquisition plan has been approved by the government, the actual flow of assets is at an early stage and it will be almost a decade when the Command would be properly equipped. The fact that the Malaysian airlines MH 370 flew over the airspace of the islands, coming quite close to the main islands, but was not detected since the main tracking stations are shut down at night reflects the state of defence preparedness.

This point should be appreciated in the light of the fact that the exclusive economic zone (EEZ) of the islands is 1,80,000 sq. km., almost one-third of India's 6,00,000 sq. km. EEZ. In earlier years, fishing trawlers from Thailand and even distant Taiwan used to regularly poach in these waters. In recent years, Myanmarese fishers harvest sea cucumbers, which serves the lucrative Chinese market. At certain times, there are over 1000 Myanmarese fishers in custody awaiting/undergoing trial, including many repeat offenders. Ever so often, desperate Rohingyas trying to reach Malaysia, Australia and other countries was upon the Andaman shores. Till now none of these have posed a threat to national interests or security. But we should not wait for an incident to the focus on the security and development challenges of the islands. The Defence Ministry should prioritise the acquisition, and transfer of assets to make the command minimally functional.

Lack of connectivity, physical and virtual, is the primary development challenge that must be sorted out. Port Blair airport used to shut down by 12 noon due to lack of ATC staff; the Navy has since added more staff. Due to lack of competition, it is often more expensive to travel to Port Blair from Kolkata and Chennai than it is to go to Thailand and stay there for three days. Most inter-island journey except in the main Andaman group is by ships. There has been inadequate investment as a result often there is crisis due to lack of ship availability. The Andaman Administration runs helicopter services linking different parts of the islands by hiring the services of Pawan Hans. And some areas are covered by an amphibious aircraft. Since there are air strips at different locations, it makes much more sense to run fixed-wing services that carry more passengers, are economic and are safer.

Internet connectivity outside Port Blair are patchy, and practically non-existence in the Nicobars. This is because the islands are on the edge of ISRO satellites' footprints. Having dedicated satellites makes little sense because of the large scale redundancy and paradoxical need for back-up. It makes much more sense to take breach cables from undersea cables running between Chennai and Singapore.

Improved connectivity would not only lead to better quality of life and improved security preparedness but can be used to leverage the growth of tourism. The tourism potential of these islands includes world class beaches, water sports, high-end diving, game fishing and dense equatorial forests. Even the tribals of Nicobar, so far sheltered from the outside world through restrictions on movement, are increasing asking for opening up tourism that would create jobs. Presently blanket one-size fits-all environmental regulations restrict development works over most of the territory, 92 per cent of which are forests. In fact the Environmental Ministry had turned down the defence request for clearance for a radar facility on Narcondum Island; fortunately the change in government had led to the clearance being given. It must be understood that smart regulation could drive growth and sustainability.

The location of the islands so close to the main shipping routes presents another opportunity, that of transhipment facilities and ship repairs at Campbell Bay (Great Nicobar Island). This port could serve ports on the eastern coast of India as well as ports in Bangladesh, Myanmar and western ports of Thailand. Government must pro-actively push economic development in the national interest.

The distorted nature of representative institutions in the islands makes for inadequate economic development. Robust panchayati raj in the Andamans (and Great Nicobar) has meant that rural roads, water supply, health and educational outcomes are far ahead of the national figures. However, lack of it at higher levels of governance, and inadequate evolution in the tribal Nicobari areas has meant that higher order development is stultified. A non-representative administration lacking in real local accountability has inherent limitations. There are tens of countries with land area and/or populations smaller than the islands that are economically self-sufficient and have higher standards of living, while it is only the generous budgetary support from the Government of India that keeps these islands going. Clearly this is an unsatisfactory, and ultimately unsustainable, state of affairs.

The bottom line is that converting the islands into an economic dynamo backed by a strengthened defence establishment would not only be India's robust outer ring, but more importantly enable India to project its power into the broader Info-Pacific space.

Shri Shakti Sinha, IAS (Retd.)
Director, Nehru National Museum and Library, New Delhi

Preface

Andaman and Nicobar Islands, one of the Union Territories of India, are situated in the Bay of Bengal. These islands, though part of India, are over 1000 km. away from the mainland of India but much closer to Myanmar and Sumatra. The International Trade Route passes close to the Nicobar group of Islands. As a result this Union Territory of India has great importance strategically. India has no option but to keep constant surveillance in order to protect her island territory from external aggression and/or encroachment. She needs to control the illegal immigration and trading of illegal goods also.

During British occupation, these islands first saw the sign of development. The establishment of Penal and other settlements during British occupation had also shown the light of development to these islands for the first time. The next phase of development took place during the Japanese occupation for a short period. But the development in the true sense, started after India's own freedom. It was a constant effort on the part of the Government to develop these islands, particularly those which are inhabited by the people. Establishment of new settlements, construction of roads, increase of the transport and communication system, development of small scale industries and power, development of agriculture etc. are definitely proofs for development. The most marked development was the establishment of an administration in true sense, after Independence, which started looking after the needs of the islanders, and accordingly it is putting further efforts for the development of the islands and the islanders.

Along with the development, the National Government also has given stress on the development of the islands' Defence establishment as well as Coast Guards in the islands territory considering their strategic importance. Growing presence of the foreign powers in the Indian Ocean, illegal immigration, illegal fishing in the Indian Sea Water and also for many such reasons, India has to promote and develop all three wings of its Defence (Air Force, Army and Navy) in these Islands.

Another important development that one finds, is the urge for political autonomy. With the spread of education, political activities, modernity etc. people here have become politically conscious. So, some of them appealed for the statehood of these islands territories so that with the establishment of a State Assembly through election, the representatives of the people can form the Government, run the administration and promote further development.

However, through this edited book we have presented before learned readers various such issues so that they can form a good idea about these new dimensions of this Union Territory of ours. The views expressed in the articles are absolutely of the author(s) and not of the editors.

Acknowledgements

This Edited book is the outcome of UGC sponsored National Conference on "Strategic Importance, Political Autonomy and Sustainable Development of A & N Islands" held in 2011. We are indebted to UGC, NABARD and NATMO for their financial support to the said Conference.

We express our sincere thanks and gratitude to the then Lt. Governor, Lt. General (Retd.) Shri Bhupender Singh and also to all other officials and defense personal and civil society, who have given their logistic and moral support for making the Conference a success. We are also thankful to former Principal Dr. Iqbal Ahmad and present Principal Dr. N. Francis Xavier, JNRM for their moral and administrative support in holding the seminar and also preparing this book. Without their help, co-operations, assistance and advice it was impossible for us to hold the seminar and publish this book.

Thanks are also due to all the authors who have contributed their articles to enrich this edited book. We are really grateful to Concept Publishing Company Pvt. Ltd., New Delhi for publishing this book.

Last but not the least, we are thankful to Shri Shakti Sinha, former Chief Secretary, A & N Administration for writing Forward of this book. Presently, he is the Director, Nehru National Museum and Library, New Delhi.

Acknowledgements

Contents

PART-III

Political Autonomy and Development of Andaman and Nicobar Islands

PART-IV

Developmental Process in Andaman and Nicobar Islands

List of Contributors

Dr. Kailash Chandra Joshi, Associate Professor, PG Department of Geography, JNRM, Port Blair, Andaman-744104.

Prof. Gopalji Malviya, (Retd.) Professor and Head, Department of Defence Studies, University of Madras, Chennai.

Dr. Swapan Kumar Biswas, Associate Professor, PG Department of Political Science, JNRM, Port Blair, Andaman-744104.

Dr. N. Francis Xavier, Principal, Jawaharlal Nehru Rajkeeya Mahavidyalaya, Port Blair, Andaman-744104.

Dr. R.V.R. Murthy, Associate Professor and Head, Department of Political Science, MGGC, Mayabunder, Middle and North Andaman-744206.

Col. Promod Sangwa, Andaman and Nicobar Command, Andaman and Nicobar Islands-744102.

Prof. R. Thandavan, Vice-Chancellor, University of Madras, Chennai.

Dr. S.S. Sreekumar, Associate Professor and Head, PG Department of Political Science, JNRM, Port Blair, Andaman-744104.

Dr. Rabindra Nath Rath (Retd.) Principal, Mahatma Gandhi Government College, Mayabunder, Middle and North Andaman-744206.

Basudev Dass, Member, Electricity Consumer Grievances Office, Port Blair, Andaman-744104.

Govind Ram, DANIC, A and N Administration, Port Blair, Andaman-744104.

Dr. Nirupama Rath, Associate Professor, Tagore Government College of Education, Port Blair, Andaman-744101.

Dr. Pearl Devdas, Associate Professor and Head, PG Department of Geography, JNRM, Port Blair, Andaman-744104.

Er. Manohar Singh (Retd.), Superintendent Engineer, Electricity Department, A & N Administration, Port Blair, Andaman-744101.

Dr. Hema Bannerjee, Associate Professor and Head, Department of Economics, JNRM, Port Blair, Andaman-744104.

Dr. Sweta Banerjee, Research Associate, National Thematic Mapping Organization, Salt Lake, Kolkata-700106.

Niranjan Dass, FE-362, Salt Lake, Kolkata-700106.

Ms. Aiman Fatima, Ph.D. Scholar and Guest Faculty, Department of Historical Studies, JNRM. Port Blair, Andamans-744104.

Introduction

India is a big country with distinct ethnic, economic, socio-cultural, political and religious diversities. India does not have one single mass entity but it consists of island territories also in both the Bay of Bengal and the Arabian Sea. Here, both ecological and ethnic variations are also markedly high. Since, time immemorial India "has given shelter to a number of people of different ethnicities, different languages, different cultures, different social organizations, different political ideologies, different religions, different economies and so on" (Coomar, Raha & Bhui, 2009). The people here are either indigenous or immigrants who have come from outside India. They are settled in different ecological zones. The immigrants have come to India as conquerors, invaders, immigrants, traders, religious preachers, missionaries or in search of habitation. Many others arrived here in search of livelihood. While many of immigrants came of their own, many others were brought in this country for some specific purposes. Many of these varieties of people ultimately settled in this great country, and finally, accepted this great country as their own. The ecological, ethnic or cultural diversities did not stand as barriers against their settling down in this country (*ibid.*: 2009).

In this regard Andaman and Nicobar group of Islands is no exception. This Union Territory has also followed the footsteps of Indian mainland. This group of islands has both indigenous as well as immigrant population living close to one another. Here also people from different parts of India and also from some foreign countries came and are still coming for various purposes. Many of these people were also brought to these islands for various reasons. Even today many people still pouring in this island territory for different reasons, have settled there permanently to lead their life in the new environment in this Union Territory.

After the colonial rulers tightened their grip on the mainland of India, they thought of establishing some settlement in Andaman and Nicobar Islands. While considering it they had in their mind the strategic importance of these islands. Lord Cornwallis, the then Governor-General of India, was keenly interested to establish a colony in Andaman Islands. He allotted this arduous task to John Richie and asked them to conduct a survey in these islands in order to examine the feasibility and potentiality of establishing a colony. Lt. Archibald Blair and Lt. Robert Hyde Colebrook also conducted another survey and submitted their reports.

The then Governor-General in Council decided in 1789 to take possession of these islands in order to establish a safe harbour mainly for the British fleet. Thereafter, first settlement was established in October 1789. In this way first ever non-indigenous settlement started functioning in Andamans. Since then till today several non-aboriginal colonies/settlements have been established and several thousand people from outside Andaman and Nicobar Islands started pouring in for permanent or temporary settlement.

Besides settlement of these outsiders in these islands, the British Government during pre-Independence era and Government of India after Independence, had shown keen interest for the development of these islands and also to look after the security and safety of these islands and people living there. After Independence the Union Government has given much importance to both development and security of these islands.

Andaman and Nicobar group of Islands is a Union Territory of India. From Basic Statistics 2011-12 of the Department of Economics and Statistics, Andaman and Nicobar Administration, we come to know that this Union Territory is situated in the Bay of Bengal about 1230 km. from Kolkata, 1400 km. from Chennai and 1278 km. from Visakhapatnam by sea. This group of Islands, which consisted of over 500 big and small islands, is situated 92 to 94 East Longitude and 6 to 14 North Latitude. This group of Islands has a geographical area of 8249.00 sq. km. with 8211 sq. km. rural and 37.92 sq. km. of urban areas. Out of this total geographical area 7170.69 (83.96%) sq. km. are forest areas.

According to 2011 Census the total population of this group of islands is 380581 of which total male population is 202871 (53.31%)

and total female population is 177710 (46.69%). Again out of the total population of Andaman and Nicobar Islands, 237093 (62.30%) live in rural areas and 143488 (37.70%) in urban centres. Out of this population of 343739 (90.32%) live in Andaman group of Islands and remaining 36842 (9.68%) live in Nicobar group of Islands. Out of this population in Andamans 182144 (52.99%) are males and 161595 (49.01%) females. In Nicobar Islands, the total population is constituted of 20727 (56.26%) males and 16115 (43.74%) females. As Nicobar do not have any urban centres, so all urban people of Andaman and Nicobar Islands live in Andaman Islands. Again, out of total population of Andaman 105593 (30.72%) live in North and Middle Andaman District. In South Andaman 238142 (69.28%) inhabitants are found to inhabit. The sex ratio is 876 females per 1000 males in Andaman and Nicobar Islands, 925 in North and Middle Andamans, 871 in South Andaman and 777 in Nicobars. The density of population is 46 in Andaman and Nicobar Islands, 28 in North and Middle Andamans, 89 in South Andaman and 20 in Nicobars, according to 2011 Census.

If we look at the growth of population in Andaman and Nicobar Islands, we see that from the population of 24649 in 1901 the same has become 380581 in 2011. Similarly, with a density of population of 3 in 1901, it has come up 46 in 2011. The literacy rate among the people of Andaman and Nicobar Islands is quite spectacular. 86.63 per cent people in these islands are literate. Among the male population while 90.27 per cent and among the females 82.43 per cent are literates according to 2011 Census. In 1971 the same rate was 51.15 per cent for population (excluding 0-4 age group), 58.82 per cent for the males and 38.29 per cent for the females.

The development and security are two essential parts of human life. The development is directly related to the achievement of poverty reduction. Development encompasses 'change' in a variety of aspects of the human condition. The simplest definition of 'development' is probably, according to the Chambers' Dictionary (2004: iii, 2-3) notion of 'good change'. The dimensions of development are extremely diverse, including economic, social, political, legal and institutional structures, technology in various forms (including the physical or natural sciences, engineering and communications), the environment, religion, arts and culture. Further, development is 'a process of historical change' in view, of 'structural transformation' and 'long-term transformations of economics and societies'. This implies a major societal shift in one dimension, for example from a rural or agriculture-based society to an urban or industrial-based society (what is sometimes called the shift from 'traditional' to 'modern' characteristics). Development has been differently defined as, progress, positive change in the economic position of the people, a community or a nation (IGNOU, 2004). Development involves changes to socio-economic structure — including ownership, the organization of production, technology, the institutional structure and laws. Development has been defined as synonymous with 'modernity' which is presented in the discourse as a superior condition.

"Development is not merely the enhancement of inanimate objects of convenience, such as a rise in the GDP; nor is it some general transformation of the world around us, such as industrialization or technological advance, or social modernization. Development is ultimately, the progress of human freedom and capacity to lead the kind of lives that people have reason to value" (Sen, 2000.). Economist Amartya Sen has further defined development as freedom where development is the way to provide capacities to people to bring out their fullest self (IGNOU, 2004). The term 'Development' refers to economic, social, political and cultural processes of change in human societies. However, it is true that the development theories based on the Western models of economic growth were intensely inadequate in Indian context. The concept of inclusive growth and development has given a new meaning to the people of the Third World. Now, the focus has been shifted in favour of well meaning individuals and communities relationships, helping them to live in harmony with nature and to live without impoverishing or endangering future generation, leading to what has come to be known as "sustainable development" (Sahoo, 2012).

Security and development are two essential and important aspects for every citizen of a country. Security refers to both internal and external. Both these are parameters of the very existence of a sovereign nation. Security provides the Government to ensure peaceful lives for its citizens. The geography of a country defines the nature of security arrangement which is required for the safety of the people. India is the gateway of Asia since time immemorial. It has 3500 km long coastal line which has been the main security challenge for the government. In addition, the Andaman archipelago in the Bay of Bengal with more than 500 islets is virtually a big challenge for our defence.

The strategic location of the Andaman and Nicobar Islands has to do with more than just sovereignty. The surveillance of Indian Navy is not restricted to just protecting territories. Close to Andaman and Nicobar Islands passes one of the busiest trade routes in the world and the responsibility of keeping them safe and sanitized is one of the chief responsibilities of the Indian Defence. But the irony of the situation is that international water surrounding these territories has to be kept safe in coordination with navies of other nations, including China. It is an undoubtedly maritime adversary. A variety of factors are proving to be challenges in the way of providing security to these islands, the main being difficult topography, inadequate infrastructure and manpower, lack of coordination, inefficient intelligence and pervasive under-development (Das, 2010). Andaman and Nicobar Islands face greater challenges to their internal security through non-conventional threats such as illegal migration from littoral States of the Bay of Bengal, poaching of marine and forest resources, arms and narcotics smuggling through uninhabited islands and natural disasters. In recent years, several such attempts and instances have created a sense of insecurity in the area. These externally sponsored security threats have now for long raised serious issues both in terms of determinable losses to life and property and non-quantifiable losses to national will and drain on scarce economic resources (Kukreja 2013).

The isolation and remoteness of these Islands from mainland India contribute to their defence lessness to both conventional and non-conventional threats. Virtually, a military threat to these islands can be possible in the form of intervention in the Bay of Bengal by some foreign countries as the Indian Ocean is the main oil import sea passage to some countries. To ensure the supply of oil such countries have developed cordial relations with Myanmar, Bangladesh, Sri Lanka by developing ports and other infrastructural facilities in the Indian Ocean nations. "It is a known fact that the Chinese have built Signal Intercepting and Intelligence stations in Andaman sea ... besides the Coco Islands in Myanmar ... The Indian Coast Guard has intercepted fishing trawlers flying Myanmar flags off the Andaman Islands and found them manned by Chinese carrying radio and depth sounding equipment for submarine usage" (Dar, 2015).

The Islands also face non-conventional threats like poaching, illegal settlements, gunrunning and use of uninhabited islands as hideaways by terrorist groups and smugglers. These islands also face natural disasters. Poaching has emerged as the biggest problem for these Islands. Several factors have contributed to the emergence of these islands as a magnet for poachers. Another serious security concern for these Islands is the issue of illegal migrants who later on got settled. The illegal Bangladeshi settlers have increased in recent years especially in the aftermath of the Tsunami Rehabilitation work. (Kukreja, 2013). Scarcity of labourers has forced the local administration to allow migrant labours for reconstruction of buildings, and other developmental activities, but they continue to reside in the Islands group permanently. Dozens of uninhabited islands of the archipelago provide safe passage for drug trafficking and gunrunning, and these remain an issue of grave concern. During surveillance under anti-smuggling operations, it is revealed that many islands of the archipelago are used as sanctuaries for gunrunners, terrorists and insurgents. Very recently, the United Nations Human Rights Commission (UNHRC) has disclosed a serious incident of crime in South East Asian region. For decades people such as traffickers have carried out profitable trade by trading Muslim minority, the Rohingyas of Myanmar and Bangladeshi in Malaysia, Thailand etc. Recently, it has surfaced that some 7000 migrants are still trapped on vessels in the Bay of Bengal and Andaman sea (*The Indian Express*, May 2015). Hence, it is a serious security challenge for our defence to apprehend this human trade in sea routes.

The islands' economy is fairly dependent on imports of various articles and household goods from mainland India through sea routes. The main economy of these islands is agriculture. Besides, local vegetables and other items are insufficiently grown. There are no big industries except limited tourism. The natural resources and vegetation including forests and sea have limited possibility of exploitation due to environmental protection rules and laws. More than 90 per cent forests are notified as reserve forests including the Tribal territory. Only about 6 per cent of land is available for development. The use of lands for agriculture and other allied activities is inadequate as per the growing demands of the population both floating and permanent. All sets of development activities are going on with due permission from Defence Department. From security point of view, the water territory of the Bay of Bengal is the main security area for the Central Government. According to Mr. Vivek Rae, Former Chief Secretary, Andaman and Nicobar Administration, the Andaman and Nicobar Islands have considerable economic potential, due to benign neglect, misplaced priorities and absence of long-term strategy for sustainable development, the islands' economy is not accelerating as expected. To ensure future development, he has suggested islands like Great Nicobar and Little Andaman should be opened up for comprehensive development efforts, including deployment of strategic assets. Both these big islands could generate a million jobs over the next two decades by harnessing the development impulses which Singapore and other Southeast Asian countries have both harnessed and generated (Rae, 2015).

Conceptually, tourism is the main sector for the future of Islands. Tourism potentiality is good and bright for the islanders. But future draft plans on that issue has to be linked with security of these islands and India at a large. Hence, the development of free ports, connectivity of Port Blair Air Port with international tourist destinations is not getting green signal from Central Government after knowing the fact that for boosting up the island's economy, the route of tourist destination nations need to be opened up. Every project relating to Islands' development and future is dependent on Islands security and security of nation. Very recently, the Lt. Governor, Lt. General (Retd.) Shri A. K. Singh has recalled the importance of the security of this zone, when he spoke in an National Seminar at Port Blair on the Tribal people of these Islands, and their future. He asked the scholars to look into the matters before drawing conclusion on the subject of tribal development issue. The points are fragile ecology surrounding the tribal territory and the whole islands should be preserved along with their welfare projects. Security of nation from defence angle should not be ignored at any level (National Seminar, ANTRI, 2014).

Development means to provide quality of life to all the inhabitants of an area where development is taking place. Development means to provide food, shelter, good health, potable water and other essential services. Development means improvement of human existence and healthy survival of all humanity. It means to provide quality of life to thc people. From Amartya Sen's Development *versus* Freedom (2000) we get how society provides each member of a society the capacity for creating his own livelihood, controlling their own affairs.

Development of a country can be ascertained from the Development of certain parameters like the industry, employment, medical and public health, transport, shipping, air service, banking etc. From the basic Statistics of 2011-12 of the Directorate of

Economics and Statistics of Andaman and Nicobar Administration, we like to cite the status of all the above during 2011-12 in order to help our learned readers to form some ideas about the development of this Island Territory.

Andaman and Nicobar Islands do not have any large scale industries. But there are a number of small scale industries. With registration of 82 micro and small scale industries in 2011-12, the total number of such industries have increased to 2121. All these industries generated 10029 employments. There are 2735 commercial establishments in Andaman and Nicobar which have given employment to 4200 persons.

But when we see the picture of industries in March 2006 we see that industries have not much on the increase. During March 2006 there were five large/medium scale industries, 1914 small scale industries, 15 industrial centres and 8 industrial estates. That means only small scale industries have increased and the industries estates by one. But at the same time, all large/medium scale industries and 9 industrial centres have possibly been closed down as no mention has been made about these in 2011-2012.

As already said the health and medical facilities are important indicators for the development as development means to provide better health services to the citizen. In 2011-12 Andaman and Nicobar Islands had 4 hospitals, 4 Community Health Centres, 22 Primary Health Centres, 5 Urban Health Centres, 114 Sub-Centres, 8 Homeopathic, Dispensary and 1 Aurvedic Dispensary. All these health units had a total number of 1065 beds. It is further see that not much of the health facility has been increased since 2009-10. Only three Primary Health Centres and 20 beds have been added during 2011-12 from 2009-10. Even such facilities have not been much increased since 2006-07. The number of Hospitals was also 4 at that time, Community Health Centres were also 4, Primary Health Centres were 20, Urban Health Centres 5, Sub-Centres 111, Dispensaries 8, Aurvedic Dispensaries 1. Total number of beds was 1045. That means from 2006-07 only 2 Primary Health Centres, 3 Sub-Centres and 20 beds have been increased in 5 years.

During 2009-10, there were 124 doctors, 50 specialists and 362 nurses serving in different health units, which include hospitals, Primary Health Centres etc. for treating the people there. But in 2000-01 there were 127 doctors and 312 nurses. That means after about 10 years the number of doctors has slightly reduced though by 2001-02 there were 137 doctors and 349 nurses. No doubt during 2001-02, we find that the people there are getting the services of 50 specialists. But during 2009-10 the presence of such specialists have not been mentioned.

In Andaman and Nicobar Islands, there were 294281 literates of which 164377 (55.86%) are males and 129904 (44.14%) females according to 2011 Census. During 2011-12 these islands had 438 educational institutions which consisted of 91051 students. They were taught by 5669 teachers. There were 428 primary and secondary schools and 10 higher and technical institutions out of these 438 educational institutions. During 2011-12 there were 86081 students enrolled in different types of schools from pre-primary to senior secondary and 4970 in higher and technical institutions. Again out of 5669 teachers there were 5373 teachers taught at different types of schools and remaining 296 teachers were employed in different types of higher and technical institutions. So the teachers-students ratio in schools of the Andaman and Nicobar Islands during 2011-12 was 19:1 in senior secondary schools, 14:1 in secondary schools, 13:1 in middle schools, 14:1 in primary schools, and 22:1 in pre-primary schools. The dropout rate was 0.87 in primary, 2.18 in middle and 4.40 in secondary schools. During 2011-12 a total of 97.49 per cent students passed 10th class examination (School Final) and 70.09 per cent in 12th class examination (Higher Secondary).

But in 1971 the rate of literacy was 51.15 per cent, in 1981 it was 60.25 per cent and 1991 the same was 73.02 per cent. Among the males the rate of literacy was 58.82 in 1971, 67.32 per cent in 1981 and 78.99 per cent in 1991. But among the females of Andaman and Nicobar Islands the same was only 38.29 per cent in 1971, 50.51 per cent in 1981 and 65.46 per cent in 1991. So the process of literacy is very significant here. In 2000-01 the number of educational institutions was 387, the number of students enrolled was 87,224 and the number of teachers were 2515. Again out of these 387 educational institutes, 380 were schools (Pre-primary, Primary, Middle and Secondary) and the rest 7 were higher educational institutions. Out of 87,224 students enrolled during 2000-01, 84,478 were students of different types of school and the rest only 2746 were students of higher educational institutions. In 2000-2001, the rate of passing the All India Secondary Examination was 69.29 per cent. In the same year the rate of passing All India Senior Secondary Examination was 72.38 per cent.

The development of transport system (air, sea and land) is an important indicator for the development of a country. For the development of a country both internal transport and transport with other states including the foreign country is essential. Andaman and Nicobar Islands also require for her development the promotions of transport system both internal and also with the mainland of India. This Union Territory being a group of islands, it requires also to develop all the three types of transports. As this Union Territory is a group of islands it has limitation to develop the land transport. It can be developed only within its territory and that too within an island. Inter-islands road cannot be feasible unless there is bridge connecting two islands or unless there is ferry services between two islands. That too is not feasible everywhere. But sea transport is most essential for connecting one island with another and also islands with mainland. Same is the case with the air transport. Now, let us examine the transport system of Andaman and Nicobar Islands. The Basic Statistics 2011-12 of this Union Territory has failed to give the total mileage of road so far been constructed in these islands. So, we shall not be able to frame any idea about the length and network of roads in this islands territory. But surely we have data about number of different types of vehicles ply.

There are a total of 76713 vehicles in this island territory which include different types of vehicles like two wheelers, lorry/trucks, bus, car/taxi, auto and others in 2011-12. As regards motor transport total number of state buses on road were 191, the length of the routes 4489 km. The buses own by private agencies was 207 and by the State, 219. Middle and North are also connected with Port Blair by Andaman Trunk Road and bus services.

As regards sea transport (shipping), this Union Territory had a total of 22 vessels and 17 other types of vessels like chartered vessels, for inter-island connection. Out of these total vessels 14 vessels and 11 other vessels are functioning as on 31 March, 2012. There are five ships, namely M.V. Nancowry, M.V. Swaraj Dweep, M.V. Nicobar, M.V. Harshavardhan and M.V. Akbar sailing between Port Blair and Kolkata, Madras and Visakhapatnam. Besides, there are another five ship which travel between Port Blair and Campbell Bay including Southern group of islands. Of course, there are other vessels those ply from Port Blair to North and Middle Andaman. In fact almost all inhabited islands are connected by some services.

Andaman and Nicobar Islands also have air services connecting between Port Blair in one hand and Kolkata, Chennai, Visakhapatnam and New Delhi on the other. Very recently Chartered flight has been started in between Port Blair and Chennai and also Kolkata for Islanders with special low fare prices. Flight connectivity is also available in between Port Blair and Car Nicobar. Everyday Inter-island Helicopter services have started also in between Port Blair and other far-flung islands for both passengers as well as emergency patients.

So far as land transport is concerned, as many as 25217 vehicles are found registered in 2000-01 in Andaman and Nicobar Islands, which include car, taxi, lorry, truck, motor cycles, scooter, moped, jeep and other vehicles. During this year 121 cars, 59 jeeps, 26 buses, 97 lorry/truck, 26 other vehicles, 1482 two wheelers and 93 autos were plying in Andaman and Nicobar Islands.

In the modern era electricity is essential commodity for development and progress of any country. For development of agriculture, industry, tourism and almost all other things power generation is possibly the first and foremost thing. The area is considered backward where is no electricity. In Andaman and Nicobar Islands the installed capacity was 83710 KW and 250353448 KW were generated in 2011-12. During this period the total consumption was 198618184 KW. In this islands territory 339 villages were electrified, and there were 91843 domestic and 15922 commercial consumers. In these islands per capita average consumption of electricity as on 31 March, 2012 was 522.75 KW. At the same time energy loss on transmission, distribution and unaccounted power loss was 18.03 per cent. But, during 2000-01 total electricity generated in Andaman and Nicobar Islands was 118558501 KW. During the same year the electricity consumption here was 89108151 KW. The installed capacity was 38805 KW.

The book on Andaman and Nicobar Islands of ours consists of seventeen articles. On the basis of the theme of the articles we have distributed these articles in five parts, each part contains one or more articles.

Part-One of this book deals with *Areas, Population and Development of Andaman and Nicobar Islands* and has one article. The theme of Part-Two is *Strategy for Security of Andaman and Nicobar Islands*. This part consists of five articles. The title of Part-Three is *Political Autonomy and Development of Andaman and Nicobar Islands*. This part contains four articles, Part-Four is on *Developmental Processes in Andaman and Nicobar Islands* and has five articles. The last Part, i.e. Part-Five entitled *Other Issues* and consists of two articles.

The article of Part-One is of Dr. Kailash Chandra Joshi, who has dealt in his article the area of Andaman and Nicobar Islands, weather condition, general population, tribal population, sex-ratio of the population of these islands. The author has linked rapid increase of population with the development of the area. The rapid growth of population has adverse effect on development and environment.

Prof. Gopalji Malviya has written about the security of the Indian Ocean, particularly of Andaman and Nicobar Islands. He has divided threats faced by these islands into two types: traditional military threats and non-traditional threats to national security issues. Apart from the traditional military threats, the non-traditional security threats like maritime piracy, Islamic militancy and fundamentalism etc. is a cause for great concern to the Indian authority. No doubt it is an extremely difficult task for the maritime security forces and the law enforcement agencies "to detect, destroy or eliminate such threats." In such a situation Prof. Malviya wants that there is an urgent need to change the attitude towards these island regions and to take appropriate policy at a highest level of the country's decision making authority.

Dr. Swapan Kumar Biswas has also discussed in his article the strategy taken by the India's defence personnel for protecting Indian Territory from external aggression, protecting her Exclusive Economic Zone from exploitation and also for barring the poachers, gun runners, and from non-Indian fishermen from illegal fishing from India sea areas. He has stressed on defence activities of some foreign countries in the neighbourhood of India who are creating much worries to our administrators, defence personnel and also politicians.

Dr. N. Francis Xavier often mentioning about the geographical and historical situations of Andaman and Nicobar Islands and also occupation of these islands territory by the foreign powers time to time, has given stress on the defence preparedness by the three wings of Indian military, i.e. Army, Air Force, and Navy.

Dr. R.V.R. Murthy in his article for this book, has also given emphasis on the illegal immigration of the non-Indian people in this island territory which often keep the security of these islands at bay. While discussing about the geo-strategic importance of these islands on the Bay of Bengal, Dr. Murthy stresses that illegal immigration, poaching etc. are the main threat to these islands. These, according to him must be taken care of.

Col. Pramod Sangwa, in his article, has pointed out that the Andaman and Nicobar Islands' proximity to "unstable littorals coupled with eventually of extra-regional players extending their influence in the region, make the Bay Islands quite vulnerable to both conventional and non-conventional threats." These have provided both challenges and opportunities to India. As a result these islands "are critical not only for protection of our interest but also power projecting." Col. Sangwa has finally given stress on the development and the security and defence of these islands.

Prof. R. Thandavan's article deals with the political autonomy and development in Andaman and Nicobar Islands. He has attempted to show the necessity for more political autonomy so as to "activate governance process and stimulate sustainable development" in order to promote prosperity of this islands territory. For this rational understanding of geo-political and strategic importance of these islands is essential. He has also given stress on two important steps are: (i) self-sufficiency in food and other essential commodities and (ii) focus of sustainable development of economy, employment opportunities, responsive and representative institutional development in this Union Territory.

Dr. S.S. Sreekumar has contributed his article on sustainable development and decentralization of governance especially for Andaman and Nicobar Islands. He has also examined the nature of participation at the grassroots level. To achieve these the emergence of a mass political culture in the rural area is a must. Simultaneously, the emergence of a strong middle class with political consciousness and vigil is necessary as only the vigilant middle class can achieve this.

Dr. R.N. Rath has also written article for this book on sustainable development and political autonomy. He has shown in his article, the long distance travelled by this group of islands from complete bureaucratization to semi-autonomy. He thinks that Andaman and Nicobar Islands are "slowly and gradually progressing in all the spheres including political autonomy." He has also stressed that political autonomy will lead to greater participation for the people and also greater prosperity.

Mr. Basudev Dass and Mr. Govind Ram have written their article based on political activities and political autonomy for this group of islands. After discussing on the political activities in this islands territory since past, they have marked the presence of "political immaturity of the larger chunk of the leaders." So, the authors think that "it will be another blunder to offer an Assembly" as demanded by many groups. According to them a Pradesh Council or some analogous institutions with some more power and autonomy would have been the right choice.

Since her journey for last two hundred years or a little more, rather since British occupation, Andaman and Nicobar Islands received a host of immigrant from different parts of the world, particularly from Indian mainland. As a result in the present day Andaman and Nicobar Islands cultural fusion is one of the special features. In the modern era these islands have adopted sustainable development for the progress and prosperity. The author of this article, Dr. (Mrs.) Nirupama Rath has tried to show these two aspects in these islands through her article.

Mrs. Pearl Devdas, through her article, has tried to highlight the development of the sustainable agriculture in Andaman and Nicobar Islands.

In his article on the renewable energy option for power generation in Andaman and Nicobar Islands, Er. Manohar Singh has given us a detailed picture for such option. With gradual dependence on these options, the administration would be able to tackle with the growing demand for more energy as there was constraints in generating power through diesel and also there are problems in transporting diesel from Port Blair to different islands, particularly during monsoons. So to him to cope with this difficult, the renewable sources is the option.

The article by Dr. Hema Bannerjee is on the need for the sustainable tourism in Andaman and Nicobar Islands. In her article she has focused on some particular areas in South, Middle and North Andaman and also Nicobar group of Islands. If these areas and also some 36 beaches are developed, then this will definitely attract a good number of tourists. At the same time, infrastructural development was also necessary. She has pointed out the problems connected with the development of the tourism spots.

The next article is of Dr. (Mrs.) Sweta Banerjee who in her paper, has highlighted the importance of development and conservation of resources in Little Andaman island. At the same time, she has given emphasis on the tourism development in Little Andaman. According to her if proper steps are taken in this direction, Little Andaman would be a very attractive venue for the tourists both from Indian mainland

and abroad. Again if resources are utilized properly and in a scientific manner, then all-round sustainable development of tourism is possible.

Mr. Niranjan Das has written his article on a very vital issue, that is Penal Settlements. He has given a detailed chronological account of development of the penal settlement since the British rulers first occupied this group of islands. He has also shown how the settlements developed in Andaman and Nicobar Islands and reached the present stage and how in different periods of time, batches of people came in these islands or are brought here to populate and also for the development of Andaman and Nicobar Islands.

In Andaman and Nicobar Islands the tribal people like the Great Andamanese, the Onges, the Jarawa, the Sentenalese, the Shompen and the Nicobarese are the original inhabitants. Mrs. Aiman Fatima through her article has tried to show the present status of the first five tribal groups who have also been declared as the PVTGs (Particularly Vulnerable Tribal Groups). She has stated the socio-economic and health status of these groups and the effects of development on them.

Through these articles we have tried to show briefly the problems of security conditions of these islands because of the external threats and encroachments faced by Andaman and Nicobar Islands and also demands for political autonomy. Development is also another key issue here which has been discussed at length in some of the articles. As a result one will get a first hand information about not only the above three major issues but at the same time, history and geographical conditions, population, development of settlement and also the tribal people as well.

BIBLIOGRAPHY

Census of India, 2011 (2013), *Primary Census Abstract, Data Highlights 2011, Andaman and Nicobar Island IIT*, Directorate of Census Operations, Port Blair, Andaman & Nicobar Islands.

Coomar, P.C., M.K. Raha and S. Bhui (2009): *Tradition and Transformation in an Immigrant Islands Society: The Keran of Andaman Islands*. Abhijit Publications, New Delhi.

Coomar, P.C. and M. K. Raha (2013): The Sherpa of Sikkim and their Land. In *Tribal Panorama of North East India* (ed.) Sarthak Sengupta, New Delhi: Gyan Books.

Dar, Muzammil Ahad, 2015: India's Maritime Security, *South Asian Politics*, May, 2015.

Das, Pushpa, 2010: *Securing Andaman and Nicobar Islands, http://www.idsa.in/event/SecuringAndamanandNicobarislandsc916.html?q=print/5199 2010*, Fellows' Seminar, Institute for Defence Studies and Analysis.

Directorate of Economics and Statistics (2014): *Basic Statistic, 2014*, Andaman & Nicobar Administration, 2014.

Dre'ze, Jean and Amartya Sen, (2013): *An Uncertain Glory; India and its Contradictions,* Allen Lane, Penguin Books.

Kukreja, Dhiraj, Air Marshal, (2013): A and N Islands: A Security Challenge, In *Indian Defence Review*, Vol. 28 (January-March, 2013).

Rae, Vivek, (2015): Tap Into The Treasure Islands in *India Today*, May, 4, 2015, Former Chief Secretary, A & N Administration.

Raha, M.K. (2002): Polyandry; Development, Distribution and Decline. In *Journal of the Indian Anthropological Society,* Vol. 37, No. 1.

Sahoo, Rudra Prasad, 2012: Development Projects and Tribals: In *Displacement and Rehabilitation*, (ed.) Nihar Ranjan Mishra, New Delhi: Gyan Books.

Singh, A.K., Lt. Governor, Lt. General (Retd.) (2014): *Seminar on Tribal Development and Future Plan* organized by Andaman & Nicobar Tribal Research Institute, Port Blair on 1st and 2nd December, 2014.

IGNOU: India, (2004): *Democracy and Development*, MPS-003, Book-2, New Delhi.

The Indian Express: People-Trafficking in South-East Asia, 18 May, 2015.

Part-I

Land, Population and Development of Andaman and Nicobar Islands

1
Area, Population and Development
A Study of Andaman and Nicobar Islands

Kailash Chandra Joshi

Introduction

The behaviour and structure of contemporary man are products of his evolution through millennia. Today man's wide distribution and abundance are evidence of how well these attributes have helped him maintaining a vital relationship with his environment. Yet despite his apparent success as a species, he now faces a crisis. The complex interrelationship between population, environment and development is sometimes known as the development paradox, while development can slow population growth, population pressure can slow development by diverting natural and economic resources. Population explosion and pressure is a matter of concern for India with 16 per cent of the world population and 2.4 per cent of the global land area, it is a problem of serious magnitude. Already there is tremendous pressure on our resources for providing even the basic needs. If the present growth of population is unchecked, there would be serious impact on our socio-economic development, the quality of life and environment.

Area Profile

As in the rest of the country, there is a mythological interpretation to the *raison d'etre* of these islands. It is believed that the Andamans were islands inhabited by the Handuman. The first reference to the Andaman Islands is to be found in the great Indian Epic, the *Ramayana*. Among western sources, the first reference to the island is in the *geographika syntaxis*, the most laudable attempt in ancient times to place the study of geography on a scientific basis. Several centuries later, we have the account of the Chinese traveller I'Chang. The truth is that, it was not until the Cape of Good Hope was discovered and ships playing the trade route around the Cape eastward bound found, the Nicobars *en route*, that the world became aware of these islands (Kaul, 1989).

Lapped by incessant white foamed crested waves, the Andaman and Nicobar Islands archipelago lies in the centre of the Bay of Bengal. The story of the islands begins when time began. Once the geological forces had created mountains, islands and oceans, living creatures evolved, until at last the earth came to be dominated by *Homo sapiens*. The rest of the world marched on, the process of evolution halted in Andaman and Nicobar Islands. The islands are, therefore, inhabited by aborigines though there are some islands that are quite uninhabited. The most geographical description of these islands was written by C. Boden Kloss when he visited the island in 1901.

A great part of these islands are composed of rocks belonging to Eocene period. The Andaman and Nicobar archipelago lies in a crescent that stretches from Cape Wegrais of Myanmar to Bande Arc of Sumatra. Collectively, the entire group of islands is the projection above the sea level of long and narrow submarine ranges which were formed at the expense of narrow but deep geosynclines against the Gondwana land in the west.

The Andaman and Nicobar islands consisting of 306 islands and 206 rocks and rocky outcrops are Lattitudinally situated between 6°45′N to 13°41′N and longitudinally 92°12′E to 93°57′E. The total geographical area is 8249 square km. with a coast line of 1962 km.

The land area of 6408 sq. km. of the Andaman group constitutes almost 90 per cent as reserve or protected forest of which 36 per cent is tribal reserve. The Nicobar group is spread over an area of 1841 sq. km. of which 1542 sq. km. are recorded forest. The Nicobars are separated from Andamans by the 10 degree channel, a wide gap of 160 km. with heavy tidal flows, making sea transport by small boats difficult.

These islands are situated in the equatorial belt and are exposed to marine influences and had a tropical climate—warm, moist and equable. The temperature ranges from 18 degree to 35 degree Celsius. The proximity of the sea and the abundant rainfall prevent extremes of heat, and these islands experience both the north-east and south-west monsoon. The average annual rainfall ranges from 3000 to 3500 mm and humidity varies from 66 to 90 per cent (Table 1.1).

The Andaman and Nicobar Islands have a unique tropical ecosystem with a wide range of diversities of a genetic nature in germoplasm and great natural beauty. The biotic conditions and the climate of the islands are congenial to productivity. The mangrove ecosystem, the coral reefs and the inaccessible type of the region along with beaches, have allowed the unique ecosystem to be preserved in its pristine form.

The physiography of these islands is striking because no where the height is more than 2402 feet which is the culminating point in the entire Andaman and Nicobar groups of islands. This height is attained by Saddle peak along the east coast of north Andaman. The general elevation of the hill ranges in these islands varies from 250 to 1250 feet. A number of ridges and spurs projected out from these hill ranges and spurs that enclose narrow and flat valleys, and at places have been cut up by streams. It is worth noticing that a major part of these islands comes below 5 degree of slope where both the rural and urban settlement and agricultural activities are confined.

Table 1.1: Climatic condition in Andaman and Nicobar Islands (2011)

Months	*Rainfall (mm)*	*Temperature (in Celsius)*		*Relative Humidity*	
		Max	*Min*	*08:30 hrs*	*17:30 hrs*
January	0.0	30.1	23.0	77	81
February	0.0	31.5	22.0	78	77
March	27.2	32.7	24.0	80	83
April	157.4	32.5	26.0	75	80
May	405.1	31.4	25.0	82	86
June	505.4	29.1	25.0	88	90
July	178.8	29.9	25.0	91	91
August	418.5	30.3	25.0	91	94
September	416.2	27.8	25.0	93	94
October	237.6	31.0	24.0	83	94
November	88.6	31.5	25.0	72	89
December	61.9	31.0	25.4	77	79

Source: Meteorological Statistics of Andaman and Nicobar Islands.

Human Resource

The survival and degradation of ecosystem depends largely on man. Within the confines of an island's ecosystem the arrival of human, especially in large number, can bring about great change. These islands show the impact of such intervention. Out of 306 islands and 206 rocks and rocky outcrops, only 38 are inhabited including 25 in Andaman group and remaining 13 in Nicobar group of islands. It is interesting to note that inhabited islands encompass about 94 per cent of the geographical area of Andaman and Nicobar Islands (Table 1.2).

As per 2001 Census, the population of the Andaman and Nicobar Islands was 356265 accounting for 0.03 per cent of the total population of India. Though the decadal population growth in this Union Territory was higher than the all India rates of 21.3 and 23.9 per cent during the nineties and eighties respectively, there has been a continuous decline in the growth rate of population since 1971. One of the main reasons behind the decline in the population growth is the decline in child population (0-6 year age group) in nineties that appears to be due to low birth rate which in turn can be attributed to improvements in literacy and life expectancy at birth and low infant mortality rates.

Although, Andaman and Nicobar Islands recorded a higher average annual population growth of 3.8 per cent during 1971-2001 compared to 2.1 per cent for all India during the same period but it is significant to note that there has been a steady decline in population growth in Andaman and Nicobar Islands since 1971 (Table 1.3).

The increase in population in this Union Territory is, to a large extent, due to the immigration of people from mainland. While the inflow of people from other countries has declined significantly over the years, migration from mainland India still continues. Of the total born population in Andaman and Nicobar Islands, one-third constitutes from the mainland (Development Report, 2008). The Census of 1991 had revealed a perceptible change in the region's demographic scene especially in its growth rate. Although the last inter-censual decade added over 90370 populations which was about 16762 more than the addition during the previous decade of 1971-81. Yet in terms of percentage increase, the decade 1981-91 recorded a growth of 3.97 as against 4.92 during the previous decade. Thus there was a fall in the growth rate of population to the tune of about 75 per cent. It signals the beginning of new era in the demographic history of the region.

Table 1.2: Andaman and Nicobar Island's Inhabited Islands

Sl. No.	*Geographical Name*	*Area (Sq. Km)*	*Population (2001)*	*Density*
A.	***Andaman Group (total)***	***5907.37***	***314084***	***53.1***
1.	Aves	0.20	2	10.0
2.	Baratang	297.80	6062	20.4
3.	Cinque	9.53	6	0.6
4.	Curlew	0.03	2	66.7
5.	East	6.10	17	2.8
6.	Flat Bay	0.14	10	71.4
7.	Havelock	113.90	5354	47.0
8.	Interview	133.40	16	0.1
9.	John Lawrance	41.98	25	0.6
10.	Little Andaman	731.60	17528	23.9
11.	Long	17.90	2199	122.8
12.	Middle Andaman	1535.50	54385	35.4
13.	Narcondam	6.80	17	2.5
14.	Neil	18.90	2868	151.7
15.	North Andaman	1376.0	42163	30.6
16.	North Passage	22.0	11	0.5
17.	North Sentinal	59.67	39	0.7
18.	Ross	0.65	Nil	–
19.	Rutland	137.20	688	5.0
20.	Smith	24.70	676	27.3
21.	South Andaman	1347.97	181949	134.9
22.	Spike	11.70	19	1.6
23.	Stewart	7.20	2	0.3
24.	Strait	6.0	42	7.0
25.	Viper	0.50	4	8.0
B.	**Nicobar Group (total)**	**1841**	**42068**	**22.9**
1.	Car Nicobar	126.9	20292	159.9
2.	Chowra	8.2	1385	168.9
3.	Teressa	101.4	2026	20.0
4.	Bompuka	13.3	55	4.1
5.	Katchal	174.4	5312	30.5
6.	Kamorta	188.2	3412	18.1
7.	Nancowry	66.9	927	13.8
8.	Trinket	86.3	432	5.0
9.	Little Nicobar	159.1	348	2.1
10.	Pillomilo	1.3	150	115.4
11.	Kondul	4.6	150	32.6
12.	Great Nicobar	1045.1	7566	7.2
13.	Thillangchang	16.8	–	–

Source: Forest Statistics and District Statistical Hand Book, Andaman and Nicobar Islands.

Table 1.3: Population growth in Andaman and Nicobar Islands (1901-2001)

Year	*Total Population*	*Decadal Growth*	*Expo. Growth*
1901	25649	—	—
1911	26459	7.34	0.71
1921	27086	2.37	0.22
1931	29463	8.78	0.82
1941	33768	14.61	1.38
1951	30971	–8.28	–0.86
1961	63548	105.19	7.20
1971	115133	81.17	5.98
1981	188741	63.93	4.92
1991	279111	47.88	3.97
2001	356265	27.64	2.37

Source: Directorate of Economics and Statistics, 2002, Port Blair.

Table 1.4 depicts the projected population for Andaman and Nicobar Islands. It is based on the assumption that average growth per annum is 3 per cent.

Table 1.4: Population growth in Andaman and Nicobar Islands (Projected)

Year	*Andaman District*	*Nicobar District*	*Total*
2001	314239	42026	356265
2005	361375	48330	409705
2010	415581	55579	471160
2015	477918	63916	541835
2020	549606	73504	623110
2025	632047	84529	716576

Source: State Development Draft Report, 2014, Andaman and Nicobar Islands.

Tribal Population

The Andaman archipelago is home of four negrito tribes—the Great Andamanese, the Jarawa, the Onge and the Sentnelese. Recent studies conducted by the Centre for Cellular and Molecular Biology, Hyderabad show that these tribes settled in these islands some 60,000 years ago. They are the last of the first people. At least two of these four tribes—the Jarawa and the Sentnelese continue to be hunter gatherers and are among the most isolated communities in the world. The Great Andamanese, consisting of 10 territorial and linguistic groups, were at one time the largest tribe inhabiting the archipelago.

It is believed that prior to the penal settlement of 1858, between 5000 to 8000 Great Andamanese lived in different parts of the Great Andaman island. These tribes fiercely resisted British incursions into their territory and suffered heavy casualties in the process. Subsequently, they made peace with the British and were introduced to addictive substance. Contact with the outside world brought with it diseases and by the beginning of the 20th century, the Great Andamanese population had dwindled to 625.

The Jarawa are among the few classic communities of foragers left in the world. They live in the area reserved for them. This negrito group has attracted more attention than any other primitive tribes of Andaman, primarily because their fate has become inextricably linked with the Andaman Trunk road.

The Onge live in a small island in the Andaman Sea. A tribe which numbered 672 at the beginning of the 20th century, today has less than 100 numbers. The Sentinelese, who inhabit the North Sentinel Island are without doubt, the most isolated community (Table 1.5).

The Nicobar group of islands are home of two tribes of Indo-Mongoloid origin. They are the Shompen and the Nicobarese. The Shompen, who live along the coast and deep inside the forest of Great Nicobar, are hunter gatherers. The Shompen are the first inhabitants of the Nicobar Island. It is believed that they came from Sumatra and settled in their present abode over 10,000 years ago. The Nicobarese are presently the largest tribal group inhabiting these islands. Unlike the other tribal groups, the Nicobarese have much greater contact with the outside world. This is the only tribal group of the islands whose population has shown a constant growth.

Population Density

Density of population has its impact upon the environment of the region and hence its quality of life. Therefore, it is of special interest for geographers to analysis the changing pattern of density of population for understanding the process of development affecting quality of life. Density is to measure the incidence of population concentration and is generally expressed in terms of persons per square kilometre of land area. Prior to independence, the increase in density was only marginal in these islands adding only a few more people to each square kilometre. The density of population in Andaman and

Table 1.5: Tribal population of Andaman and Nicobar Islands

Tribes/Year	*1901*	*1911*	*1921*	*1931*	*1941*	*1951*	*1961*	*1971*	*1981*	*1991*	*2001*
Great Andamanese	625	455	209	90	–	23	19	24	26	45	43
Onge	(672)	(631)	(346)	(250)	–	(150)	129	112	97	95	96
Sentinelese	(117)	(117)	(117)	(50)	–	–	(50)	(82)	NE	(100)	(39)
Jarawa	(468)	(114)	(114)	(70)	–	(50)	(500)	(275)	31	(280)	(240)
Nicobarese	5962	7991	8248	9589	12252	11902	13903	17874	21984	26000	28653
Shompen	(348)	(375)	(375)	(200)	–	20	71	92	223	250	398
Total	–	–	–	–	–	**12145**	**14762**	**18102**	**22361**	**26770**	**29469**

Bracket—Provisional, NE—Not Enumerated.

Source: Directorate of Economics and Statistics, Port Blair.

Nicobar Islands had only 3 persons per square kilometre till 1921 as the Union Territory experienced very low growth of population. It saw an increase of only one person per square kilometre in 1931 which remained constant till 1951. During the year 1961, it saw a two-fold increase in the density of population from 4 to 8 persons per square kilometre.

The 1991 census revealed an average density of 34 persons per square kilometre for the region. It implies an addition of 11 persons to the island's density of 23 in 1981. An addition of the burden of 11 persons to each square kilometre area of the region, which have very much fragile ecosystem and are distantly located from mainland, in a short span of a decade is really alarming. It reflects the magnitude of increasing strain on the area's limited resources. It warrants rapid mobilization of the region's resources if the standard of living is to be improved and if the number of those slipping below the poverty line is to be arrested (Table 1.6).

Table 1.6: Population Dynamics of Andaman and Nicobar Islands

Year	*Density (persons Per sq. km.)*	*Sex-ratio (females Per 1000 males)*	*Literacy*
1901	3	318	–
1911	3	352	–
1921	3	303	–
1931	4	495	–
1941	4	574	–
1951	4	625	–
1961	8	617	–
1971	14	644	33.52
1981	23	760	43.59
1991	34	820	60.25
2001	43	846	73.02
2011 (P)	61	877	81.29
2021 (P)	74	–	–

Source: Directorate of Economics and Statistics, Port Blair.

Unevenness of distribution is another typical feature of the population in the region. Wide disparities in the index of concentration of population are observed at micro level. The region is having nine tehsils in all. Highest concentration of population is in Port Blair (about 40 per cent of the total population) followed by Diglipur and Ferranganj. The remaining tehsils show less concentration of population. Broadly speaking, agriculturally prosperous areas, which have had a long history of settlement and is now experiencing urban development, display high incidence of population concentration. By contrast, the areas which suffer from some kind of physical hardship of terrain, subsoil water etc. exhibit a low degree of population concentration.

Urban Population

The process of urbanisation is an intrusive dimension of economic and social development and in consequence, both developed and developing countries are going through the process of shifting from predominantly rural to predominantly urban societies (Shrivastava, 2004). Urban areas and urbanisation have been increasing ever since the emergence of first urban agglomerated settlements. The trends of urbanisation in Andaman and Nicobar islands reveal that there was no urban area in this Union Territory up to 1941. During 1951 Census, Port Blair town, the capital of these islands, was first treated as urban area which had only 7789 persons covering about 33 per cent of the then total population of Andaman and Nicobar Islands. Gradually, the urban population increased to 14075 in 1961, 26218 in 1971, 49634 in 1981 and 74955 in 1991. Urban population of these islands reached 116198 in 2001 and finally 135533 in 2011 Census elevating to that of a city.

Urbanisation is a process of great demographic significance. It transfers population to a very different socio-economic and physical environment. It also transfers people into a very different demographic environment one that is itself often changing rapidly with further social and economic consequences.

As the population of this Union Territory has increased remarkably since 1961, remarkable increase has also been noted in the urban population. The percentage share of urban population to the total Union Territory's population during 2001 has been recorded 32.62 percentages which is 6 percentages higher than that of 1991 Census and it further reached up to 35.66 percentage of the total population. This may be mainly due to the extension of the boundary of Port Blair town and due to the inclusion of two census towns—Garacharma and Bambooflat—in the urban area. The main characteristics of urbanisation of population in these islands are the changing trend of migration of population from rural to urban areas.

Sex-Ratio

In any study of the population analysis, the sex composition plays a vital role. The sex composition of the population is affected by the differentials in the mortality conditions of males and females, sex selective migration and the sex-ratio at birth. Sex-ratio is defined as the number of females per 1000 males. It is one of the reliable indicators of the states of women in a society. Sex-ratio in Andaman and Nicobar Islands though improved from 820 females per 1000 males 1991 to 846 in Table 1.7.

Table 1.7: Rural and Urban population of Andaman and Nicobar Islands (1901-2011)

Year	*Rural*	*Urban*
1901	24649	–
1911	26459	–
1921	27086	–
1931	29463	–
1941	33768	–
1951	23182	7789
1961	49473	14075
1971	88915	26218
1981	139107	49634
1991	205706	74955
2001	239954	116198
2011	244411	135533

Source: District Statistical Hand-Book, 2010-11.

It is low when compared to all India ratio (933). However, sex-ratio of 0-6 year age group population in Andaman and Nicobar Islands is higher at 965 as compared to 933 for all India.

Conclusion

Any development has an impact on the ecosystem. The relationship between population dynamics and the ecosystem on which the survival and well-being of people depend, will be decisive in achieving sustainable development. With growing population, existing land must be subdivided into even smaller plots. Where plots are too small for even subsistence farming, farmers are forced to destroy forest cover to get more land. As population pressure breaks down fragile ecosystem, people are forced to move elsewhere to survive.

With the continuation of the present trend of increase of population, the total population of these islands will reach up to approximately 541835 persons in 2015(P) and about 716576 persons in 2025 with a density of more than 74 persons per square kilometre. The existing environmental conditions are not conducive to go along with this ever increasing population of these islands which may ultimately deteriorate the existing fragile ecosystem of Andaman and Nicobar Islands.

According to an estimates concluded by the Food and Agricultural Organisation of the UN, Andaman and Nicobar Islands can support 3 persons/hectare at an intermediate level of agriculture and 5 persons/hectare at a level of intensive and technologically advanced agriculture. The 1989 production rate did not a significantly increase since then. Currently increase in population trends clearly indicates that the agricultural carrying capacity of these islands has been well surpassed (Sirus, 1999).

Andaman and Nicobar Islands are famous tourist resort and producer of timber, coconuts, spices etc. But unprecedented population growth within a short span of the past few decades has created manifold complex problem and environment degradation. The bulk of the valuable land resources have been rendered unproductive by erosion and deforestation. The demographic and technological threats pushed by the man on the fragile ecosystem, have caused widespread pollution in the region. In encountering the environment in these areas for making it more favourable, man has over stepped his limit and the results are painful disastrous.

Recent decades have witnessed an increase in developmental activities in these islands. These activities have simultaneously given rise to a growing concern over their adverse environmental impact. The environmental conditions and the consequences of development in the Andaman group of islands are sufficiently distinct from those of Nicobar group. An ecological sustained management policy is needed for the sustained development of environment.

BIBLIOGRAPHY

Ali, R., H.V. Andrews and I. Das (2002): *Ecology, Floristic and Socio-Economics of three Protected areas in the Andaman Island*, ANET, Tech. Report.

Andaman and Nicobar Administration (2005): *Draft of State Development Report of Andaman and Nicobar Islands*.

Andrew, H.V. and K. Shankar (2002): *Sustainable Management of Protected Areas in the Andaman and Nicobar Islands* (eds.), New Delhi: ANET, FFI, IIPA.

Directorate of Economics and Statistics (2010): *District Statistical Hand-Book*, 2010-11.

Joshi, K.C. (2014): Environment and Human Ecology: A Study of Andaman, *Practicing Geographer*, Vol. 18, No. 1, Summer, Kolkata, pp. 118-129.

Meteorological Department (2011): *Climate and Weather Reports of Andaman and Nicobar islands.*

Paul, R. (1989): *Andaman and Nicobar Islands in the Sun*, England: Spantech Publisher.

Planning Commission (2008): *Andaman and Nicobar Islands Development Report*, New Delhi: Government of India.

Shrivastava, A.K. (2004): *Population Development Environment and Health*, New Delhi: APH Publishing Corporation.

Sinha, P.C. (1998): *Population Explosion*, New Delhi: Anmol Publishing Pvt. Ltd.

Sirus, H.S. (1999): *A Rapid assessment of threat to the coastal environment and their Root causes in the Andaman and Nicobar Islands, A Component of IND/95/G41 (UNDP)*, unpublished Report, New Delhi.

Part-II

Strategy for Security of Andaman and Nicobar Islands

2
Strategic Contours of Andaman and Nicobar Islands

Gopalji Malviya

Indian coast line and islands encounter a plethora of security challenges in the Indian Ocean particularly Andaman and Nicobar (ANI) Islands. These threats could be categorized into traditional military threats and non-traditional security issues. These emerging trends and security environment in the maritime domain pose serious changes to India's national interests. It is in this context, the security development and governance of Andaman and Nicobar Islands could be visualized with India's emerging status and its role in the region in consonance with its Look East Policy. The role of Andaman and Nicobar Islands has increased many fold, and this requires special attention towards enhancing its economic potential and fine tuning the governance to meet a modern requirement. The overall development of Andaman and Nicobar Islands is the key for securing the region's prosperity that would also be integral to India's emerging regional power status. Therefore, the urgency requires the synergy between tri-services with true sense of jointness, civil administration and identifying economic potential of Andaman and Nicobar Islands region. A robust security apparatus to control and dominate the region particularly oceanic sea bed keeping India's national security and interest in mind.

The Andaman and Nicobar region in India's far east has long been perceived as a key vulnerability particularly due to geographical distance from the main land and the history of its repeatedly 'slipping away' syndrome from the Indian main land. Since the past decade several measures have been taken to enhance its defence capability in the region, and accordingly an integrated Andaman and Nicobar Command was established in 2001. These steps were meant to translate India's geo-strategic vision that would enable Andaman and Nicobar Command to play a vital role in the security India's maritime interests in the region.

India's forward presence in the eastern IOR is enabled by Andaman Islands. The location and geography of these islands impart them with immense strategic advantage. The propinquity of these islands to the busy shipping lines is specially Malacca Straits not only opens up an opportunity for India in controlling and commanding this oceanic highway but also provides proximity of the archipelago to the South East Asian neighbours. This provides excellent opportunity for trade, diplomacy and other maritime engagements.

The Andaman and Nicobar group of islands straddles the strategic seaway leading to the Malacca Straits. The Archipelago comprises 572 islands, islets and rocks of which only 37 are inhabited. It accounts for 30 per cent of country's EEZ, has vast marine resources and a potential reserve of natural oil and gas. Notwithstanding the distance of the Andaman and Nicobar Islands from the mainland, which is more than 1200 kms, these islands have a close proximity to a number of littoral states. Apart from possessing the abundant natural resources, these islands are our national assets for India's 'Look East Policy'. This policy fuels the engine that drives the functioning of the Andaman and Nicobar Command.

While the Andaman contributes large part of EEZ to India's total oceanic areas, various species, untapped marine life and high value seafood are located in and around this region. This region has potential for seafood export to Southeast Asian countries if appropriate infrastructure facilities and expertise are developed. Port Blair could also be developed as an international trade centre and oil terminal and transhipment port to meet the increase of maritime activities.

The non-traditional threats to national security have emerged as a significant feature of the security calculus. Assessing the risk of threats to human and ecological security is a complex task. Today, states grapple with non-obtrusive attacks on the core values and cultural systems without the faintest idea of how these threats can manifest themselves in a variety of national and regional sectors which stroke the embers of violent conflicts, large scale migration and social unrest. Even if these issues do not lead to violent conflicts, they can and do constitute a risk to regional stability and security. It is in this context the security of Andaman and Nicobar Islands need to be analyzed. Continued maritime piracy and other oceanic crimes have now spilled over to the Bay of Bengal region. The rise of Islamic militancy and fundamentalism is causing considerable security concern, the thick forest is spread over 550 Islands, its terrain and topography makes it ideal place or perhaps a sanctuary for insurgents and terrorist groups operating in this region. Also it becomes an extremely difficult task for maritime security forces and law enforcement agencies to detect, destroy or eliminate such extensions and movements.

In the light of the foregoing, it is important for India, as a regional power and emerging global player, to make a risk assessment in its area of influence which at this point of time and in the midterm would be the Indian Ocean Region. In conceptualization such a risk assessment, a multidisciplinary approach that identifies the challenges to each component of national power, which is diplomatic, informational, military and economic, is now a necessity. Assessing of risk is an intellectual process of constructing, communicating, accepting and even opposing particular geo-cultural and popular concepts of danger, hazards and security. The process has both temporal and spatial dimensions. Risk assessment in accordance with one model envisaged risk to be a product of severity, probability and exposure. Risk management with respect to non-traditional threats to security in the region requires convergence of different elites at the levels of the individual, government, non-government and inter-state actors. A convergence of perceptions through social solidarities would go a long way in addressing these issues.

In the current strategic environment probability of a conventional threat to these islands from immediate neighbours appears remote. However, the Chinese strategic threat looms large in the form of possible military interventions, influence, collaborative engagement through an adversary or any other form to destabilize the region. With the increase of its prowess the power projection efforts of the Chinese Navy has increased its activities in the Indian Ocean Region (IOR). Its non-military benign activities also need to be viewed through the prism of displaying 'strategic reach and sustenance' in the backyard of India. The Chinese military presence in Andaman and Nicobar and Oceanic region around, its declared agenda, its military might clubbed with its collaborative strength has continued to be a cause of concern for Indian security establishment. The question thus arises about the actual Chinese designs in the Indian Ocean Region (IOR). China is currently working for great power status. The Chinese attempt to adopt a containment strategy against India, the 'string of pearls', encompasses the strategy to build leverage points in areas that lead to Indian Ocean and also to strategically surround India.

This region falls within the Chinese strategy and its focus. The Chinese declaration of 'sting of pearls' strategy is one that needs to be countered appropriately. According to this strategy China seeks to setup bases at outposts across the region. Strategically located along its energy supply lines and also to monitor and safeguard its energy flows. Each 'pearl' in the string of pearls construct is a link of China's geopolitical influence and its maritime presence. In the IOR the string passes through Myanmar and towards Chittagong in Bangladesh and thereafter to Sri Lanka. The string that further moves west into the continent of Africa *via* Gwadar deep sea port on Pakistan's Makaran coasts. This ambitious plan exists to link the post with Karakorum highway thereby providing China with the gateway to the Arabian Sea.

India's rigorous diplomatic exercises in Southeast Asia can also be traced from the Chinese presence in the region. China has been developing a powerful nuclear submarine base in the Hainan Island in the South China Sea which is only 2,000 nautical miles from Andaman Islands. It also occupies the Paracel Islands seized from Vietnam and has built naval facilities. Its strings of pearls in the Coco Islands in Myanmar and the Gwadar Port in Pakistan add anxiety over the real intent of China.

While New Delhi must wait and watch, it cannot ignore the fact that both North Korea and Pakistan are the closest allies of China and going through unprecedented domestic challenges that could intensify concerns for neighbours in South Asia alike. Pakistan has been accused of giving North Korea crucial nuclear technology. The Sino-Pak-North Korea nuclear designs and its covert missile proliferation agenda is well known to the strategic community all over world. Any illicit trade of nuclear armament or technology from Pakistan to North Korea goes through these waters. Hence, Andaman and Nicobar Islands region and its strategic command need to be strengthened for surveillance, intelligence gathering and have the capacity to intercept such delinquent ships in AN region. As far as

Indian strategic thinking is concerned, Beijing has promoted these two unstable regimes on its periphery to keep neighbours like Japan and India off balance. Their instability and uncertainty could revive old weapons and nuclear proliferation ties between Pyongyang and Islamabad that would have a direct bearing on India's security.

Traditionally a marine nation, India's coastal vulnerabilities have increased manifold despite of technological advances. The key to the security of these islands in particular and the main land in general lies in the rapid infrastructural build up thereby facilitating growth of commerce and trade, the benefits of which will be reaped by the locals up to the grassroots level and will ensure greater participation in the overall security matrix as their economic stakes grow. Overall development is the key to these challenges and is integral to India's emerging status as a regional power. For this, the need of the hour is to have synergy not only within the Armed Forces but also with the civil administration. Jointness is the quintessence of strength and the Andaman and Nicobar Command serves as a role model for jointmanship.

Major Challenges: Non-traditional Threats to A&N Islands

- Remote location from Indian mainland with large number of uninhabited islands and Inter/Intra Islands connectivity problems.
- The islands location in the most challenging seismic-zones on the earth.
- Illegal immigration from the Littorals. The need to maintain cultural, ethnic and religious balance on the islands.
- Proximity to unstable littorals of which some have radical outlook amongst its populace. Proximity to the Golden Triangle that is prone to drugs/gun running and piracy.
- Oceanic Crimes/Piracy and Armed Robbery.
- Maritime Terrorism
- Phantom Ships
- Cargo Fraud
- Smuggling of Small Arms
- Drug-Trafficking/Gun Running
- Illegal Exploitation of Marine Resource
- Marine Pollution
- Insurgency/Illegal Migration

- Natural Disasters.
- Illegal fishing and poaching.

With India's emerging status and its role in the region in consonance with its 'Look East Policy', the role of Andaman and Nicobar Islands has increased manifold. In addition to the need for harnessing its economic potential, the islands face the challenges of the growing Chinese influence in the region, increase in maritime trade activities, unstable Littorals in the neighbouring, illegal immigration, drug peddling, poaching and piracy. India's diplomatic skill in Southeast Asia is particularly visible in the context of the Malacca Straits. This sea lane carries major stake for India as a prominent share of ships pass through the Straits.

Almost 70 per cent of the world's commercial traffic passes through this area. Development of South Eastern tip of Nicobar as a Transhipment Port for container handling, bunkering and refuelling of international/national ships would provide great economic and strategic potential. This port could provide an alternative to Singapore and Colombo and become a major strength for India. Such an initiative will also help the country in fulfilling our growing ambitions in the fields of regional co-operation with South East Asia and the issues of the "National Look East Policy."

There is sufficient potential for industrial and socio-economic development by harnessing available resources on sustainable basis while having a balance between environmental concerns and the development requirements. This balanced growth would envisage without disturbing the ecosystem of the Islands. These Islands chain is vast store house of timber and its adjoining water contains various species of marine life. The Islands would also become an attractive place for trade and investment and also tourist paradise. This may require sufficient infrastructure development with upgraded air and sea links currently the revenue generation largely depends on tourists. The handicraft industry could be encouraged, to its optimum potential, this sector would be key to provide development and employment generation capacity. Private players could also be encouraged, and there is sufficient place for these players to contribute economic development of these Islands.

Another thrust area for development of these Islands is guided by its potential to tap the natural resources, achieve agriculture, self reliance and creating modern facilities for preservation and export promotion for sea food. Improved means of communication and alternative source of power would provide value addition to the development of these Islands. The growing population and their aspirations require creation of modern infrastructure and development of new vistas in health care, sanitation, hygiene, due to possibility of biological threats, disease like malaria, cholera, dengue, HIV, SARS etc., that could affect the population. Primary and higher education requires serious attention to provide opportunity for Information Technology knowledge resource for the island population and to open up research activity for the scholars. This would further enhance the capacity building of youthful population and provide equal opportunity with their counterpart in the mainland. The best option of governance of these tiny Islands would be the existing status of Union Territory, while the democratization of its local governance is essential, and this could be reviewed to provide greater opportunity to the citizens within certain amount of autonomous status. However, any over ambitious dream or short-sighted plan of statehood may prove to be disasterous in the present context. Limits of growth in the AN Islands is strictly conditioned by the geographical factors.

The Andaman and Nicobar Command (ANC) was created in October 2011 with its Headquarters at Port Blair. This Command functions under the direct control of the Chief of Staff Committee. The broad functions of the ANC could be divided into three major categories, i.e. Military, Diplomacy and Policy. The military role involves maintaining deterrence through maritime domain, ensuring physical presence of the tri-service in this region, protection of India's interest and also conducting joint naval exercise with friendly neighbouring countries. On diplomatic level conducting the naval exercise, initiatives like *MILAN* for the purpose of promoting regional cooperation and mutual understanding and addressing maritime issues and concerns. Policing functions primarily involve enforcement of the rule of law at sea, checking smuggling, collecting information, conducting low intensity maritime operations to prevent poaching, illegal migration, narcotics and arms smuggling in the region, although, the ANC charter did include protection of sea lanes and surveillance of EEZ. It is more oriented towards 'territorial defence' of the Andaman and Nicobar region. Security of widely scattered islands of Andaman and Nicobar is always a difficult task. The ANC could also be seen India's acquisition of power projection capabilities. It would be better if the ANC could be transformed as theatre command. This could be the synergy role of the Navy, Coast Guard, Air force, Army, and the theatre command would provide a robust security arrangement to deal with traditional and non-traditional threats in and around these waters.

Considering various dimensions of micro and macro issues of security concerns there is a need for a change in India's attitude towards Andaman and Nicobar region. Instead of mere defending it, it should be viewed as the first line of defence. The main objectives of India's security perspectives should be to assess the threats especially from some neighbouring countries and evolve appropriate strategic apparatus to counter them. This would require highly efficient surveillance network to monitor non-conventional threats emanating in the region. The advance communication network would also have to be developed to carry out surveillance and monitoring. This will require skill and trained human resources and most modern state of art equipments. The implications for policy and operation thus have become pertinent agenda for a comprehensive academic discourse on maritime security issues and concerns. An intense debate among the strategic fraternity would be fruitful for appropriate policy formulation at highest level of the country's decision making establishment.

3

Military Strategy in Indian Ocean

With Special Reference to Andaman and Nicobar Islands

Swapan Kumar Biswas

"To be secure on land, we have to be supreme at sea."

—*Jawaharlal Nehru*

Since long, from security and military points of view, the importance of the Indian Ocean in general and the Andaman and Nicobar chain of islands in particular, has been taken into account at various points of time by many scholars, defence analysts as well as governing authorities. The British occupied these archipelagos not to transport hundreds of soldiers of Sepoy Munity in 1857, but they realized its strategic importance. The Chief of Staff under the Ministry of Defence of the British Government in a conversation with the Viceroy before his departure from India, had emphasized on the importance which they attached to these islands as an essential link in the chain of Commonwealth air and sea communications. It is vitally important not to be deprived of the use of these islands for strategic purposes (Tamta, 1992).

Even at the time of transfer of power to India by the British Crown, the Defence top brass desired that Andaman should come under the British Government, because of their strategic importance as a potential naval and air base. Even over a century back in 1777 John Ritchie drew the attention of the Viceroy Warren Hastings on "the great utility" of these islands. Archibald Blair, who first surveyed these archipelago in 1788 stressed on the strategic location of these islands and its vulnerability from naval point of view. In the later period, when question was raised about the evacuation of these islands or closing down of the penal settlement in Andaman as recommended by the British high level committee, the matter did not materialize for many reasons. Some of the important ones are: (1) *the existence of about 3000 "Local Born"(the descendents of convicts) who could not be repatriated to any particular provinces of India*; (2) *the commercial value of the forests*; (3) *the strategic importance of the islands*; and *(4) the large amount of money spent on establishing the settlement* (Mazumder, 1975).

Burma (now Myanmar) and Malaysia wanted to set up colonies in these islands. All these factors forced the British Emperor to occupy these islands. Their primary objective was to exercise maritime hegemony over the Indian Ocean (Chowdhury, 2004). During Second World War, the Japanese occupied these islands. They also realized the strategic importance of these islands from war point of view. They utilized these islands as vital military base for an advanced war strategy in their favour. During their short stay in Andaman, particularly at Port Blair, the capital of the Japanese forces, they had built hundreds of bunkers around the sea coast/belt of South Andaman. Their military preparations and building of these bunkers signified the importance of these Islands for the Japanese Emperor, who did not want to lose this area during war.

During post-Independence period the government has also come to realize the importance of Indian Ocean and Andaman and Nicobar Islands from security point of view and also the International Trade route. Time and again, there have been series of diplomatic activities with neighbouring countries in South-East Asia and countries in the Indian Ocean, regarding the safety and security of these islands which has become a vital issue for our government. This chain of islands lies in the Bay of Bengal as gateway of international sea route of the Indian Ocean. It is one of the busiest trade routes for the Gulf Countries, who are the exporters of oil to the entire South-East Asia, of which China is the main trader. China has become a big player in the area of international trade and wants to play a crucial role among small South Asian nations including nations like Sri Lanka, Maldives etc. China has realized the importance of these islands nations.

As the Indian Ocean is the main sea route for all these nations, this sea territory has become a haven for sea piracy, smuggling, gun running, narcotic drug peddling and illegal fishing. All these illegal trade links ultimately sensitize the question of Indian security. However, India's security is directly linked to her small neighbouring countries, i.e. Bangladesh, Bhutan, Maldives, Sri Lanka, Myanmar, Thailand and Pakistan. Defence analyst Commodore C. Uday Bhaskar said, "The Andaman and Nicobar Islands are crucially located offering a strategic view over the shipping traffic between the Gulf and the Malacca Straits" (Indian Foreign Policy 1996, World Focus).

It is a safe passage for narcotic drug trafficking through the Golden Crescent in which traffickers from countries like Pakistan, Iran, Afghanistan including Myanmar, Thailand are involved. The extremists of Pakistan and also extremist groups of some other neighbouring countries are also active in drug trafficking and gun running by using wide sea territory and also sometimes sea ports of some countries to supply arms to North-East secessionist groups active in India. In December 2000, Lt. General T.S. Shergill, the General Officer Commanding, 3 Crops based in Nagaland's Dimapur town, while briefing the Press in Agartala, and said "We have information that arms consignment worth 750000 US Dollar which comprises AK series rifles, mortars, landmines, stenguns and high powered explosives, is coming into the Northeast from Cox Bazar" (Chaudhary, 2004). On their way, they even use few small islands in North Andaman as routes of halting. The coastal areas of the neighbouring countries have become a safe area for terrorists in the shipment of drugs and arms.

The well known naval expert, the US Navy Admiral Alfred Thayer Mahan said that whoever controls the Indian Ocean, dominates Asia. "This Ocean is the key to the seven seas in the twenty first century, the destiny of the world will be decided in these waters" (Sharma, 2010). The Indian Ocean has always been the nerve centre of international scenario due to its geo-strategic significance. It is the busiest route of cargo transportation. On an average, more than 300 ships traverse the sea route. Forty super tankers also pass through the water territory. Each year crude oils worth 250 billion US dollars passes through the straits of Harmuz and 70 million US dollars worth through the Malacca Straits to Japan and China. The Indian Ocean is a gateway for heavy international maritime traffic that includes half of the world's containerized cargo, one-third of its oil shipment.

During 1980s, the container traffic was 36 million, which has gone up to 300 million containers in 2009. The Malacca has strategically important point as world's busiest sea route covering over more than 70 per cent of world sea trade transaction. It finds its due consonance in India's *Look East Policy,* whose security is to India's vital economic and military interest in the vast Indian Ocean region area (Sharma, 2010). The main strategy of China is to have a good and cordial relations with Myanmar, Sri Lanka and other countries in the Indian Ocean route by offering infrastructural development projects, like construction of national port at Hambantota, coal power plant at Norachcholai in Sri Lanka. The Hambantota happens to be very close to India. The construction of this port will bring China within the breathing distance of India's southern coast where installation of sensitive power plants has been made. It would also help China in keeping a track of India's nuclear space and naval establishment in South India.

China has assisted Myanmar in the modernization of its naval infrastructure and building oil and gas pipeline connecting it to the port of Kyankpya on the Bay of Bengal, rail link *via* Myanmar to Chittagong port. With the construction of Sona-deep sea port at Cox Bazar, development of existing facilities at Sittwe near Bangladesh border and the development of radar facilities in the Coco-Island at a distance of only 30 nautical miles from the Andaman Land fall Island. India's primary concern is to counter the threat posed by China's "encirclement", i.e. her growing presence in the Bay of Bengal, especially its new foray in Bangladesh, Sri Lanka and Myanmar. However, India's interest to recognize Indian Ocean as a Zone of Peace is also aimed to ensure the security of its maritime boundaries and to guard its interests in the vast water territory. The newly built Andaman Nicobar Command (ANC) is intended to stop the Chinese from the east of the Malacca Strait.

According to Pankaj Dadh, "The geo-political setting of Coco-Island to Indian southern boundaries which is strategically located between the Indian Ocean and the Andaman sea in North of Andaman Islands, has put additional security pressure on Indian Defence from the Bay of Bengal. The Coco island, therefore, provides an ideal location for China to observe Indian naval and missile defence launch facilities in the whole of Andaman and Nicobar Islands and activities of the Indian navy on entire eastern Indian Ocean. Today China operates a signals-intelligence collection facility from the great Coco islands." Long back, Jawaharlal Nehru also justified the importance of Indian Ocean to India. He stated "The road to Asian hegemony goes through Indian Ocean" (Dadh, 2009).

India alone is facing multi-faceted challenges to make the Indian Ocean free from War zone. America's presence in Diego-Garcia is an additional problem for India in the road map to declare Indian Ocean as free peace zone. Moreover, it is a hectic exercise for Indian Defence and sea surveillance force to launch operations against poachers, who often illegally fish in the Andaman sea. The regular capture of foreign trawlers in Andaman water territory shows the presence of poachers in North Andaman Islands and also some other islands. Varieties of sea fishes and other valuable sea wealth in the water territory of the Indian sea, are the main attraction of neighbouring poachers. Every year, hundreds of poachers are arrested along with their fishing boats giving an alarm to our defence and our surveillance force to save the vast sea wealth from sea piracy, fishermen and hunters. The illegal hunting, fishing and poaching by foreign nationals in the tribal reserve areas in the Jarawa territories in the west coast of South Andaman, Sentinal Island and Little Andaman, Terresa. Trinket and Telang Chang islands in Nicobar group of Island are the major concern. These poachers often visit these remote and isolated islands and exploit resources meant for this tribal communities. The statistics of last ten year show that 3240 persons were apprehended along with 85 trawlers by the Coast Guard's anti-poaching forces. All were engaged in fishing, clandestine activities and extracting timbers in Andaman areas. These poachers were from Myanmar, Indonesia, Sri Lanka, China, Thailand and Bangladesh (*The Daily Telegram*, July 2009, Port Blair).

Defence Establishment in these Archipelagos

Due to the growing presence of the Chinese threat in the Indian Ocean, the Government of India has put its sincere efforts to protect its long sea water from foreign illegal presence. Of late, the Indian Navy and Coast Guard have established their units in Andaman Territory. Presence of paramount Military establishment started in 1978 not only to protect 6033 km. long coastal line of the mainland, about 2000 km. of these islands from poaching and infiltration and to safeguard nearly 2 million sq. km. of her exclusive economic zone but also to thwart militant organizations for using scattered, isolated islands for nefarious activities (Chaudhary, 2004).

Serious views over arms and drug trafficking in the Bay of Bengal was recorded in *Outlook* magazine published on 26 March, 2001. The article highlighted that due to slackness in surveillance of the defence activities and leniency towards the Myanmar and LTTE rebels, the seas off the Andaman are not only being used in the drugs-arms trade but also the deserted Landfall Island and St. Martine Island of the Andaman groups are obtrusively misused as two main transit points in the trade (Gokhali, 2001).

The Andaman and Nicobar Command (ANC) was set up on 8 October, 2001 by three wings of Indian Defence Forces—Army, Navy and Air Force including Coast Guard under a command of Commander-in-Chief of Indian Defence Forces. The formation of ANC for these islands reveal its strategic importance and ensures impregnable surveillance and security in the Bay of Bengal. This unified Command assumes great importance and serious challenges in view of global problems of terrorism, narco-terrorism, drug trafficking, gun-running etc. during normal times. Moreover, it has also been protecting the economic and commercial interest of the country by its constant vigilance in the territorial water as well as the Exclusive Economic Zone (EEC) (Choudhary, 2004).

"Dr. Manmohan Singh (former Prime Minister) consistently defined India's maritime strategy in terms of economic links with its major trading partners spanning the rim countries of the Indian and Pacific oceans. The idea that the Indian and Pacific oceans, and the region connecting them, was an important strategic space for India, given the flow of goods and energy, was implicit in Dr. Singh's view of Indian maritime strategy. India had created the Andaman and Nicobar Command (ANC) to keep an eye on this region and to police it" (Bharu, 2014).

The cutting of trees and other forest materials is totally banned in Island's forests. The Hon'ble Supreme Court of India has imposed a ban on deforestation to protect the ecology and marine life, fauna and flora of these islands. But ironically, sometimes the foreign nationals are illegally cutting and logging the valuable commercial woods and forest items from remote islands of North Andaman and destroying our environment. The serious thing is that the foreign poachers are also entering the Jarawa reserve areas and Sentinel Islands as well as Little Andaman and exploiting forest resources from these areas. The local poachers are also active in destroying forest and marine resources. Illegal fishing in our water territory by the people from the foreign nations like Myanmar, Bangladesh, and Thailand has become a regular feature. Every year crores of worth of fishes are caught by foreign fishermen from our sea. In spite of strong vigilance by the Coast Guard and Naval wing the illegal fishing in our sea water has not come under control. As a result India is losing a substantial amount of her national wealth.

It has also become a difficult task for the local police to keep them in custody and start judicial proceedings against them. On one or two occasions, these foreign nationals have tried to escape from jail. Illegal fishing is a serious threat for our security agencies, especially the Coast Guard and Navy. Every year from 2000 to 2009, more than 300 foreign nationals were apprehended with their trawlers from Andaman sea. During the same period, 83 trawlers/fishing boats with modern equipments for fishing were captured by our surveillance forces.

India's the then Foreign Minister Shri S. M . Krishna had informed Parliament on 31st August, 2010 that "The Government of India has come to realize that China has been showing more than a normal interest in the Indian Ocean affairs." However, India's interest to recognize Indian Ocean as a Zone of Peace also aimed to ensure the security of its maritime boundaries and to guard its interests in vast water territory. The newly built ANC is intended to stop such foreign countries like China from the east of the Malacca Strait.

A serious view has been recorded in the daily local newspaper *The Andaman Sheekha* (25.12.2014) "the presence of foreign nationals in the Bay Islands which is posing a serious threat to our national security from military point of view." It is quoted by the daily news as the Home Ministry has told the Parliamentary Standing Committee on Home Affairs that The A & N Islands have possibly been used by Sri Lanka, Myanmar, Bangladesh citizens as their community people are already settled in various islands. The Home Ministry has informed that the "The UT government is of the view that left out LTTE cadres may look for safe havens in the near vicinity and may take advantage of our uninhabited islands for their temporary hideouts." A large number of islands are scattered and difficult to access and these are possibly good places to hide for anti-nationals. The Standing Committee further informed that "In fact the geographical locations and conditions make these islands an ideal place for providing safe havens for terrorist groups for jungle warfare training and even dumping grounds for arms and ammunitions." On many cases illegal Bangladeshi nationals have been booked in Bengali settlements. These Bangladeshis often intrude into this sea territory. It is sometimes, difficult for the local police to identify them as their language and other physical appearances are similar to Indian Bengali settlers in these islands. It is reported that these islands consist of deep tropical jungles, and the remoteness of these gives the advantage to go deep into the creeks and jungles to take shelters.

BIBLIOGRAPHY

Bharu, Sanjaya (2013): *The Accidental Prime Minister: The Making and Unmaking of Dr. Manmohan Singh*, p. 170, 2014. New Delhi: Penguin Books India.

Dodh, Pankaj (2009): Emerging Sino-India Relations in Indian Ocean Region in the Context of Recently Opened Deep Water Port at Gwadar and its Strategic Implications to India's Maritime Security in *South Asia Politics*, Vol. 8, February.

Mazumder, R.C. (1979): *The Penal Settlement in Andaman,* New Delhi: Government of India, Ministry of Culture.

Ray Chaudhary, Rabin (2004): *The Black Days; Japanese Occupation in Andaman*. New Delhi: Manas Publishing House.

Sharma, Sourabh Jyoti (2010): Indian Ocean in the 21st Century: Formulating a Futuristic Maritime Strategy for India in *South Asia Politics*, Vol. 9, May, 2010.

Tamta, B.R. (1992): *Andaman and Nicobar Islands,* New Delhi: National Book Trust of India.

Bhaskar, Uday C., (1996): Indian Foreign Policy, *World Focus*.

Andaman Sheekha (2014): The presence of foreign nationals in the Bay islands, Local Daily News Paper, 25.02.2014, Port Blair.

The Daily Telegram, I and P, A & N Administration, July 2009, Port Blair.

4
Strategic Importance of the Andaman and Nicobar Islands

A Historical Perspective

N. Francis Xavier

When we look at the map of India we several times miss out the long line of dots in the Bay of Bengal that lies closer to Burma (now Myanmar) and Thailand than to mainland India. Not many are aware that Indira Point, the southernmost tip of the archipelago, is also the southernmost point of India, being further down the latitudes than Kanyakumari (Cape Comorin). The northern most tip of the Andaman and Nicobar chain is only 103 km. away from the Myanmar's territory of Cape Negrais. The southernmost Indira Point is just 144 km. away from the northern tip of Sumatra. It also abuts one of the busiest shipping lanes of the world leading to the Malacca Strait.

At an average distance of about 1200 km. from any part of mainland India on the eastern seaboard, the Islands become the farthest outpost of our country. A quick glance at the map shows that Sri Lanka is 1400 kms, Chennai 1130 kms, Vizag 1200 kms, Calcutta 1255 km, Bangladesh 1367 km, Myanmar 600 km, Thailand 450 km, Malaysia 600 km, Indonesia 163 km. and the Coco Islands 60 km. from the Andaman and Nicobar Islands. This 700 km. long chain of 572 "islands, islets and rocks" is a Union Territory governed by the Centre. There is hardly any revenue earned from the Islands but still, the Government of India spends about 1000 crore of rupees every year on these Islands. The reasons are obvious. The Islands form a long bulwark in the middle of the Bay of Bengal against any misadventure by an enemy country. They are strategically located in an area traversed by ancient trade routes. Ships of the various kingdoms of India plied regularly to countries in the east with merchandise and Indian culture. Buddhism and Hinduism travelled along these routes all the way to Thailand, Cambodia, Vietnam, China, Korea and Japan. The Balinese temples are examples of Hindu influence in Indonesia.

The earliest references to the islands, therefore, are found in mythology, that too for strategic reasons. Some believe that Lord Rama first thought of using the islands to launch his attack on Sri Lanka. The name Andaman seems to have originated from the name Hanuman, Lord Rama's trusted follower, which in Malay is pronounced Handuman. However farfetched this argument may appear that it is evident that the world knew about their existence long before many countries have been discovered.

The Islands figure in one of the earliest maps of the known world prepared by Ptolemy…or Claudius Ptolemaeus, the famous Egyptian astronomer, mathematician and geographer. Ptolemy calls these islands by the name Agadaemon, a land of cannibals. The presence of the Islands on the 1st century A.D. map clearly shows that these were well known to ancient seafarers. The Islands find mention in the writings of I-Tsing the seventh century Chinese Buddhist pilgrim, who seems to have visited both the Andamans and the Nicobars. This clearly shows that a sea route linking China with India passed through the Islands even in those times. As the trade route passed by the ancient kingdoms along the Sunda and Malacca Straits, their rulers tried to participate in the trade and also exert their influence as the route passed through their territories.

Sri Vijaya the 7th Century Buddhist Kingdom of southern Sumatra controlled the Straits for a long time and levied tributes on the shipping that passed through. Sri Vijaya's hegemony lasted till the 11th century when the Chola Kings of India attacked it repeatedly and established their own power over the trade routes. The Chola King Rajendra had inscriptions written in which he claimed to have conquered the Nicobars, which he called as Nakkavaram or the land of the naked.

That the shipping has increased much between China and India with the passage of time is evident from the writings of Marco Polo, the thirteenth century Venetian traveller. Marco Polo sailed past the Islands on his way to China from Venice. He called the Andamans 'Angamanian and the Nicobars as Necuverum and described the people as cannibals with faces like dogs. China's Mongol Emperor Kublai Khan sent a fleet to the Java Sea in 1293 to demand tribute from the Straits kingdoms. This is again an indication of the growing strategic importance of the islands that lay along the India-China trade route.

Between the 14th and 16th Centuries the Islands did not attract much attention, but, with the emergence of the Portuguese, Spanish and the English explorers looking for new lands to conquer and colonize, ships started plying in large numbers through the Malacca Straits.

With the invention of instruments which can measure the longitude and latitude accurately travelling by sea became easier and less hazardous. By the seventeenth century 'Hydrographers', whom we may today call surveyors of the sea, started sailing across the hitherto uncharted seas of the world, preparing excellent navigational charts and almanacs. Their aim, ostensibly, was to make shipping safer, but there was a hidden motive also. They wanted to find safe harbours and havens where the expanding fleets of the empire could assemble, shelter and refit. They could also control the busy shipping lanes, keep them free from pirates, and, perhaps, set out on a conquest. Surveyors and Hydrographers like John Ritchie (1777) and Archibald Blair (1789) explored the Islands and made extensive and accurate maps. John Ritchie was the first to mention "the great utility" of the Islands in a letter to Warren Hastings, the Governor General of India.

Blair founded the settlement first at present day Port Blair and then shifted it to Chatham Island in North Andaman, which was named again as Port Cornwallis, ostensibly for the purpose of setting up a naval arsenal there. It was while the work on the settlement was in progress that the strategic location of the Islands was put to use for the first time. On 13th June, 1793 news was received that England was at war with France. Maj. Kyd who was in charge of the settlement at once put it on a state of high alert. Fortifications and armaments were put in place. Proposals were sent to acquire artillery and arm the ships attached to the settlement. The aim was to protect the settlement against attacks by the enemy country and also to deny it access to the shipping lanes. All the recommendations of Maj. Kyd were approved by the Governor General, although the reinforcements never arrived. The settlement, however, had to be disbanded due to the extremely high rate of sickness and mortality.

The second time the strategic location of the Islands was put to use was during the First Anglo-Burmese War (1824-1826). Port Cornwallis became the rendezvous for assembling a fleet for the invasion of Burma. The fleet carrying the army of Sir Archibald Campbell, a veteran of the Mysore Wars, to Rangoon assembled in the capacious harbour of Port Cornwallis. Thanks to this vantage point the British were able to carry the war into the enemy territory, which would have taken a long time *via* the land route. The army on the Chittagong front could make little progress, meeting stiff resistance from the Burmese. However, the expeditionary force of 5000 soldiers sailed stealthily from Port Cornwallis, entered the Rangoon River and anchored off the town of Rangoon on 10th May, 1824.

The ships' guns battered the city defences before the soldiers were landed. Rangoon was taken in twenty minutes! The Andaman Islands were successfully used as a launch pad for striking at the enemy and taking him by surprise. Regular supply of weapons was also possible along the sea route. When besieged in Rangoon the British could get a supply of rockets which were used both for offence and psychological effect.

In 1844 another incident occurred emphasizing their strategic location and the need to have a garrison of some sort there, which can come to the aid of ships in distress. Two British troop ships— The *Briton* and the *Runnymede*, sailing from two different points on the globe, ran aground on John Lawrence Island on the same day during a terrible storm. The ships carried soldiers and their families numbering 620. Following military discipline and making optimum use of materials salvaged from the ships the survivors spent 54 days on the desolate island. During the period they cleared the forest, laid a vegetable garden, fought off the aborigines and built a boat that was sent to bring a rescue ship. In spite of the hardships only seven adults and some children died.

The arrival of the convict mutineers in 1858, after the First War of Independence of 1857, started a new chapter in the history of the Andaman and Nicobar Islands. The old harbour has been named Port Blair and a penal colony of self-supporting convicts came up with Ross Island as its headquarters.

A jail and gallows were erected on Viper Island. Soon the Nicobars were also annexed by the British and another penal colony came up on the island of Kamorta. European and native troops were stationed at both places. With the advent of steam engine the waters around the islands were patrolled more frequently by ships of the

Royal Navy. Using the Islands as a transit base they could extend their power over the Strait Settlements also. Frequent incidents of piracy in the Nicobars were put down by the Naval frigates. The waters were made safe for merchant shipping. It is believed that some ships from the naval garrison at Port Blair were sent to China during the Second Opium War.

However, with growing rivalry between England and Russia concern was voiced about the defenceless state of the Andaman and Nicobar Islands in 1885 itself. Col. Cadell, then Chief Commissioner and Superintendent of the Settlement, in his confidential letter No. 119 dated Port Blair, the 23rd April, 1885 wrote, "In view of the apparently not improbable eventuality of war with Russia I deem it my duty to bring the defenceless state of this settlement to the consideration of the Government of India." He felt that, "If no means are taken to protect the settlement, Port Blair might become a very convenient rendezvous for the enemy cruisers sent to prey on the commerce of the Bay of Bengal." (This apprehension proved to be true a few years later when the German raider Emden attacked and sank many ships and shelled coastal towns and cities during the First World War. Her presence in the island waters has been recorded by its sighting by Rani Lachmi of Nancowry.)

Cadell went on to say that the harbour should be protected by torpedoes and the garrison strengthened with more troops. Going further he says that perhaps I shall not be considered as going beyond my province if I venture to express my opinion that Port Blair might be used as a very important strategical centre for the operations of our men of war. He strongly lobbies for laying a telegraph cable between the Islands and Calcutta by saying that the squadron at Port Blair, being in a centrically position could act in any direction on receipt of reliable news by wire, all ports around the Bay, of course, telegraphing their news daily to the Senior Naval Officer at Port Blair. We may see that Cadell in his wisdom as a military strategist and veteran of the First War of Independence of 1857 has foreseen and planned what we were able to implement more than 100 years later.

However, Cadell's proposal were struck down by the cost-conscious British Indian government of those days. Replying his letter Mr. A. Mackenzie, Secretary to the Government of India wrote that the "Governor General in Council, after reconsidering the question of the establishment of telegraphic communication with the settlement, is not prepared at the present time to incur the large expenditure which the construction and maintenance of the cable would involve." But, the question of the defence of the islands had been taken seriously and the Inspector General of Military Works was asked to "depute an officer of experience to visit Port Blair for the purpose of preparing a full report of the means that should be adopted, and the probable cost that should be involved in placing that port in a fair state of defensive security." (Letter No. 479, MW., dated Simla the 21st May, 1885).

When the First World War broke out there was not much activity in the Islands or the sea around them except for stray incidents. No reinforcements were stationed at Port Blair during the period. The Andaman Sea was open for the lone German raider Emden which sank a number of merchant shipping in the waters before it was sunk off the Keeling Islands.

Due to the absence of British war ships in the Bay of Bengal and the Indian Ocean Emden could strike with impunity at the busy steamer lanes between Singapore, Calcutta, Madras and Bombay. On 22nd September, 1914 Emden attacked Madras and fired 130 shells, setting on fire the fuel stocks in the city and sending a wave of panic, leading to a mass exodus from the city. It is believed that Emden passed close to Nancowry Island when Rani Lachmi, the tribal leader in charge of the island, hoisted the Union Jack mistaking it to be a Royal Navy ship. Emden thought there might be British presence nearby and sailed away.

Even after the First World War and the Emden incident the British did not think it proper to use the Islands for strategic purposes. Perhaps they thought that the heavily fortified Singapore was sufficient to stop any advance from the East. The Japanese, however, realized the importance of the Islands. Under the guise of pearl divers Japanese spies had been visiting Port Blair in the late 1920s and carefully mapping the seabed for a future invasion. Two Japanese photographers and a Japanese dentist living in Port Blair at that time were supposed to have supplied vital information to the Nippon army. They were arrested on suspicion and deported to Fort William. But it was already too late. When the Japanese landed in Port Blair on 23rd March, 1942 each soldier was armed with a map of the city. The landings took place without any resistance.

The British had left already. But the Chief Commissioner CF Waterfall and a couple of his personal staff stayed back. The next three years of the Japanese occupation is remembered with dread even today by the local population as a reign of terror. The most gruesome incident during the period was the public beheading of Maj. A.G. Bird, Supply Officer and Secretary to the Chief Commissioner.

The strategic location of the Andaman was put to maximum use by the Japanese. They built solid coastal defences and laid roads. A chain of pillboxes and bunkers, many of them still in pristine condition, rings Port Blair and surrounding areas. Huge naval guns removed from Singapore were mounted at strategic locations on the Port Blair coast.

Anti-aircraft defences were mounted around vital installations. Bunkering and supply facilities for ships and submarines were provided. The aim was to use the Islands, as the British did during the First Anglo-Burmese War, as a springboard for an invasion of mainland India *via* Burma. The Japanese almost succeeded in their objective, reaching up to Nagaland but with heavy attrition on both sides.

The Japanese did, however, use the islands effectively during their three-year occupation, maintaining their supremacy in the waters. It was only towards the end of the war that stray British submarines and Allied bombers managed to inflict some damage on the Japanese installations in the Islands.

The visit of Netaji to the Islands in December 1944 was an important event during the occupation. The Japanese tried to convince the local population about their future plans for a 'co-prosperity sphere', in which the Asian people can be united under one banner and overthrow the western colonial yoke. However, the atrocities on the local population increased towards the end of the war. Many local people were condemned to death in many 'spy cases', and summarily executed.

At the end of the war the Japanese garrison surrendered to an Allied force that landed at Port Blair on 7th October, 1945. The formal surrender ceremony took place on 9th October, 1945 at the historic Gymkhana ground. Brig. A.J. Solomon, commanding the 116 Brigadc took the surrender on behalf of Admiral Louis Mountbatten, Supreme Allied Commander, South-East Asia.

The Second World War brought to fore the important role the islands could play in times of war. After the war, when the plans for granting independence to India were being drawn the British thought of retaining the Andaman and Nicobar Islands as a 'Crown Colony'. A little known fact was that Pethick Lawrence, the Minister of State

(India) wrote to the Viceroy that in the opinion of Chief of Staff Committee, the Andaman and Nicobar Islands must be retained under the hegemony of Great Britain. On 18th March, 1947 The Chief of Staff Committee expressed their plan to build airbases at Port Blair and Car Nicobar and to keep them under their control.

Although it was already decided that the Andaman and Nicobar Islands would form a part of Independent India, some desperate attempts continued to be made by Britain to retain the Islands under one pretext or other, obviously because of their strategic importance in the post-Second World War scenario and the changing geo-politics of the region. On 19th June, 1947 Frank Turnbull, Assistant Secretary to Draft Committee stated that the Committee had taken a decision to retain the Andaman and Nicobar Islands with Britain. The Muslim League felt that a part of the Islands should go to Pakistan. On 20th June, 1947 the Burmese press urged the Government of Burma to stake a claim for the ownership of the Islands since geographically the Islands were closer to Burma and have been administered from Burma for a long time. On 25th June, 1947 Lt. Gen. Hollice wrote a letter to the British Minister of Defence explaining the strategic importance of the islands and emphasizing on the British interest to build up Naval and Air Bases.

Even the Australian Government requested His Majesty's government to keep Australia informed of the negotiations with India for defence facilities on the Andaman and Nicobar Islands and to take into account the vital concern of Australia in the Indian Ocean line of communications, in view of the strategic importance of the Islands. It also advocated long-term lease of the islands' facilities including the right to station troops and maintain naval and air bases. The fate of the Andaman and Nicobar Islands hung in balance due to the conflicting claims of India, Pakistan, Burma and Britain over their ownership. Finally, due to the strong objections of Pandit Jawaharlal Nehru, on 4th July, 1947 Prime Minister Clement Atlee announced in the House of Commons that the Andaman and Nicobar Islands would be an inseparable part of India.

After Independence the need was to settle people in the remote territories, which were hitherto uninhabited, mainly with a view to discourage infiltration from neighbouring countries and to develop defence infrastructure. Under the settlement scheme settlers from West Bengal, Kerala, Madras, Burma, Mahe and Pondicherry and Ranchi were brought to the Islands from 1949 to 1954 and settled on North

Andaman, Middle Andaman, Baratang Island and South Andaman. Settlement in Great Nicobar was planned on the lines in which NEFA had been settled after the Indo-China conflict. Two batches of ex-servicemen settlers hailing mainly from Punjab were brought in 1969-70 to colonize the southernmost part of the island chain.

Upgradation and addition of defence facilities in the Islands also progressed at a brisk pace after Independence. First to be upgraded were the naval facilities. The naval base has been reinforced with the commissioning of INS Jarawa in the 60s. A couple of patrol vessels under the Eastern Command at Visakhapatnam were stationed for short intervals at Port Blair. INS Kardip at Kamorta followed. New FACs (Fast Attack Crafts) have joined the fleet recently.

In the 1980s INS Utkrosh, Naval Air Station was commissioned. A squadron of Island's aircraft of the Navy was stationed in the Islands along with Chetak helicopters for search and rescue operations. Slowly more facilities like ship support units, jetties, floating dry dock etc. were added. The ageing Islanders were replaced by Dorniers. New hangars and night landing facilities have been provided. The runway has been extended. COMAN (Commander A & N Islands) was re-designated as FORTAN or Fortress Commander A & N Islands. After the creation of Andaman and Nicobar Command a Commander-in-Chief of the rank of Vice Admiral looks after the defence related matters in the Islands.

During the Indo-Pak War of 1971 the Indian Navy's aircraft carrier INS Vikrant was positioned in the waters to deny access to Pakistani Navy from reaching East Pakistan. During the Second Gulf War Indian warships stationed at Port Blair were used to escort American warships passing through the Malacca Straits. Naval ships and aircraft were extensively used during the rescue and rehabilitation efforts after the Tsunami of 26th December, 2004.

The Second World War airstrip at Car Nicobar continued to be under the control of the IAF. However, the facilities were used by the RAF till the late 50s, mainly for refuelling. IAF transport aircraft ran a courier service to serve the small unit stationed there. During the 80s a Mi 8 squadron was positioned there. Hangars and residential facilities were built. The runway was extended and strengthened to take fighter aircraft. It became a proper airbase.

After the creation of the Unified Command for the Islands the air base has been equipped to operate the most modern fighter jets. A regular AN 32 courier service connects the base with Port Blair and

Tambaram (Chennai). It has night landing facilities. Although badly damaged by the Tsunami of 26th December, 2004, the base has been rebuilt and brought back to operational readiness in record time.

In the early years after Independence the Army maintained a token presence at Port Blair. In the 70s plans were drawn to develop a cantonment in the outskirts of Port Blair. A full-fledged Brigade Headquarters has come up accordingly. Army units are also involved in the combing operations searching for foreign poachers.

A Coast Guard Regional Headquarters also functions under the A & N Command. They are equipped with helicopters, Dorniers and one OPV.

During the 1980s when construction of facilities for a naval base with Chinese support was detected on Cocos Island of Myanmar, which lies close to the northern most tip of the island chain, there was tension between the two countries. Aerial reconnaissance revealed what appeared to be submarine berths. The matter was denied by the Chinese. But recent reports of the presence of the Chinese spy ships in the waters around the islands once again raises fears of the Chinese interest in the waters as they are now a global power, both militarily and economically. In this connection the little known visit of the Chinese Ambassador to the Islands may be recalled. The author of this paper was assigned the job of liaison officer to the Ambassador.

During his visit to Port Blair in May 1998 the then Defence Minister George Fernandes said, "As far as the discussions between China and India are concerned, they should go on in a spirit of good-will and there are no outstanding issues between us which cannot be settled through a dialogue." He was commenting on the Chinese objection to his earlier statement about "Beijing constituting India's main threat and the Burmese denial about Chinese surveillance station at Coco Island (*Andaman Herald*, May 8, 1998).

Consequent upon the 'Look East Policy' of the Government of India a combined Naval exercise of littoral states, named 'Milan' is being held every two years. Navies of Thailand, Myanmar, Sri Lanka, Indonesia, Malaysia, Bangladesh and Singapore join the exercises. Sometimes, Australia too sends its military attachés as observers. Milan 2005, cancelled due to the Tsunami, was held in 2006. Apart from Milan 'Ind-Indo CORPAT', a joint patrolling exercise of the Indian and Indonesian Navies, aimed at checking poaching and piracy, is held periodically. Goodwill visits from neighbouring navies are held regularly. After the BIMSTEC (Bay of Bengal Initiative for Multi-

Sectoral Technical and Economic Cooperation) declaration the importance of the islands has further increased as the BIMSTEC countries, except for Nepal and Bhutan, lie close to the Islands. In the present geo-political scenario of growing ties with Myanmar, China, Thailand and Indonesia the Islands have an important role to play as India's closest frontier to these countries.

An important step in highlighting the future development of the Islands was the seminar: Andaman and Nicobar Islands Vision 2025. The two-day seminar held on 25th and 26th August 2005 by the Andaman and Nicobar Command was attended by a galaxy of eminent speakers drawn from civil and military as well as local officials of the A & N Administration.

The objective of the Seminar was "to define the roles the Islands would play in coming years, keeping with our 'Look East' and 'Maritime Projection' policies and thereafter quantify infrastructural needs to support these policies.

The five sub-themes of the Seminar were:

1. Post Tsunami Review,
2. Economic Development,
3. Strategic Perspective,
4. Changing roles, and
5. Force and Infrastructural Development.

At the conclusion of the Seminar The Vision Statement stated the summary of recommendations as "To develop A & N as 'Islands of Excellence', endowed with world class tourism infrastructure, a marine produce export hub and centre for organic farming, thereby achieving self-sustaining revenue surplus model economy by the year 2025."

In the recent time the world super power United States of America has also started showing interest in the islands. The visit of USS Defender and earlier visits by other ships are indications of growing interest of the US in the region.

It is clear that the Islands are poised to play a major role in India's 'Look East Policy' because of their strategic location. They, no doubt, are a bulwark for the entire eastern seaboard of India, and, at the same time, an extension of India's power deep into the Far East. In the times ahead the Islands are destined to serve as a key hub for implementing our foreign policy towards our South East Asian neighbours. The future of the Islands is bright and full of hope, and their name "Islands of Good Fortune" as mentioned in ancient maps may come true.

BIBLIOGRAPHY

Andaman and Nicobar Command (2005): *Andaman and Nicobar Islands Vision 2025*. The two-day seminar held on 25th and 26th August, 2005. Port Blair.

Andaman Herald, Friday, May 8, 1998.

Letter No. 479, MW., dated Simla, the 21st May, 1885.

5
Illegal Immigration and its Impact on Security of Andaman and Nicobar Islands

R. V.R. Murthy

Introduction

The region of Andaman and Nicobar islands is characterized by vast distances across the sea between continental landmass but dotted with atolls and relatively small clusters of islets and islands, prone to illegal immigration and poaching activities since its existence on political map of world. The 572 islands and islets make up the region into 8,326 square miles, in general terms and the area is spread into 745 kilometres long from north to south. Many of these islands were consolidated by the British in the aftermath of 1857 revolt to transport nationalist and hard core criminals.

The purpose of this article is to briefly discuss the magnitude of illegal immigration and alarming threat to strategic importance of Andaman and Nicobar Islands situated in the middle of the Bay of Bengal, particularly in the context of changing global security scenario. A subtle shift of defence orientation in the post-September 11 attacks on USA; presence of terrorist in the Ache province and piracy, its constant threat to the International Sea Lanes (ISLs) within the geo-strategic realm of the Andaman and Nicobar Islands, draw more attention to the foreign policy makers to safeguard the region from illegal migrants, poachers and drug-smugglers.

Geo-Strategic Importance of Andaman and Nicobar Islands

The strategic location of the island region in the midst of the Bay of Bengal has placed within easy reach of many sensitive areas including Indonesia (90 nautical miles), Myanmar (170 nautical miles); Thailand (270 nautical miles) and Fareast Asia. Similarly the strategic location of the Malacca Strait almost at the end of Island region gives central position in littoral countries of the Bay of Bengal politics. In recent years world has witnessed significant development in the field of intensification of trade-linked developments; essentially sea-borne trade has grown due to the globalization of the world economy including energy, capital and access to the markets, which forms new order of the day. This changed perception was reflected in series of policy initiatives, which came to be known as the "Look East" policy and BIMSTEC-RC. In this process of rapidly changing world, India is developing a more holistic and focused approach in keeping with its security and strategic perspectives in relation to the littoral states of the Bay of Bengal.

Illegal Migration: A Major Security Threat

Most littoral countries of the Bay of Bengal in particular are dogged by internal problems that bear an uncanny resemblance to their external problems. A number of extremist groups under the cover of Islamic movement, have become active in drug trafficking, gun-running and anti-Indian activities. It is widely acknowledged that Pakistan ISI has nurtured a number of extremist Islamist groups, such as the Harkat-ul-Jehad-al-Islami, in the port city of Chittagong and put a number of secessionists rebels from India's northeast in touch with this terrorist network. As a result, north of Andaman Islands, Bangladesh coasts areas have become a nest of terrorists involved in the shipment of drugs and arms. A pattern of arrests and seizures indicate that arms are brought by the terrorists from Laos, Cambodia, Thailand and Chittagong from where they are transported northward by land to Bhutan. The route from Kalikhole in Bhutan to Cox's Bazaar passes through the northern Bengal, Assam and Meghalaya and on into Chittagong. The most dealings occurred in the Bay of Bengal region. Drug trafficking leads to money laundering and funds from the sale of drugs are used to mobilize gun-running, insurgent and terrorist activities. Added to these is the transnational security concerned linked to human smuggling that has multiple effects, ranging from funding terrorism to illegal immigration causing socio-political instability in the region.

In recent years a large influx of foreigners into the islands by illegal means reported into media[1], and there were occasions where large scale illegal migrants were arrested by patrolling vessels in the mid-sea. One such incident draws the attention of the reader that 412 Bangladeshi illegal migrants left Chittagong by six mechanized boat to enter illegally into Malaysia. But these boats were intercepted and detained by the Thai Navy in high seas for about four weeks for preliminary investigation. Subsequently, these illegal migrants were transferred to a non-mechanized boat with some bags of rice and released in the high seas off Thailand coast. 102 persons of Bangladeshi and Myanmar nationals after 12 days reached Little Andaman coast. As per prevailing security scenario, the Coast Guard immediately launched "Operation Suraksha", to determine the veracity of the intelligent input. Accordingly, the CG vessels and Helicopters embarked on it and finally, they found that there were 88 persons on board the ill fated boat about 40 miles away of Little Andaman. The Joint Operation Cell (JOC) at Headquarters, Andaman and Nicobar Command (ANC) immediately jumped into action and sighted several dead bodies of north of Sandy Point. In its press release Coast Guard informed that 411 persons were abandoned at mid-sea in a non-mechanized boat. After 12 days of journey, some 300 persons reportedly jumped into the sea hoping to swim across to shore but almost all of whom are feared dead or missing[2]. How to deal with hundreds of these illegal migrants is a question to which there are no easy answers, particularly, if political parties support and provide asylum for consolidating vote bank.

Considering the islands huge strategic importance, New Delhi is coordinating the joint patrols with Indonesia in the Andaman Sea since 2002, occasional joint Naval exercises with Thailand to boost cooperation in curbing arms smuggling since 2003, are steps in the right direction and naturally succeeded by creating common states in the maintenance of peace and stability in the region. In fact, it would tend to encourage more organized anti-India outfits, such as the Pakistan ISIs and outside linked Maoists, to exploit these networks and weaken India's eastern flank. Currently, non-state threats to sea-lines in the Bay of Bengal pose the principal challenges. It is imperative for India to engage the Bay of Bengal and the Andaman sea particularly littorals in a calibrated manner. Another area that merits special attention in the context of India's security interest in the region is that a substantial part of India's external trade and energy supplies pass through this region.

Micro-Level Observation

The major challenge for the A & N Islands is to check illegal immigration. The immigrants are mainly shipped from Bangladesh, Myanmar and Sri Lanka (Tamils). While the demographic characteristics of these islands make it easy for these 'outsiders' to merge with the local populace in the short period, it eventually leads to socio-economic tensions, criminal activity and polarization of society on communal lines. There are also apprehensions of the ISI and China infiltrating these groups for subversive activities[3].

Demographic invasion from Bangladesh, has assumed serious security dimension. In many of the Bengali settler areas it has brought about a total demographic transformation, forcing the original inhabitants to leave their resources to illegal migrants from Bangladesh. Large scale Muslim infiltration from Bangladesh through West Bengal actually started in 2004 for Post-Tsunami reconstruction of damaged southern group of Islands. Most of them have come to Islands in search of jobs and some of them opted to come through contractors to execute construction work in Islands. They have acquired ration cards, enlisted their names in voter list, and even some of them managed to get Islanders Card through local patrons. It is also learnt that some of them marrying local Bengali women; these marital or family relations are often used to serve sinister purposes. Some local administrative machinery members of the politically motivated seems to be remain silent spectators in this regard. Consequently, the internal security of island territory and social harmony are in peril.

There is another side of this story, which is no less disturbing and no less dangerous. The Andaman and Nicobar Islands police have apprehended three illegal migrants of Bangladesh from Port Blair (South Point). This recent incident is evident that Bangladeshi people were coming to these islands illegally in large numbers; most of them remained unidentified for years. Only massive drive by local authorities can check this unwanted influx. This ceaseless increase of population through infiltration and other means assumes a new dimension when it slowly and steadily takes the shape of demographic invasion. The consequent socio-political disturbances can possibly destabilize the entire Andaman and Nicobar islands.

This large diaspora is no more only a cause of demographic changes, but, denial of economic opportunities and civic amenities to islanders. It provides convenient alibi and sheltering facility to the terrorists and fundamentalists who are now increasingly using the islands as a new and safe base. Thesc migrants also bring with them deeply grouted anti-indianism and seeds of fundamentalism. The islands are porous and the infiltration from the littoral states get full support from China particularly stationed at Great Coco Islands provide strategic guidance and financial support to enter into island region. Sources are also revealed that the Chinese are pushing illegal migrants to islands to collect necessary defence information and inputs of stationing of defence establishment in Andaman. The above scenario presents a formidable challenge to Island administration and Government of India. Numerical response of accretion in force levels, upgradation of the weaponry and equipments of the security forces, strengthening protective cover for targeted entities, are important but not adequate.

Poaching: Serious Threat to EEZ

The major role of defence forces stationed in Andaman and Nicobar Islands to protect the Exclusive Economic Zone (EEZ), a vast area of 5,95,217 sq.km, roughly 30 per cent of total EEZ of the country. There are two basic types of poaching activities prevailing in the region, i.e. poachers from neighbouring countries venture into the Andaman sea in small boats to the coast for collecting sea-cucumbers, timber, and fishing and crocodile hunting. Secondly, poaching by modern mechanized trawlers of littoral countries was actively involved in drug smugglers and gun runners. Every year poaching activities by foreign poachers usually starts from the first week of June.

The Navy and the Coast Guard are thc two maritime security agencies those were tasked with the security of the oceans, the coast and the Exclusive Economic Zone. The illegal Bangladeshi infiltration into Andaman and elsewhere in the region has changed its demography, and now it has become a serious threat to the future survival of the primitive tribal groups and also the internal security problem for the island region. The defence forces stationed in the Andaman Islands catching 15-20 per cent of the poachers as a large number of them were the Myanmarese and the Bangladeshis (See Table 5.1). The poachers usually come in small boats at night and escape in bigger vessels that are lurking outside India's territorial waters. In many occasions the patrolling vessels of the Coast Guard and ANC are unable to catch since they possess high speed boats and other satellite communication devices for navigational use. A massive drive is essential to destroy the permanent bases and hideouts set up by the poachers, but many more continued to exist in some remote islands. Poachers from Myanmar are increasingly preying on the fragile marine ecology of India's remote A & N Islands and have even set up hideouts. Sources revealed that there

Table 5.1: Illegal Poachers Apprehended in Andaman Waters

Year	*No. of Persons Apprehended*	*No. of Trawlers Apprehended*	*Nature of Crime*	*Nationality*
2001	208		Fishing, extracting timber and illegal activities	Myanmarese, Indonesian and Sri Lankans
2002	302	12	Fishing and clandestine activities	Myanmarese, Indonesian and Sri Lankans
2003	389	15	Fishing and illegal activities	Myanmarese
2004	300	13	Fishing and clandestine activities	Chinese, Myanmarese and Sri Lankans
2005	384	10	Entered into tribal reserved area and fishing	Myanmarese and Bangladeshi
2006	357	11	Fishing and extracting timber	Myanmarese, Bangladeshi, Sri Lankan and Indonesian
2007	390	9	Illegal activities and fishing	Myanmarese, Thai, and Sri Lankan
2008	412	8	Illegal Migration	Bangladeshi
2009	500	5	Fishing and illegal activities	Bangladeshi, Myanmarese and Sri Lanka*

* Five Sri Lankan boats along with 28 crew apprehended for illegally fishing in Andaman waters. (*The Daily Telegrams*, dt. March 16, 2009)

Source: *The Daily Telegrams*, Port Blair, A & N Islands.

is nexus between the Bangladeshi illegal migrants and the Myanmarese Rohingyas. Authorities are step up a battle against the rising number of boats sneaking in from Myanmar.

The Andaman and Nicobar Islands have been attracting foreign vessels that illegally fish in its waters, particularly those from the neighbouring Southeast Asian littorals. The 'fetch' from these waters, which abound in varied species of seafood and other marine organisms, is sold back home at very high prices. The easy availability of hi-tech nautical equipment in these countries (radar, refrigeration plants and GPS) miniaturized for small boats, facilitates evasion, endurance and precise navigation. Poaching by the foreign fishermen, if unchecked, could lead to depletion of fish stock and ecological imbalance, besides their attendant security implications. Such a threat from non-state actors pose a daunting challenge — if such activities are not interdicted at sea, it would become extremely difficult to take corrective measures.

The entry of foreign poachers in the Tribal Reserve is major concern, and there is strong feelings of discontent among the tribal population of southern part of Nicobar Islands. Poachers from littoral countries often visit these remote islands to exploit resources meant for the tribal people and such contact in the past became devastating because of the spread of epidemic disease, and sometimes created violent conflict with unsympathetic poachers conducting illegal timbering operations. The invasion on their land by poachers from outside and inside poses a serious threat to the primitive tribes, depleting wild foods on which the tribes are totally dependent. Entry to the tribal reserve by outsiders is illegal. This tragedy must surely galvanize the Andaman administration to act in order to keep illegal migrants off the tribal land.

New Delhi is fostering relations to build "bridges of friendship" with the maritime neighbours to check the menace. Indeed, particular importance is the need to engage Myanmar and Bangladesh, where China's influence is growing. This would also serve to enhance India's naval presence in the northern Bay of Bengal. India's interactions with Myanmar and other littoral countries will enhance to curb illegal migration and terrorist movement within geo-strategic realm of the Bay of Bengal. In order to prevent illegal fishing and to check on infiltration in the Andaman Islands, New Delhi embarked upon bilateral agreements for coordinated patrols with Myanmar, Bangladesh, Indonesia and Thailand. Although the maritime surveillance and policing capability of Andaman and Nicobar Islands has lately been improved considerably in the context of Mumbai attacks.

Repatriation and Goodwill Gesture

As a goodwill gesture to reciprocate the friendly ties between India and Myanmar have already vastly improved. India has always been trying to improve its relations with its neighbouring countries especially with politically torn states of the Bay of Bengal region. The Indian government encouraged the illegal migrants to repatriate to their respective countries since 2005. The following table will enable us the number of poachers so far repatriated to their respective countries.

Table 5.2: Year-wise Apprehended Poachers Repatriated

Year	*No. of Poachers Repatriated*	*Nature of Crime*	*Name of the Country the Poachers Belonging*
2005	129	Illegal fishing	Myanmar
2006	Not available		
2007	213	Illegal fishing	Myanmar
2008	360	Illegal fishing	Myanmar
2009	384	Illegal fishing	Myanmar

Source: Andaman and Nicobar Command (ANC) and *The Daily Telegrams*, July 19, 2009.

An official estimate in the year 2003 reveals that 50,000 foreigners have taken illegal shelter in the Andaman and Nicobar islands. Indeed the unofficial figures are much higher than this. A large number of them were Bangladeshis. As most of them were few technical skills and the Andaman have little demand for them in any case, they turn to smuggling and other unlawful activities. In 2001, according the Indian Army officials, the security forces launched a wide ranging operation to clear illegal poachers in some 300 uninhabited islands and found huge catch of arms. The arms are said to belong to the LTTE and other terrorist groups. The search and destroy operation was carried out by the Indian government after repeated request from Colombo in the early part of the year 2000. Similar search operations were conducted by the littoral countries of the Bay of Bengal to destroy the terrorists' hideouts.

India cooperating with the Myanmar in areas such as border

management, control of illegal trafficking of narcotics and border trade. A security dialogue with Myanmar has been maintained. The relationship is widening into a number of developmental areas. India already entered with Thailand to build a Dewei (Tavoy) Kanchanburi road link for ocean-*cum*-overland inter-state model transit from Indian ports. Recent Indo-Thai agreement to link the Andaman Sea and the Gulf of Thailand with an oil/gas pipeline and to link Port Blair with Phuket to encourage international tourism is a milestone in improving relations with littoral countries of the region. These initiatives could mark the beginning of the new era in keeping with the prevailing global security paradigm; 'territoriality' was in the forefront of India's perception of external security. This probably explains the erstwhile wariness and insecurity of the Indian political leadership with regard to the geographically distant Andaman Islands.

The Andaman and Nicobar islands have immense strategic value, and these could be used as a springboard for engagement of the eastern neighbourhood, i.e. ASEAN countries. This would also facilitate building political trust and reinforcing economic ties. Diplomacy and confidence-building would foster security bonds with the maritime neighbours to jointly combat common threats including illegal migration emanates from littoral countries.

BIBLIOGRAPHY

Andaman and Nicobar Command (ANC) and *The Daily Telegrams,* July 19, 2009.

Maitra, Ramtanu (2005): Trouble in India's Islands, www. atimes. com. February 13, 2005.

The Daily Telegrams (2008): December 28 and 29, 2008.www.andaman. nic.in

Yosef Bodansky, Beijing's Surge for the Strait of Malacca, www. geopolitics

6
A Strategic and Developmental Perspective of Andaman and Nicobar Islands

Pramod Sangwa

Global Overview

The world at large is in a state of flux. The last two decades have witnessed an unprecedented rise of China, both economically and militarily. There has also been relative decline in American power, because of financial meltdown, and US getting overstretched strategically, even though it maintains military and technological dominance. China poses challenge to its economic and strategic dominance most importantly in Asia and to a limited degree in Africa. Relative economic decline of the European Union further tilts the balance of power equation in Chinese favour. Though Russia is showing signs of resurgence, it remains ambivalent with its political and economic power in relative decline.

Geo-economic considerations call for greater collaboration but these may lead to conflicting geo-political interests. Energy and resource crisis is looming large leading to competition and conflicts. The financial imbalances could lead to extreme protectionism, autarchy, trade wars and perhaps a worldwide military (?) confrontation. There appears to be a clear economic power shift from Atlantic powers to Asia.

World today is witnessing growing clout of non-state actors and their increasing nuisance value, with an upsurge of radical forces — fundamentalism, and religious extremism leading to fawning terrorism. Increasing reliance on sea for trade and resource exploitation has given rise to incidents of maritime terrorism and piracy.

New range of competition dynamics has emerged, which covers: enemy, adversary, competitor, partner/ally and friend. Earlier peace time situation may be renamed as competition state. A partner/ally may also become a target, being a competitor in any key strategic aspect.

Regional Overview

India is located at the centre of the arc of instability. Neighbouring regions, West Asia, CAR and SE Asia score very high on the failing states index. All countries of South Asia except India have been categorized as highly failing states. India has two largest drug growing areas of the world in its periphery. Fundamentalist terrorism, separatism, sectarianism, ethnic, regional, religious/civilizational rivalries coupled with drug trafficking, arms running and organized crimes are on the rise causing concerns for one and all. Ongoing proxy war, aided and abetted from across the borders, insurgency in NE and LWE all add up to the woes of progressive India. Almost all our neighbours are grappling with their own internal issues. China's challenge in its newer and massive dimensions with Red Dragon is steadily increasing its presence and in India's neighbourhood, is undeniably inimical to our interests.

Andaman and Nicobar Islands

The Andaman and Nicobar Islands with her sun soaked and pristine beaches, incredible corals and marine life, an intriguing colonial past and the remnants of a stone age culture is not just a major tourist attraction but a paradise for strategic planners. A & N Islands present options for India to project its power and influence in consonance with its emerging status and role in the region. They also provide an ideal spring board for India to play a far more telling role in the area. Proximity to unstable littorals, coupled with the eventuality of extra-regional players extending their influence in the region, make them vulnerable to both conventional as well as sub-conventional threats. This translates into challenges and opportunities for India.

Opportunities

(a) Economic Potential:
   (i) Vast EEZ and its implications.
   (ii) Development of tourism without compromising security.
   (iii) Implications of development of fishery, shipping, natural resource exploration and commerce.

(b) Strategic Location.

Geographically closer to South East Asia, at the confluence of vital and busiest sea lines of communication, these Islands straddle the Ten and Six degree Channels leading to the Malacca Straits making the region one of great strategic relevance in India's geopolitical and geostrategic milieu. These Islands are our gateways to the East, and their significance in our national strategic calculus is increasingly being realised, as they fit perfectly in the context of India's 'Look East Policy'.

Challenges

(a) Remote location and the large number of uninhabited islands.
(b) Coupled to above, is the location of the islands in one of the most challenging seismic zones on the earth.
(c) Long extended monsoons with related problems of connectivity and communication, both inter and intra.
(d) The location of the islands lends its self to be the alternate destination for illegal immigration from the littorals, Bangladesh and Myanmar amongst others.
(e) Proximity to the Golden Triangle lends to the hostile mind, an added charm of drugs, gun running and piracy.
(f) China is fast emerging as a prominent sea power and its interests in the area are large and many. The dragon is fully dependant on the energy flow on the SLsOC, thus she would start making far and frequent forays into the IOR with rightful excuses to keep her assets deployed in the Indian waters; she has her interests to protect.
(g) In addition to all the above, there is a need to maintain

cultural, ethnic and religious balance here on the islands. The whole issue is weaved delicately with the thread of harmony which needs to be nurtured and preserved. How?

(h) Apart from the diversity and distance from the mainland the proximity of these islands to the unstable littorals has its own dynamics. The closest littoral is a nascent democratic state with a radical outlook amongst its populace. We need to be wary of the developments in our neighbourhood, more so in light of the ongoing 'GWOT' which may change form towards clash of civilizations.

The Andaman and Nicobar Islands need to be viewed through a multi- dimensional framework, comprising, Security, Economic and Environmental dimension.

Security Dimension

The location of these islands, deep in the Bay of Bengal provide invaluable strategic reach over the South East Asia region and the Straits of Malacca and Sunda, therefore, providing a significant strategic and security dimension. Islands function as Eastern bastion of the country and are at Gateway to IOR, located close to Indonesia, Thailand, Malaysia and Myanmar.

The islands are critical not only for protection of our interests but also for power projecting. Whether we need to look outward or inward depends to a large extent on how the geo-political landscape in the region evolves over the next decade. It will also depend on our capabilities and capacities to give shape to our intent. The security environment is a function of internal and external threats. The internal threats are dependent upon economic scenario, social equity and level of inclusive growth. The external threats are dependent upon events and interplay between countries having interests in the region. In the security perspective the major threats in A & N Islands are:

(a) Audacious terror attacks.
(b) Drug trafficking, Gun running, Piracy and Poaching.
(c) Occupation of uninhabited islands.
(d) Securitization of SLsOC.
(e) Conventional threats.

The islands have been traditionally treated as an outpost and have remained at the periphery of India's strategic thinking. We believe that the time has now come for a shift in the perception of the role of these islands in the Indian vision of the future. This shift is necessary not only to meet military threats but also to protect our economic interests. Trade with our neighbours, especially with ASEAN countries and China are increasing at a rapid rate. The islands are the key to ensure that this trade does not suffer. Here we share common interests with our neighbours in making sure the commercial shipping and trade routes are protected.

For the strategic options to remain viable, the development of the basic military and civil infrastructure of the islands becomes essential. It is also necessary that this development be clearly visible to our neighbours. We believe that this calls for a significant increase in our investments and resources allocated to the Islands. While we are certainly making some investments along these lines, these need to be enhanced significantly in the next few years.

(a) We have to have an all-round surveillance capability to cover ingress into IOR.
(b) In order to maintain a dissuasive deterrent, we need to develop present airports, into full length all weather, all aircraft capable runways have to be implemented on priority.
(c) It is imperative to have a visible, strong and deterrent military capability at these island. A self-sustaining military capacity should be permanently positioned on the Islands with expeditionary capabilities.
(d) We have to have an all-round surveillance capability to cover ingress into IOR.

Economic Dimension

The second dimension and one that occupies the attention of strategic thinkers and policy makers the most, is economic development. The islands are no exception to this need, and therefore, we need to address the question of the economic development of these islands.

The Andaman and Nicobar Islands appear small *vis-à-vis* Indian land mass, but they have huge economic potential which is yet to be tapped. Notwithstanding, their comparison with main land India, these islands constitute a considerable large land mass when compared with tropical island nations. With an area of 8249 sq. km, the Andaman and Nicobar Islands stand eight in size among 28 tropical island nations in the world and are larger than Trinidad and Tobago (5128 sq. km), Maldives (300 sq. km), Seychelles (451 sq. km) and Singapore (707 sq.km). They are almost as big as Jamaica (10830 sq. km).

Exploration of oil and other natural resources, fishery, forestry and tourism are areas offering great potential. The islands also contribute about 600,000 square kilometres to India's Exclusive Economic Zone (EEZ), which needs to be protected, preserved and managed. The development agenda for the EEZ should be determined by knowledge, and there should be no exploitation of resources without a sound understanding and intimate knowledge of these resources and their inter-relationships. If we compare with a country like Seychelles while the per capita income due to economic development is higher at $ 16600, the forest cover is only 66 per cent as against a forest cover of 90 per cent for our islands.

Fishery

The islands have a vast potential for fishery and marine products. Fishery has been identified as a priority sector for socio-economic development of the islands but there is a wide gap between the level of exploitation and the estimated fishery potential. Thus there is a need for developing offshore fisheries with provision of large deep-sea fishing vessels even while providing facilities for small scale fishermen near coasts and providing linkages with the South East Asian markets.

Eco Tourism

There is a need for promoting the Andaman and Nicobar Islands as an eco tourism destination. However, here, there is a need to ensure that these islands should be promoted exclusively for high value-low volume tourists, as is being done by Bhutan and Maldives. If we have exclusive destinations and develop them with exotic overlays with fast and comfortable vessels then automatically we will be steeping into the elite domain of high value tourism. In addition to this, there is also a need for developing new tourism linkages with the entire South East Asian region.

Natural Resources

The seas around the islands of A & N have huge deposits of oil and gas. Exploration has already been started in the region, a major oil or gas find shall change the complete geo-political balance in the region.

Development of a Transhipment Port on A and N Islands

Almost 70 per cent of the world's commercial traffic passes through this area. Development of South Eastern tip of Nicobar as a Transhipment Port for Container handling, bunkering and refuelling of international/national ships would provide great economic and strategic potential. This port could provide an alternative to Singapore and Colombo and becomes a major strength for India. Such an initiative will also help the country in fulfilling our growing ambitions in the fields of regional co-operation with South East Asia and the issues of the Look East Policy.

Unlike other parts and areas of India there are certain aspects that are specific to the islands that may dictate a different route for development. The development of the islands in our view should be conditioned by the two requirements of preserving security and preserving the environment.

Environmental Dimension

As a hot-spot of bio-diversity, with unique flora and fauna, both marine and terrestrial, and a high degree of endemism, these Islands have a significant environmental and ecological dimension. The great advantage that the islands provide from a fundamental research or knowledge point of view comes about once again from their geography. The islands are living laboratories for major initiatives in the study of the natural and social sciences. There is a need for a multi-disciplinary science-based approach to understand what we possess. The various tribes located on different islands are the living relics of humankinds past. The tools they use, the languages they speak and their links to languages spoken elsewhere are obvious areas of interest. Some of the tribes have made the transition into modernity whilst others have not done so. Comparative sociological and anthropological studies are once again themes of great interest.

In-depth studies of the flora and fauna on the islands are needed before we talk about harnessing the potential of the islands for development. If we do not do this there is a danger that we will destroy something that could turn out to have great value. Botany, Zoology, marine life studies, studies on coral islands and reefs are domains of knowledge requiring specific attention. The islands are located in an active seismic zone. Barren Island has the only active volcano in India. The creation of a multi-disciplinary research institute based on the special resources and problems of the islands and devoted exclusively to studies of each and everyone of the islands, seems to be a necessity. Developmental initiatives on Islands require sea, air and land based infrastructure, the same is also required for preserving security. This aspect has to be accorded top priority.

Effect of Climate Change

Tourism and prosperity in the islands is almost entirely depend on their natural ecosystem like coral reefs, mangroves, beaches etc. Climate change is known to have profound impact on the fragile ecosystems like coral reefs and mangroves. We have to undertake a wide range of measures to make sure these are protected. Not all islands will experience the same type of hazards and even those experiencing the same hazards will not experience the same severity of hazard. The severity of a hazard will vary by island depending on geo-physical, social and economic characteristics.

Conclusion

Andaman & Nicobar Islands have immense strategic and economic value. However, we need to bridge the gap between potential and reality. These Islands need impetus for indigenous growth and development. Location of GNI capping Six Degree Channel provides good opportunity to harness geo-political and economic advantages. Security concerns emanating from China compel early development of security infrastructure on the Islands.

The way ahead logically is development. Easier said than done; the issues of development have their own dynamics on these islands. Also development needs to be balanced with the ethnic and local life. Preservation, morals and ethical issues are linked to this fundamental aspect of development. The challenge lies in harnessed development and prevention of skewed vectoring of a hurriedly put erroneous development plan which may for posterity wipe away treasures preserved till today's modern era.

The security and defence of the island territories remain the fundamental building block. The islands are also the show windows of our intentions and power projection. This is also linked to capacity building and other related developments which form the crust of the civil military puzzle of jointmanship. The littorals of the IOR need to unite through 'Regional Forums' and confidence building measures for which a strong democratic and stable country like India serves as an ideal launch pad. The A and N Islands are perhaps, the best example of civil-military cooperation in promoting regional growth and security, contributing substantially to the best interests of the country. The freedom, safety and prosperity of these Islands and their occupants coupled with safeguarding of vital national intent will always remain the primary task of this unified Command—today, tomorrow and always.

Part-III

Political Autonomy and Development of Andaman and Nicobar Islands

Part-III

Political Autonomy and Development of Andaman and Nicobar Islands

7

Governance, Political Autonomy and Sustainable Development in Andaman and Nicobar Islands

Some Perspectives

R. Thandavan

Introduction

An attempt has been made in this presentation to analyze the need for more political autonomy that would activate governance process and stimulate sustainable development in Andaman and Nicobar Islands.

Historical Background

The Andaman and Nicobar Islands, also known as the Bay Islands or the Emerald Islands, are an archipelago of 572 islands situated in the Bay of Bengal. They are situated 1200 km. off the southeastern coast ot the Indian mainland. They are spread over an area of 8249 sq.km. in a north-south direction. These historically significant islands, of which only 36 are inhabited, are a treasure trove of nature's bounty, beauty and resources. Mythologically, the name Andaman is presumed to have derived from the monkey-God "Hanuman", who was known to the Malayas as Hanumans. The name Nicobar seems to be a corruption of the South Indian term

"Nakkavaram" (Land of the Naked) as indicated in the great Tanjore inscription of 1050 AD.

Historically, the islands were well known to geographers and travellers like Ptolemy, Marco Polo and some Chinese travellers. Their maps have references to these islands and their inhabitants. Ptolemy talked of "Andaman islands" (Islands of Good Fortune), implying thereby that these islands were being visited by the Western and then Arab merchants going to the Far East. However, it was after the British period that these islands gained disrepute. The British took control of Andaman group of islands in 1790 and the Nicobar group in 1869. In 1858, the British founded a penal settlement here; there started development history.

The Nicobar group, it may be noted, was under the Dutch colonialists in between 1758 and 1869. Be that as it may, under the foreign rule, the islands became more famous (or notorious?) as "Kalapani", meaning island of black water. The Cellular Jail, Ross Island and Viper Island were used by the British to imprison and punish the prisoners from the mainland, majority of whom were fighters for Indian freedom, particularly after the 1857, the year of India's First War of Independence. During the Second World War, the islands fell under the Japanese. The British regained them in 1945. Despite opposition from Pakistan, the Andaman and Nicobar Islands became part of India when the British left the subcontinent over six decades ago. But the Andaman remained away from public glare as the government developed the mainland. The strategic importance of the islands was first realized during India's 1971 war with Pakistan, when the Indian Navy used them as a base to blockade and attacks the Naval bases at the East Pakistan, now Bangladesh.

Geographical Context

Geographically, the Andaman and Nicobar groups are separated by 160 km. of sea, the former lying to the north of 100 channels and the latter to its south. The Andaman Group comprises from the North, the North Andaman, Middle Andaman and the South Andaman, which also has the Capital of the entire Union Territory, Port Blair. The Northern most point, called the Land Fall Island, is barely 190 Nautical Miles, or approximately 300 kilometres from the Myanmar mainland. From the Coco Islands, which house, today, the Chinese maintenance and berthing facilities, it is just 18 kilometres. The Coco channel divides Land Fall Island from the Coco Island.

The Nicobar Group consists of Car Nicobar in the North, and the Little Nicobar and the Great Nicobar Group of islands further south. The last is the Southern most of the Indian territories with the southernmost tip called the Pygmalion point (also called the Parsons Point) and now renamed as Indira Point which is just 150 or so kilometres from Sumatra. "Six Degree Channel" separates Great Nicobar from Sumatra. This distance equals that between Delhi and Agra! In fact, the southernmost point of India is Indira Point, not, as per the general perceptions, Kanya Kumari. Similarly, Phuket in Thailand is only 273 nautical miles away from Indira point, which is less than the distance between Chennai and Madurai. These aspects of the geographical location of the Andaman and Nicobar Islands are all the more significant when one realizes that their distance from any part of the Indian mainland is about 1200 kilometres (1255 km. from Calcutta, 1190 km. from Chennai and 1200 km. from Visakhapatnam).

Demographic Profile

As per 1901 Census, the population of Andaman and Nicobar Islands was 24,649. This increased to 30,971 in 1951 census and has jumped to 3,56,151 as per the 2001 census. This accounts for a miniscule 0.03 per cent of the total population of India. It is to be noted that 88.2 per cent population of the Union Territory lived in Andaman District out of which 37 per cent were in urban areas. The density of population of Port Blair was 5301 in 1991whereas it was 859 persons per sq. km. in 1951. Nicobar District does not have any urban areas. The population density in A & N Islands has increased from 34 per sq. km. in 1991 to 43 per sq. km. in 2001.

Tribal Population

There are six tribes in Andaman and Nicobar Islands. The Andamanese, Onges, Sentinels, and the Jarawas are found to live in Andaman Islands and the Nicobarese and the Shompens reside in the Nicobar Group of Islands. There is a distinctive racial difference between the Andaman Tribes and their counterparts in Nicobar. The former are Negrito while the later are Mongoloid. The Andaman tribes are primitive hunter gatherers while the Nicobar tribes are mainly horticulturalists and herders. As 2001 Census the ST population in Andaman & Nicobar Islands was 29469.

Slow Growth Syndrome and Need for Autonomy

In fact, a slow tempo activity, based on piecemeal planning has failed to deliver the goods for Andaman and Nicobar Islands. India's first Prime Minister Pandit Jawaharlal Nehru believed that the development of the tribal island economics like Andaman and Nicobar requires gradual tapping of indigenous resources like forest wealth and other natural attributes. The result was that during first forty years (1950-90) of planned development of the Indian mainland, Andaman and Nicobar was virtually outside the orbit of the centralized planning mechanism. In fact, Andaman and Nicobar opted for slow, step-by-step development, as a result of which a serious imbalance was created between the development tempo of mainland India and the eco-systems of Andaman and Nicobar.

We have had a glance of historical, geographical and demographic profile of Andaman and Nicobar Islands. Let us now come to our main focus, i.e. "Political Autonomy."

Need for Political Autonomy and Participative Governance

Autonomy in a political sense, limited to self-government, short of independence, of a political state or, more frequently, of a subdivision. The term is also used for other self-governing units, such as a parish, a corporation, or a religious sect. A test of autonomy is the recognition that the group may make the rules governing its internal affairs. Political autonomy is frequently based on cultural and ethnic differences. As such, Andaman and Nicobar Islands lack in political autonomy.

As a unit of administration, Andaman and Nicobar Islands (ANI) is a Union Territory of India since 1956. It is administered by the President acting through an Administrator presently designated as Lt. Governor. In 1979, thirty members indirectly elected representatives in the Pradesh Council which was constituted by promulgation of the Andaman and Nicobar (Administration) Regulation, 1979 to advice the Administration. In 1982, the post of Chief Commissioner was upgraded to that of Lieutenant Governor. With the passage of 73rd and 74th Amendments to the Constitution, in 1994, the Municipal Boards Regulation 1957, and the Gram Panchayat Regulation, 1961 were replaced by the Andaman and Nicobar Islands (Municipal) Regulation, 1994 and Andaman and

Nicobar Islands (Panchayat) Regulation, 1994. Andaman and Nicobar Islands have now one member in the Lok Sabha. Till 1967, the Member of Parliament from the Islands was nominated by the President of India.

The Lieutenant Governor and Lack of Participative Governance

In the above context, the scope for popular participation is limited, hence the feeling of absence of representative democratic institutions. Lieutenant Governor (L.G.) is appointed by the President of India under Article 239 of Constitution. The Lieutenant Governor is the most important figure in the government and politics in Andaman and Nicobar Islands. In the absence of a formal legislative council, the Lieutenant Governor looks after the entire legislative structure of the state. The various departments work under his supervision. The government departments of the state operate on both directorate and the secretariat levels, and take care of the state executive. The presence of many Central Government organizations also helps in enhancing the administrative as well as governance profile of Andaman and Nicobar.

The Government and Politics of Andaman and Nicobar Islands operate in a way that is slightly different from the governance of most states and Union Territories of India. The first notable thing about the Government and Politics of Andaman and Nicobar Islands is the lack of a legislature. The Lieutenant Governor is himself the chief Executive in the Government of the Andaman and Nicobar Islands. The Executive wings run under his supervision and remain under direct monitoring from the heads of the various departments. The state judiciary falls under the supervision of the Calcutta High Court.

Major Andaman and Nicobar Islands Political Parties

The major political parties at Andaman and Nicobar Islands arc the ones with prominent national presence. The major political parties of Andaman and Nicobar Islands are:

- Indian National Congress (INC)
- Bharatiya Janata Party (BJP)
- Bahujan Samaj Party (BSP)
- Nationalist Congress Party (NCP)

- Communist Party of India (Marxist) (CPM)
- Communist Party of India (Lenninist) (CPIML)

Politics of Andaman and Nicobar

Although there is no legislative council in the state, it does participate in the general elections. The nominal presence of a state party and a couple of extreme regional parties characterize the politics of Andaman and Nicobar. However, it is the national level parties that really rule the roost in Andaman and Nicobar's political scene.

If given statehood, preferential treatment must be given like Mizoram, Arunachal Pradesh and Manipur where 90 per cent central fund are given and only 10 per cent revenue is to be generated by the state. Political autonomy and democratic empowerment could perhaps help in enhancing the popular will and promote greater involvement of people in day-to-day administration. The Andaman and Nicobar group of islands is an example of harmony, assimilation of culture and language, secularism and accommodation. Hence, Andaman and Nicobar group of islands is known as "Miniature India."

Justification for Statehood

In the Andaman and Nicobar administration people have no say in administrative and development process. If democratic gates are opened in the line of Puducherry Union Territory, people will have their own representatives, and the administration and development decision will reflect the aspiration of the people through their representatives in the assembly.

The statehood means enlarging the top hierarchy, Legislative Assembly, democratic participation through election and elected representatives. Statehood has been given to a few Union Territories including National Capital Delhi, Goa and Puducherry. The same yardstick can be followed and attempt must be made to provide statehood to Andaman and Nicobar islands taking the following three factors:

- Geo strategic position,
- Lack of legislature and long term neglect, and
- Contemporary relevance.

Topography, composition of multi-ethnicity, lack of communication, and distance from mainland particularly from the Capital necessitate statehood for decentralized planning and for administrative cohesiveness. Now we shall discuss the dynamics of local governance in Andaman and Nicobar Islands.

Local Governance

The Andaman and Nicobar Islands had only one district until 31st July, 1974. In 1994, the Andaman and Nicobar group of islands has been statutorily provided 67 Gram Panchayats, 7 Panchayat Samities and 1 Zilla Parishad. The remaining areas have traditional tribal councils. As mentioned earlier, in conformity with the Constitution (73rd Amendment Act), the Andaman and Nicobar Islands Panchayat Regulation, was set in motion in 1994. Nicobar District is excluded from the application of this Regulation. These Regulations outlines the powers and functions of the Panchayats in respect of development planning and implementation of the programmes of economic development and social justice. Seats are reserved for Scheduled Tribes and women according to the Regulation.

The only available democratic means is Municipal Councils (Single Tier) till 1994 then three-tier system of PRIs. The Nicobar Islands were constituted as a separate revenue district with its Head-quarter at Car Nicobar. In August 2006, Andaman District was bifurcated into South Andaman District and North and Middle Andaman Districts. There are 6 Sub-Divisions, 9 Tehsils and 9 Development Blocks. As mentioned, a three-tier Panchayati Raj system exists in the Union Territory comprising 69 Gram Panchayats, 7 Panchayat Samities and 2 Zilla Parishads. Elections to the officers of Gram Pradhan (Village President) are held directly. The tenure of Gram Pradhan, Pramukh and up-Pramukh is for five years, while the office of Adhyaksha for the first and third year of the Zilla Parishad is reserved for women.

Presently, there are 69 Gram Panchayats, 7 Panchayat Samities and 2 Zilla Parishads. Committees have been constituted to deal with grassroots level planning with the mandate to consolidate the plans of PRIs. Activities and schemes of the 29 subjects listed in the 11th Schedule have been transferred by the line departments. A number of officials have been transferred to the Panchayats and some new posts have also been created.

Some headway has been made in the field of administrative and financial devolution. These steps are listed below. The Chief Executive Officer, Zilla Parishad, Executive Officers, Panchayat Samities and Secretary, Gram Panchayat have the following control over the staff transferred to the PRIs.

- Controlling officer for tour diaries, attendance and annual reports.
- To call for reports/returns.
- Distribution of work in accordance with their qualification, experience and expertise, prescribe field duties and approve tour programme.
- To recommend leave.
- Reporting a performance of the staff to their authorities in respect of their performance of duties.
- Elected Head of PRIs have been given the power of ACR writing.

Therefore, it seems that at local government level, there is autonomy due to decentralization, hence autonomous State would help in sustainable development.

The Pradhan of a Gram Panchayat has power to accord administrative approval and expenditure sanction for works up to Rs. 10 lakh. The Pramukh of a Panchayat Samiti has the power up to Rs. 25 lakh. The Adhyaksha of Zilla Parishad has the power up to Rs.75 lakh. Funds for developmental activities are directly given to the PRIs. PRIs have been endowed with the powers to levy and collect taxes and to impose penalties and to undertake any such voluntary works that may benefit the community in general. With the passage of the 74th Amendment to the Constitution, the Municipal Council of Port Blair was set up in 1994 replacing the Port Blair Municipal Board. This is the only urban local body in Andaman and Nicobar Islands and its jurisdiction is 26 sq. km. The Municipal Council aims at providing basic urban services like sanitation and conservation, distribution of drinking water, street lighting, disposal of carcasses, civic amenities such as parks and gardens and social service centres like community halls, auditoriums, public grounds. They also set up shops and shopping complexes, run urban poverty alleviation programme, regulate construction activities and slaughter houses. An important subsystem of sustainable development is the educational institutions, now we shall concentrate on it.

Educational Development

It seems that, in the Andaman and Nicobar Islands, state education has a very strong network of schools and centres of higher education. The Education Department of Andaman and Nicobar is devoted towards enhancing the education profile of the State, specially the comparatively deprived tribal regions. As a result of their tireless work and efforts, Andaman and Nicobar is presently a Union Territory with one of the highest literacy (80%) rates in the country. About 200 primary schools comprise the Andaman and Nicobar Islands state education. A number of vernacular schools are also a key feature of the state education. Various Ashram schools have been established in the tribal areas to propagate education among the tribal populace of the islands. But, as an advocate of education, I prefer more vocational curriculum orientation in schools.

Higher Education of Andaman and Nicobar Islands State Education

Similarly, it also has a great infrastructure for higher education. The colleges of Andaman and Nicobar were originally affiliated to the Rangoon University. However, the cessation of Burma from India brought about a change. The colleges thereafter became affiliated to the Calcutta University. The higher education of Andaman and Nicobar State education includes two training institutes, two polytechnic colleges, a government B.Ed. College and a government college. Each Andaman and Nicobar Government College is under the supervision and direct control of the directorate of education in the region. There being no university in the area, the affiliations of every government college in Andaman and Nicobar Islands changed from time to time. However, presently it is settled under the affiliation of the Pondicherry University.

Here, I strongly feel that efforts must be taken to establish a central university for Andaman and Nicobar islands. Further, feasibility for starting a technology university to train and educate a stilled population also is probed.

Strategic Significance and Sustainable Development

The enhanced attention being paid to the Eastern Command is

prompted in part by apprehensions over China's looming naval presence in the Bay of Bengal and the Indian Ocean. But, it is part of India's two decades-long effort to focus its diplomatic, economic and military energies eastward as part of its "Look East" policy. Besides, the navy's new eastward orientation is also aimed at enabling India to emerge a significant player in the emerging Asia-Pacific security architecture.

A tri-services command was set-up in 2001 at Port Blair in the Andaman and Nicobar Islands. India's east coast faces six littorals—Sri Lanka, Bangladesh, Myanmar, Thailand, Malaysia and Indonesia—across the Bay of Bengal. The Andaman and Nicobar Islands are scattered midway between its east coast and the Straits of Malacca. China, though not a Bay of Bengal or Indian Ocean littoral, has been able to secure for itself a presence in these waters by building strong political, economic and defence relationships with several littoral states, including building commercial/naval port infrastructure there that have dual civilian and military use.

There is an imperative need to eguard the energy interests and voicing the concerns of India in the era of globalization particularly, the presence of the Sea Tigers, pirates, smugglers, gun runners and the Muslim fundamentalists in the region are posing threat to India's sovereignty. This is the time to critically examine the relevance of the geographical location of the Andaman and Nicobar Islands near to Malacca Strait which gives ample scope for free port, transhipment port, ship repair base and offshore bunkering facility for International Sea Lanes (ISLs). To create potentially a very strong maritime power and felicitator in the region and to eliminate the sea piracy, drug trafficking and gunrunners in the region, the Andaman and Nicobar Command (ANC) formed recently, is playing decisive role in promoting cooperation among littoral countries of the Bay of Bengal.

In the ultimate analysis, the success of India's "Look East" policy depends critically on the monitoring and containment of the growing triangular relationship among China, Myanmar and Pakistan on the one hand, and accelerating the momentum of multidimensional engagement with other Asia-Pacific countries on the other. And in task, the Andaman and Nicobar Islands are destined to play a vital role. Secure and stable Andaman and Nicobar Islands (this requires, apart from military augmentation, infrastructural development and social stability) could be the staging post for an India looking to rediscover its great maritime and civilizational influence in the Asia-Pacific.

Discussion and Suggestions

- There needs to be a change in India's attitude towards Andaman and Nicobar. Instead of defending it, the Andaman and Nicobar Islands should be viewed as the first line of defence.
- The main aim of India in Andaman and Nicobar region should be to assess the threats from China and Pakistan and build measures to counter them.
- The importance of the trade routes surrounding the archipelago is bound to increase as India's trade with China and ASEAN is set to increase in future.
- India has not fully realized the importance of the 10 Degree Channel and 6 Degree Channel, while China is fully aware of the importance of these two important trade routes.
- The isolated location of these islands is the major problem that India faces.
- A highly efficient surveillance network is a must to monitor non-conventional threats.
- The communication network needs to be developed to carry out efficient surveillance and monitoring.
- More manpower and modernization of equipment are a must.
- People are as vital an aspect as they can be in the region and genuine attention needs to be paid to grievances of the tribal people of Andaman and Nicobar Islands.
- The internal political disturbances in South East Asian nations could have a spillover effect on the archipelago.

Conclusion

Before planning a sustainable strategy for overall development of the Andaman and Nicobar Islands several factors must be considered. Despite the fact that there is no immediate alien terrorist threat to Andaman and Nicobar Islands, a long term strategy must be devised to keep away of vested interest, and patriotic feeling of Andaman and Nicobar people must be mobilized.

Rational understanding of geo-political and strategic importance of the Andaman regions is very much essential, as it has access to the Indian Ocean, Pacific Ocean, Bay of Bengal etc. Obviously, the Andaman and Nicobar Command is an asset for India and has several significances for Indian defence system. It would help in curbing terrorist's movements, trafficking, and intrusion of alien power and so on.

Two important steps:

(i) Self-sufficiency in food and other essential commodities is essential.
(ii) Sustainable development must focus on economy, employment opportunities, responsive and representative institutional development in the Andaman and Nicobar Islands.

APPENDIX

Package of Incentives Available for Development of Industries in Andaman and Nicobar

A. The Andaman & Nicobar Islands Administration is committed for balanced industrial development. In order to promote industries, the Industries Department has drawn out an unique package of incentives for the small scale Industries. These include:

1. Loan to Tiny Cottage and SSI Industries at reduced Rate of Interest

A composite loan up to a maximum of Rs.5.00 lakh is made available to tiny cottage and SSI Units at the rate of 7 per cent of the interest on term loan and at the rate of 10 per cent on working capital per annum for purchase and erection of plant and machinery, construction of factory, sheds, wells, tanks and other civil works, purchase of raw materials and for land development. The promoter's contribution shall be subject to a maximum of 15 per cent of the project cost.

2. Built up Sheds and Developed Plots in the Industrial Estate

There is one Industrial Estate at Garacharma and three more industrial estates, one each at Dollygunj (South Andaman), Bakultala

(Middle Andaman) and Campbell Bay (Great Nicobar) are being developed. A total of 33 hectares of land is covered under these estates wherein more than 150 sheds will be built in the next few years. Also an Industrial Estate exclusively for coir products is planned in South Andaman. The entrepreneurs are being charged nominal rents for the sheds and the plots.

3. Interest Free Loan for Procurement of D.G. Set/In-house Water Harvesting Equipments

All SSI units registered with the Directorate of Industries are eligible for a loan up to 90 per cent of the actual cost of the D.G. Set and in-house water harvesting equipments subject to a maximum of Rs. 2.75 lakh for the purchase of D.G. set and Rs.1.00 lakh for in-house water harvesting equipments. Entrepreneur is, however, required to contribute 10 per cent of the total cost of the equipments as margin money.

4. Mainland-Island Transport Subsidy Scheme

Ninety per cent of the freight charges are reimbursed to the eligible small scale industries for transporting raw materials from mainland ports to the location of the Units and for transporting finished goods from the location of the units to the mainland ports. The units which are eligible under the Central Transport Subsidy Scheme of Government of India, are not eligible under this scheme.

5. Inter-Island Transport Subsidy Scheme

Ninety per cent of the freight charges are reimbursed to the eligible small scale industries for transporting raw materials from any inter-island port/jetty of A & N Islands to the location of the unit and for transporting finished goods from the location of the units to the Inter-Island port/jetty.

6. Island Capital Investment Subsidy Scheme

Capital investment subsidy of 25 per cent subject to maximum of Rs.25 lakh is being given to the Small Scale Industrial units and the Small Scale Service and Business enterprises which are registered with the Directorate of Industries/Department of Industrial Policy and Promotion, Ministry of Industry, Government of India. Only such units which are set up after 1.4.1995 are eligible for subsidy under the scheme. Units which go in for providing their production capacity, if increased by 25 per cent, are also eligible for subsidy.

8. Interest Free Loan for Promoters Contribution for Industrial Units Marketing its Products on Mainland

All Small Scale units registered with the Directorate of Industries are eligible for interest free loan upto 10 per cent of the project cost towards promoters margin subject to maximum of Rs. 50,000 provided they market at least 30 per cent of their products in mainland. The promoters own contribution shall be 5 per cent of the project cost.

9. Interest Subsidy to PMRY Beneficiaries

The PMRY beneficiaries are eligible for an interest subsidy of 7 per cent subject to the condition that the payment of principal as well as interest installment to the Banks is regular and timely.

10. Financial Assistance and Awards to Crafts Persons for Development of Innovative Design

In order to encourage craftsmen to develop new designs in handicrafts, the department implements a scheme awards as a measure of recognition of the expertise. Besides, best craftsmen are also awarded prize money and certificates every year.

11. Credit Guarantee Scheme

It has been the experience that the local entrepreneurs face problems of providing collateral security to obtain loans from Nationalised Banks/Financial Institutions. The Administration has guarantee to the Banks/Financial Institutions to cover bad debts up to Rs. 10 lakh per unit.

B. Fiscal Incentives

There is no sales tax in this UT and the industries avail this concession.

Octroi is exempted for the SSI Units on plant and machinery/ equipments used for industrial purposes. The relief and concession extended by the Government of India for the industrially backward areas Category 'A' like a five year tax holiday for new industrial undertakings, concessional excise duty etc. are also made available to the units set up in these Islands.

BIBLIOGRAPHY

A People in peril, *Frontline*, Volume 16, Issue 9, April 24-May 7, 1999.

Government of India, *Perspective Plan for Tourism Development in Andaman and Nicobar Islands*, Ministry of Tourism and Culture, 2003.

Government of India, *Andaman and Nicobar Islands Development Report*, Planning Commission, 2008.

Murthy, R.V.R., *Andaman and Nicobar Islands: A Geo Political Strategic Perspective*, 2007.

www.mittalpublication.com, *Sustainable Growth for an Island Economy: A Case Study of Andaman And Nicobar islands*. www.and.nic.in

8
Sustainable Development and Decentralised Governance

A Study in the Context of Andaman and Nicobar Islands

S.S. Sreekumar

Introduction: Conceptual Framework

In the last four decades there is a growing awareness and activism relating to worsening environmental situation at the local, national and global levels. The emerging environmental concerns led to reconsideration of goals and strategies of development. As a result of this, the concept of development has experienced a paradigm shift. Till the beginning of the 1980s in many countries of the world, ecology was not integrated as an essential element of development planning. And hence, it was not seriously considered as a major issue. The economic expansion in the last century and half had alarming consequences for global environment. Depletion of ozone layer, air pollution, loss of forests and bio-diversity extinction of plant and animal species, loss of marine life, soil and water pollution have occurred at an alarming rate. On realising the importance of environmental variations, problems created by them and their impact on human settlement, quality of life, developmental problems and changes in fertility, mortality and morbidity, the concept of ecology acquired prominence during the 1980s. It brought forth the realization that the ecosystem had to be protected for betterment of life in general.

In 1972 the UN Conference on Human Environment took place in Stockholm. The Stockholm Conference was historical in the sense that environmental problem received a formal recognition for the first time. In 1983, The UN set up a World Commission headed by Gro Harlem Brundtland, Prime Minister of Norway, as an independent body. Its objective was to re-examine the critical environment and development problems on the planet and to formulate realistic proposals to solve them, and to ensure that the human progress will be sustained through development without bankrupting the resources of the future generations. The WCED published its report titled *"Our Common Future"* in the year 1987. This report presented the first official definition of the concept of sustainable development. The contribution of *Our Common Future* is threefold: (i) it offers the first official definition of sustainable development, (ii) it suggests, for the first time, an international strategy for confronting the crisis of modernity, and (iii) to brings about a paradigm change in conventional thinking regarding the notion of "development" (*World Commission of Environment and Development*, 1983:30-38).

The theme of the Stockholm Conference had been the 'human environment'. But the Brundtland Commission had to consider environment and development together. This was a crucial difference, because it meant focusing on the ways in which both rich and poor societies damaged the environment (for different reasons). It also meant reconciling two opposite concepts: for on the one hand, it was precisely human activities — especially those stemming from the mode of industrial production synonymous with 'development' — which lay behind the deterioration of the environment; and on the other hand, it seemed inconceivable not to hasten the 'development' of peoples which did not yet have access to decent living conditions (*Ibid.*). To overcome this dilemma, the Commission proposed the following concept of 'sustainable development.' "Humanity has the ability to make development sustainable — to ensure that it meets the needs of the present without compromising the ability of future generations to meet their own needs. The concept of sustainable development does imply limits — not absolute limits but limitations imposed by the present state of technology and social organization on environmental resources and by the ability of the biosphere to absorb the effects of human activities. But technology and social organization can be both managed and improved to make way for a new era of economic growth. The Commission believes that widespread poverty is no longer inevitable. Poverty is not only an evil in itself, but sustainable development requires meeting the basic needs of all and extending to all the opportunity to fulfill their aspirations for a better life. A world in which poverty is endemic will always be prone to ecological and other catastrophes" (*Ibid.*). The term sustainable development has been defined by Brundtland Commission as "*Development that meets the needs of the present without compromising the ability of future generations to meet their own needs*. The term 'sustainable development' gained wide international currency in recent years with the growth of ecological understanding at local, national and international levels not only among the communities and movements but also, among Nation-States and Governments. Ensuring environmental sustainability the 7th Millenium Development Goal requires achieving sustainable development patterns and preserving the productive capacity of natural ecosystems for future generations (UNDP, 2002:28).

Since the publication of the report of the Brundtland Commission, the environmental problems which received some attention by national governments and which have been incorporated into national policies during the latter part of the 20th century, are: pollution control, population planning and energy conservation. But the small-scale and marginal changes that are constantly occurring on our plant, and which have clear local and regional dimensions, have not yet been given adequate attention. All these incremental phenomena may hardly seem important by themselves; but they have severe environmental impacts and, therefore, necessitate more coherent planning (Sundaram, 1997:111). According to one view, development became unsustainable because of the collapse of a "co-evolutionary development process," entailing the elements of knowledge, values, social organization, technology and resource system. Development is a 'patchwork quilt' of these elements. Each patch is a complex one. No one way of understanding it is sufficient. A holistic view and a multi-disciplinary approach are needed. It has been argued that development became unsustainable "not simply because the use of hydro-carbons has been destroying the environment, but because there has been a cultural implosion. Value systems have been collapsing. Knowledge has been reduced to Western understanding and social organization and technologies have become increasingly the same around the world (Nogaard, 1988). Sustainable development is, therefore, interpreted as a method of returning to the co-evolutionary development process "with the diversity that remains and the deliberate fostering of further diversity to permit adaptation to future surprises." According to Norgaard, the policy challenge of sustainable development consists of finding a path towards a positive social and ecological co-evolution (*Ibid.*).

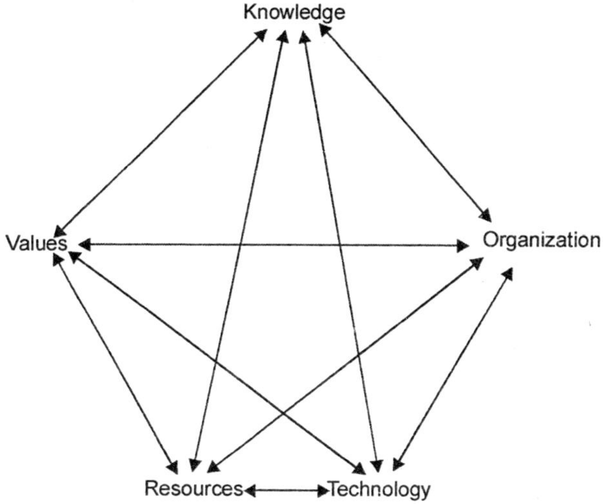

Fig. 8.1: A Co-evolutionary View of Development

Source: Richard B. Norgaard, "Sustainable Development: A Co-evolutionary view" in *Futures*, Vol. 20, No. 6, December 1988.

In this conception, no system will dominate another; none will provide a more obvious starting point for understanding the whole, and each can only be understood in the context of the others. This would mean that not only is each subsystem related to all the others, but each is changing and affecting the evolution of the others. In a sound and sustainable development, therefore, with each subsystem putting selective pressure on each of the other subsystems, they "co-evolve" in a manner, whereby each reflects the others. This, in other words, is a holistic view of development, which is nothing new and which has been expressed before in other contexts. However, it needs to be re-stated in the context of sustainable development. In practical terms, the return to co-evolutionary development at the regional and local levels would mean that (a) environmental dimensions should be consciously incorporated into regional and local level planning, and (b) a systems approach to planning should be adopted, in which knowledge, values, social organization, technology and resources are treated as more or less symmetrical (*World Commission of Environment and Development*, 1987:30-31). In arguing for sustainable development, the moral basis is that the next generation should have access to at least the same resource base as the previous generation. This would mean that a sustainable economy should serve the interests of justice. The three types of justice involved here are:

- Justice to people within a generation, i.e. intra-generational justice;
- Justice to people between generations, i.e. inter-generational justice; and
- Justice to nature.

All these three types of justice imply that sustainable development has to be conceived in a long-term perspective and in the context of the following goals:

- Equity (within and between generations, and to nature);
- Survival (durability as well as resilience); and
- Welfare improvement (raising average standards of welfare).

Sustainable Development: Requirements

The World Commission on Environmental and Development, 1987, highlighted the important requirement of "sustainable development" as given below:

> Sustainable development requires meeting the basic needs of all and extending to all the opportunity to satisfy their aspirations for a better life ... the promotion of values that encourage consumption standards that are within the bounds of the ecologically possible and to which all can reasonably aspire .... That societies meet human needs both by increasing productive potential and by ensuring equitable opportunities for all .... demographic developments are in harmony with the changing productive potential of the ecosystem .... At a minimum, development must not endanger the natural systems that support life on Earth: the atmosphere, the water, the soils, and the living beings.... the world must ensure equable access to the constrained resource and reorient technological efforts

> to relieve the pressure .... that the rate of depletion of non-renewable resources should foreclose as few future options as possible. .... the conservation of plant and animal species ...... that the adverse impact on the quality of air, water, and other natural elements are minimized so as to sustain the ecosystem's overall integrity" (*World Commission on Environmental and Development*, 1987a:30-31).

Regarding the strategy for sustainable development the Commission appoint the following way in the specific context of the development and environment, the pursuit sustainable development requires: (i) a political system that secures effective citizen participation in decision making, (ii) an economic system that is able to generate surplus and technical knowledge on a self-reliant and sustained basis, (iii) a social system that proves for solutions to the tensions arising from disharmonious development, (iv) a production system that respects the obligation to preserve the ecological base for development, (v) a technological system that can search continuously for new solutions, (vi) an international system that fosters sustainable patterns of trade and finance, and (vii) an administrative system that is flexible and has the capacity for self-correction. These requirements are more in the nature of goals that should underlie national and international action on development (*Ibid.*). At the core of sustainable development is the need to consider *three pillars* together—*Society, Economy and Environment*. No matter the context, the idea remains the same — people, habitat and economic systems are interrelated (Strange, 2010:27).

Sustainable Development and Governance

The challenges to sustainable development include de-forestation, threat to bio-diversity, effects of climate change, increasing population levels, ground water depletion and pollution, poor health and literacy rate. The biggest challenges to make development sustainable is to create governance system that promotes facilitates and formulate such policies and strategies that strive for human development, resource conservation and uphold the rule of law over the allocation and judicious utilization of development resources. This brings into sharp focus the need to discuss various methods and instruments available to assess the sustainable development in the context of governance within a political economy construct. Various countries with almost similar kind of natural resources, viz. land, water, arable soil, minerals, climate etc. have during the past few decades shown noticeable difference evidence of economic and social progress. In spite of comparable social structures it is the nature of "governance" that has made the critical difference and come to the forefront of the debate over development policy.

The National Human Development Report, 2001 states that "governance for human development relates to the management of all such processes that, in any society, define the environment which permits and enables individuals to raise their capacity levels, on one hand, and provide opportunities to realize their potential and enlarge the set of available choices, on the other". The Report also reiterates that the State is responsible for creating a favourable political, legal and economic environment for building individual capabilities and encouraging private initiative. Governance, therefore, requires the states to exercise their power through various designated bodies and pursue the said goals through an equitable, socially sensitive, non-discriminatory and participatory approach involving people at large. The most important factor is the accountability of the state in governance. While the Western countries have successfully incorporated this in their governance, the State Accountability, in India, is more or less negligible. The relevance of good governance policies and strategies is lost when the State Accountability factor is uncared for and does not mirror the aspirations of the population of a nation (Government of India, 2001).

From the above narration of the concept, it can be observed that the fundamental principles that characterise sustainable development are:

(i) Conservation of natural resources and biological diversity;
(ii) Deterrence of harmful effect on environment;
(iii) Integration of environment and economy;
(iv) Training and awareness programmes on environmental protection; and
(v) Cooperative and participatory approach.

Thus, there is a predestined link between governance and sustainable development; there is a need to integrate the dynamics of society, ecology and economy through the use of environmentally compatible technologies. Above all, there is a need to sustain development in urban and rural areas by providing basic amenities and good standard of living.

Role of Local Communities in Participation

In order to ensure efficiency, transparency and sustainability of the development initiatives, the *local participation* should be encouraged as it not only bring in the democratic approach but also ensures implementation of the projects. Participatory management and techniques need to be adopted towards achieving development. If the earth's resources are to be protected from excursive human intervention, there is a need to adopt sound and stringent penal measures. The involvement of local communities, panchayats, cooperative societies and women is a must towards creating sustained and self reliant communities. Studies conducted in participatory watershed and soil conservation programmes in various states in India have shown how a diversity of institutional arrangements and technological innovations in very different environment can lead to substantial benefits for the local peoples (Hinchcliffe *et al.,* 1995; Chatterji *et al.*, 1994; Devarajan, 1994). Linkages between non-government organizations, government agencies and local communities are resulting in:

(a) the breakdown of hierarchy in bureaucracies,
(b) the resolution of conflicts in and between communities,
(c) the recuperation of barren lands,
(d) an average doubling of crop yields,
(e) increased crop diversity,
(f) improved well water availability,
(g) greater social cohesion,
(h) alternative forms of credit management by local groups,
(i) the federation of local groups to ensure influence over high-level institution, and
(j) political interests (Jules, 1996:17-18).

The study of 95 projects in countries of East and Southern Africa (Angola, Botswana, Ethiopia, Kenya, Lesotho, Malawi, Mozambique, South Africa, Tanzania, Uganda, Zambia, and Zimbabwe) discovered that improvements are now occurring for at least 230,000 farming families (IIED,1996). Over 6 million hectares are being farmed with sustainable agriculture, and on an average crop yields have slightly more than doubled. all the projects are using resource conserving technologies and are working in a participatory fashion with local people.

The sustainability of development projects and programmes is in a large measure due to the participation of the target group needs no reiteration. The success ratio of projects where the local populace have been involved, has been widely documented and publicized with the result that government and non-government agencies have come to accept people's participation as a major component in project/programme formulation, implementation and monitoring. However, involving the people has been largely limited to the implementation stage. The built-in mind-set of the planner/administrator formulating the ideal plan, communicating it to the people and involving them in its implementation with a view to long term sustainability, still persists. This, perhaps, accounts for the petering out of many ambitious projects even when the target group was involved in their implementation. The practice of imposing a plan from above, although based on detailed survey and data analysis often results in imposing unwanted projects on the local people, when their priorities may lie in a different direction. This is particularly so in the case of urban based planners whose perceptions of the problems in an altogether alien rural environment may be less than realistic. The problem becomes even more complex when gender differences are taken into consideration (Nira, 1996:34-35).

The local institutions are important for sustainable development as they not only mobilize local resources and regulate their use in a most efficient and sustainable manner, but also encourage people to take a longer-term view by creating common expectations and a basis of cooperation that goes beyond individual interest. However, it should be recognized that local institutions and groups can also produce practices which do not favour sustainability (Upholf, 1992). It is important to recognize the difference between organizations and institutions. Whereas an institution is a complex of norms and behaviours that persists overtime by serving some socially valued purpose, an organization is a structure of recognized and accepted roles. However, institutions can be organizations and *vice versa* (Upholf, 1993). Though there could be many levels of decision-making for a particular activity, but three of them—localities, communities, and group—should be considered local as they have face-to-face inter-personnel relationships in all of them which are more frequent and intense within groups. The fact that people know each other, creates opportunities for collective action and mutual assistance and for mobilizing and managing resources on a self-directed and self-sustaining basis. In such communities, monitoring is easier, and the social sanctions are easier to implement through reputation mechanisms and multiplex relationships of face-to-face communities (Bardhan, 1993:633-639).

For sustainable development, it is not institutions and organizations which are important *per se*, but sustainability of these mechanisms of development. The sustainability of a local institution can be judged by its (a) financial autonomy in terms of whether it is able to stand on its own feet financially; (b) administrative autonomy defined as the capacity of its leaders and members to determine of the institution and the direction to achieve these objectives; and (c) managerial autonomy in terms of their capacity to manage their day-to-day operations by themselves. According to Shah a local institution can be sustainable only if it serves purposes important to its members (Shah,1993).

The Case of Andaman and Nicobar Islands

On the background narrated above it is worthwhile to examine the nature of participation at the grassroots level in the territory of the Andaman and Nicobar Islands. Before examining the nature of participation at the local level, a brief profile of the study area has been presented.

The Union Territory of the Andaman and Nicobar Islands is cut off from mainland by vast stretches of sea. The Andaman and Nicobar Islands is situated in the Bay of Bengal between 6° to 14° north latitude and 92° and 94° east longitude. There are two groups of Islands, i.e. Andaman and Nicobar separated by 10° channel which is about 144 km. wide and 400 fathoms deep. The total geographical area of the Andaman and Nicobar Islands is 8249 sq. km. The geographical area of Andamans is 6408 km, and that of Nicobar is 1841 sq.km (Census of India, 1991:8). The Union Territory consists of more than 306 named and unnamed Islands and 260 named and unnamed rocks. However, only 36 islands are inhabited. Of these 24 are located in Andaman District and 12 in Nicobar District. At present there are three revenue districts, i.e. South Andaman District, North and Middle Andaman

District and Nicobar District. Nicobar District is mostly inhabited by tribes and is declared as tribal area. There are seven tehsils and 547 revenue villages (Andaman and Nicobar Administration, 2007: 1).

The population of these islands can be classified into two categories—the aborigines and immigrants. As per 2011 Census the total population of the Islands comes to 3,80,581 and of which 2,02,871 are males and remaining 1,77,710 females recording a growth rate of 6.86 per cent. The sex ratio of the islands is 876. The density of population is 46. The literacy rate registered in this UT is 86. 6 per cent (male literacy is 90.3 per cent and female literacy 82.4 per cent). The population of tribes has shown a decline from 29469 in 2001 to 28530 as per 2011 Census, registering a decrease of 3.19 per cent. The population of tribes comes to 7.5 per cent of the total population (Census of India, 2011:13).

Decentralised Governance in the Island Territory

Local self-governing institutions began in the islands in 1957 with promulgation of Andaman and Nicobar Islands (Municipal Boards) Regulations, by the President of India. Under the Regulation, a Municipal Board at Port Blair, the loan urban area, was established. This body started functioning in 1958. Majority of its numbers were elected. To cater to the civic needs of rural area, the Andaman and Nicobar (Gram Panchayats) Regulation, 1961 was promulgated. The regulation provided for establishment of Gram Panchayats and Nyaya Panchayats in these islands. Since the population of the Nicobar Group of Islands is predominantly tribal, they have their own traditional Panchayats and village captain who are authorized to settle local matters and problems amicably.

With the passing of the 73rd and 74th Constitutional Amendment, further decentalisation was introduced in the islands in the 1990s. In 1994, the Municipal Regulations of 1957 and the Panchayat Regulation of 1961 were repealed by the Andaman and Nicobar (Municipal) Regulation, 1994 and the Andaman and Nicobar (Panchayat) Act, 1994 respectively. The Port Blair Municipal Council consists of 18 wards. As per 73rd Amendment of the Constitution of India, the new Panchayati Raj Institutions (PRIs) began to function with a three-tier system. Accordingly there are 70 Gram Panchayats at village level, seven Panchayat Samitis at Block-level and two Zilla Parishads at district level. Provision for reservation for women has also been effected as provided in the constitutional amendment.

First election to the Institutions (PRIs) of these islands was conducted in September 1995. Second time elections were held in September 2000. 3rd election to Panchayati Raj Institutions in the islands was held in September 2010 and the forth one in 2015.

Participation at the Grassroots Level

Studies were conducted in the context of decentralised governance reveal the following observations relating to participation at the grassroot level:

(a) Majority of the elected representatives are *not fully aware* of various aspects of decentralized governance. Field experience reveals that their knowledge is limited to *symbol but not in substance*.

(b) Those who are elected to PRIs second and third time are to some extent acquainted with techniques of dealing with public, meeting officials for articulation of demands and to solve the problems of the public.

(c) The researcher's own experience and interaction with the functionaries from NGOs working in the field of rural development reveal that member lack a *participatory approach*. They hesitate to come forward and not really interested to participate in socio-political activities. They do not take much interest in knowing socio-economic problems, though these affect them.

(d) NGO such as ACANI was having plan to introduce scheme in the field of agriculture in the Islands. When this NGO approached Panchayat bodies, many Panchayat Raj bodies were not ready to provide necessary data for preliminary survey. Due to this apathetic attitude, the NGO could not move further, and hence they dropped the plan.

(e) Many members of the PRIs in the islands lack capacity for decision-making. Whenever, they face any problem, they place the matter before the Secretary of the Panchayat and simply accept the decisions of the Department Officials.

(f) Majority of the members of the PRIs are not in a position to mobilize sources of income for the panchayats. They depend upon Grant-in-aid from the Government. Consequently, the panchayats lack sustainability.

Suggestions

1. *Creating awareness* regarding decentralized governance and the need for participation is one suggestion. Activating in the circulation newspaper in the rural area and strengthening the scheme of mobile libraries and starting libraries in rural area are positive steps to be taken in this regard. Accessibility to mass media.
2. There is an urgent need to assess *training needs of members of PRIs*. As per the training needs analysis, orientation programmes have to be started especially for newly elected members. Training has to be imparted in such a way that the members should obtain knowledge and skill related to matters such as scope of decentralized governance, role of PRIs, duties and responsibilities of the elected representatives of PRIs and also the rules and regulations in general. Priority has to be accorded for developing decision-making capacity of elected representatives.
3. Another suggestion that can practically applicable in the island context is that the elected representatives can be provided with chances to share their experiences with others. Platforms for this can be formed at Taluk and District levels.
4. Dissemination of information through mass media has been found successful in many places. Exposure of elected representatives through media both print as well as electronic, can play an important role in generating awareness. Publishing of the News Bulletin also helps in dissemination of views, opinions and ideas.
5. Women should be encouraged to organize themselves. Mahila Mandals in the villages can be effectively used as instruments to mobilize them. Women's organizations can also act as catalytic agents for encouraging women's participation in social and political activities.

Concluding Observations

Sustainable Development is the process of improving the quality of human life while living within the carrying capacity of supporting ecosystems. It carries the premise of development that can be achieved without an undue exploitation of the natural resources. The management of natural resources needs massive efforts to workout modalities of achieving the goal of sustainable development. The governance for sustainable development should include an integrated approach of economic and environmental concerns in the development strategy, keeping in view not only the quality of life that has to be offered to its citizens but also an equal distribution of it with 'social equity' as its goal. Governance should also safeguard a citizen's right to develop simultaneously holding the environmental concerns at a high pedestal. There are numerous challenges such as loss of biodiversity, depleting natural resources, pollution of land, water and air as also poor health, poor literacy and environmental sustainability. The decentralized governance helps in promoting human and environmental concerns alike. To ensure sustainable development, *inclusiveness of sustainable development* is a must. It has to be ensured that skills are dispersed uniformly during the growth process through adequate education, healthcare etc. For the purpose, significant acceleration in employment generation is imperative. This requires initiatives to build competence of the poor, especially in the under-developed countries. Effort is required to create mechanisms and institutions that encourage innovations and creativity, provide equal growth opportunities to everyone, and a framework for all citizens to contribute and achieve to their potential. Capacity of all sections of the society has to be built so as to enable everyone to participate in the cause of sustainable development. The government and the non-government organizations will have to work towards making the growth more participatory and inclusive so as to ensure sustainable development. There has to be a change in the mindset of politicians and bureaucrats to ensure that governance is viewed and shaped to extend to the grassroots to foster well-being of all sections of the society.

In the context of the Andaman and Nicobar Islands, a *mass political culture* in the rural area has to emerge. For this, interest groups, political parties and their frontal organizations can play a crucial role. Emergence of a strong middle class with political consciousness and vigil can help to initiate a change from subject to participant political culture. Only a vigilant middle class can help in the formation of public opinion, influence policies and make demand for favourable and appropriate legislation necessary for socio-economic development.

Creating a favourable and conductive environment for making the youths politically conscious and to inculcate democratic values, to a certain extent help to socialize politically. The political parties and interest groups have to be activated so as to educate the public as well as mobilise public opinion. Since majority of the rural mass residing in the island territory are found to be unaffiliated with any formal organization, (i.e. cultural and professional organization) an emerging need of this territory is to develop ***social capital*** which will help to contribute collective action. Collective action practically does not exist in the islands.

BIBLIOGRAPHY

Andaman and Nicobar Administration (2007), *Basic Statistics, 2005-2006*, Port Blair: Directorate of Economics and Statistic, Andaman and Nicobar Administration.

Bardhan, P. (1993) 'Analytics of Institutions of Information Co-operation in Rural Development', *World Development*, 21(4).

Chatterji, J. Kumar Das, P. Chakravarty, S. Singh, H, and Agarwal, R.P., (1994) *Scaling-up of Soil and Water Conservation Efforts in Chotanagpur Plateau, Eastern India, Paper for IIED Conference, New Horizons: The Social, Economic and Environmental Impacts of Participatory Watershed Development*, November, Bangalore.

Census of India,1991 (1992) *Andaman and Nicobar Islands, District Census Handbook, Part XIII, A & B,* Directorate of Census Operations, Andaman and Nicobar Islands, New Delhi: Controller of Publications.

Census of India, 2011 (2013), *Primary Census Abstract, Data Highlights 2011, Andaman and Nicobar Islands UT,* Directorate of Census Operations, Port Blair, Andaman and Nicobar islands.

Devavaram, J. (1994), Paraikulum Watershed, Tamil Nadu, *Paper for IIED Conference, New Horizons: The Social, Economic and Environmental Impacts of Participatory Watershed Development*, November, Bangalore.

Government of India (2001), *National Human Development Report, 2001*, Planning Commission, New Delhi: Government of India.

Hinchcliffe F., Gujit I., Pretty, J.N. and Shah, P. (1955) *New Horizons: The Economic, Social and Environmental Impacts of Participatory Watershed Development.* Gatekeeper Series SA 50, London: IIED.

IIED (1996), *Sustainable Agriculture and Food Security in East and Southern Africa: A Report for Swedish International Development Authority*, Stockholm, London: International Institute for Environmental and Development.

Norgaard, Richard B. (1988), "Sustainable Development: A Co-evolutionary View", *Futures,* 20(6), December.

Ramachandran, Nira, and Anil K. Dimri, (1996) "Participating in the Planning Process — A must for Sustainable Development", *Social Change*, Vol. 26 (1).

Shah, T. (1993): *Institutional Dimensions of Agricultural and Rural Development in India,* Working Paper No. 42, Anand: Institute of Rural Management.

Strange Tracy, and Anne Bayley (2010), *Sustainable Development, Linking Economy Society and Environment,* New Delhi, Academic Foundation.

Sundaram, K.V. (1997), *Decentralized Multilevel Planning, Principles and Practice, Asian and African Experiences*, New Delhi: Concept Publishing Company.

UNDP (2002), *Human Development Report, 2002, Deepening Democracy in a Fragmented World*, New Delhi: Oxford University Press.

Uphoff, N. (1992), *Local Institutions and Participation of Sustainable Development, IIED Gatekeeper Series, No. 31*. International Institute for Environmental and Development (IIED).

Uphoff, N. (1993): Grassroots Organizations and NGOs in Rural Development: Opportunities with Diminishing States and Expanding Markets, *World Development*, 21(4).

World Commission of Environment and Development (1987), "Towards Sustainable Development", *Science Age*, August.

World Commissioner of Environment and Development (1987) a, *Ibid.*

Web site

1. http://dsp-psd.tpsgc.gc.ca/Collection-R/LoPBdP/BP/bp317-e.tm.

9
Sustainable Development
A Transition to Political Autonomy

R.N. Rath

Sustainable development has become an unavoidable reality at all levels of economic integration. The support of most governments for the concept of sustainable development makes strong action in environmental matters all the more necessary and legitimate. The implementation of sustainable development presupposes compliance with certain conditions (democracy, autonomy, fairness, interdependence, responsibility and accountability) and with certain fundamental principles (environmental and economic integration; maintenance of biological diversity and conservation of natural resources; precaution, prevention and evaluation; cooperation, partnership and participation; and education, training and consciousness-raising).

The concept of sustainable development implies, first, the integration of environmental issues with the imperatives of economic development in order to meet the immediate needs of populations today without undermining the aspirations of future generations. However, the definition of the term "sustainable development" has been expanded to include the ideas of fairness and interdependence, not only between generations, but between the countries and peoples of the Earth. Social, cultural, economic and natural environments, whose harmonious development is essential to the welfare of humanity and of nature, are also included in the concept.

Sustainable development can only be achieved in a long-term perspective. However, this cannot be done reactively, but rather through applying the principles of proactive and strategic planning and management. It is, therefore, essential to establish clear principles at all levels of participation and decision-making, together with clear objectives and measures that are part of a long-term approach and take into consideration the various countries' ability to act and to pay.

Although they need not absolutely be linked, sustainable development can hardly be initiated or implemented in the absence of genuine democracy. It is hard to see just how to provide fairly for present needs, and without compromising the future of generations to come, without underlying mechanisms and institutions in which all can participate. Thus, all human beings, no matter what their country of origin, may legitimately aspire to clean air and water, sufficient food, comfortable housing and satisfying work in an atmosphere of peace and respect for differences and diversity. At the same time, they must be able to ensure the protection and survival of their natural and cultural heritage. In short, all human beings enjoy a fundamental right to an environment that is of high quality and is healthful. By democracy, we must understand respect not only for individual rights, but also for collective rights, and in particular the right of women and first peoples to participate actively and fully in the march towards sustainable development.

While sustainable development must be achieved in a democratic context, the autonomy of governments, peoples and ethnic groups in making their development choices must also be respected. This does not mean that governments must operate in isolation; on the contrary, they must adopt a global view of development and development planning by taking an active part in international forums and processes for determining major common objectives for sustainable development.

The concept of fairness is central to the entire issue of sustainable development, being based on recognition of the global and common nature of our environment and on the need for the planet's resources to be shared in a sustainable way. Achieving fairness in sustainable development must be addressed at two levels: (i) within populations or states, (ii) between populations or states.

Keeping these parametres as essential ingredients for sustainable development it seems democracy and autonomy are of paramount significance. Before reaching in any conclusion we must know about the long path travelled from complete bureaucratization to semi-autonomy and aspiration for more autonomy in the form of legislative assembly.

Table 9.1: Administrative set up

District	3
Sub-Division	6
Tehsil	9
CD Blocks	9
Municipal Council	1
Municipal Ward	24
Gram Panchayat	69
Panchayat Samiti	7
Zilla Parishad	2
MP	1
Lt. Governor	1

Source: Basic Statistics, A & N Islands.

The British governed the Andaman and Nicobar Islands under the provisions of the Scheduled Districts Act, 1874. The Andaman and Nicobar Islands Regulations, 1874 was the first regulation, which was promulgated for the governance of the Islands. In 1876, this regulation was replaced by another improved and amplified regulation. The new regulation generally made provision for the administration of justice within the islands, regulation of arrival and departure of vessels and landing of passenger and goods, residence in the settlement and miscellaneous matters concerning convicts in respect to their marriage, escape from detention etc. Except for the provisions concerning administration of justice, all the other provisions of the Regulation were incidental to the status of Andamans being a penal settlement (Table 9.2).

Subsequently, under the Government of India Act, 1919 and 1935 (Sections 58 and 94 respectively), these group of islands became a Chief Commissioner's province. The Act of 1874, however, continued to apply till its repeal by the adaption of Indian Laws Order, 1937. Under the Government of India Act, 1935, the Chief Commissioner's provinces were units of the Federation, but they were under the direct administration of the Federal Government (Section 94). They were governed by the Governor General acting in his discretion through a Chief Commissioner appointed by him. The Federal Legislature was empowered to legislate in relation to Chief Commissioner's provinces without any limitation as to subjects. After the enforcement of the Constitution, special provision was made for the administration of the Andaman and Nicobar Islands. Under Article 243 (now repealed) it was laid down that the territories included in part 'D' of the First

Table 9.2: Designated Heads of the Andaman and Nicobar Islands in the Pre- and Post-Independence Period

Pre/Post Independence	*Year*	*Designated Heads*
Pre-independence	1858-1872	Superintendents of Andaman and Nicobar Islands
	1872-1942	Chief Commissioners of the Andaman and Nicobar Islands
	1942-1945	Japanese Military Commanders of the occupied Andaman and Nicobar Islands
Post-independence	1946-1982	Chief Commissioners of the Andaman and Nicobar Islands
	1982-till date	Lieutenant Governors of the Andaman and Nicobar Islands

Source: Administrative Report, A & N Islands.

Schedule (only the Andaman and Nicobar Islands in Part 'D') were to be administered by the President acting through a Chief Commissioner or other authority to be appointed by him. Under the Representation of Peoples Act, 1951 the Islands were allotted one seat in the Lok Sabha to be filled by a person nominated by the President, Subsequently under the Union Territories Direct Election to the House of People Act, 1965; this provision was changed to that of direct election.

On the recommendations of the State Reorganization Commission these Islands were constituted into a Union Territory without Legislature, through the Constitution (Seventh Amendment Act, 1956). Thereafter the Territory was being administered by the President acting through a Chief Commissioner. Under Article 24 of the Regulations, the President is empowered to make regulations for the peace, progress and good government of Andaman and Nicobar Islands. The regulation has the same force and effect as an Act of Parliament. Such Regulations can also repeal or armed any Act made by Parliament or any existing law which is for the time being applicable to the Union Territories (Table 9.3).

The first elected MP was K.R. Ganesh, who held that seat for two terms, from 1967 till 1977.

Representation of the people at local level came early. The Andaman and Nicobar Island (Municipal Boards) Regulation was promulgated in 1957, formalizing an arrangement that had been in existence since the 1930s, and giving it popular representation in

Table 9.3: Democratic Evolution

Year	*Acts/Regulations/Event*
1948	Chief Commissioners Advisory Council was constituted with 4 members
1950	Declared as Part D state
1951	Nominated MP
1956	Declared as UT (Article 239)
1957	The Andaman and Nicobar Island (Municipal Boards) Regulation was promulgated
1958	Chief Commissioners Advisory Council was constituted with 5 members
1958	The first election to the Municipality of Port Blair was held
1961	Chief Commissioner's Advisory Council was supplemented by the Home Ministers Advisory Council (body of 6 persons)
1961	Andaman and Nicobar (Gram Panchayats) Regulation
1967	Home Ministers Advisory Council (body of 7 persons) constituted
1967	Elected MP
1979	Pradesh Council indirectly elected was constituted with 30 members
1994	The Municipal Regulations of 1957 and the Panchayat regulation of 1961 were repealed by the Andaman and Nicobar Islands (Municipal) Regulation 1994 and the Andaman and Nicobar (Panchayat) Act, 1994, respectively, which were drafted to give effect to the greater autonomy and powers envisaged by the constitutional amendment, and to ensure that elections were held regularly for these bodies.

Source: Administrative Report, A & N Islands.

1958, when the first elections to the municipality of Port Blair were held. The town then had a population of approximately 14,000 and nine wards. Of its strength of thirteen members nine were elected and four nominated by the Chief Commissioner, The Deputy Commissioner functioned as the *ex-officio* Chairman of the Board.

In the rural area, which comprise to this day entire territory outside the area of Port Blair, the Andaman and Nicobar (Gram Panchayats) Regulation of 1961 brought in popular representation and a growing say to their people in the contact of their affairs. The Regulation came with a clause that made it inapplicable to the tribal areas—all the Nicobar Islands except the Campbell Bay area, and thus allowed in those areas the internal systems of village administration to continue undisturbed. In Andamans, the Jarawas, the Onges, the Sentinelese, and the Great Andamanese were also excluded from these systems—In the non-tribal areas, the territory was divided into forty-four Panchayats, forty-two in the Andaman and two in areas of Great Nicobar. At the apex level, administrative arrangement continued to move surely towards democratization. The visit of the Home Minister to the Island in 1963 led to the decision to reconstitute the CCAC, on the ground that the HMAC met only twice a year and local views needed to be taken into account more frequently. The reconvened CCAC was a Committee (22nd July, 1963), with six members, two *ex-officio* members of the HMAC also finding representation in it. In 1967, this membership was enlarged to 12 to provide representation in it of another non-official member of the HMAC as well a tribal member nominated by Government of India, and three representatives of village Panchayats nominated by the Chief Commissioner. From that to a Territorial Council, which had been a consistent demand for almost a decade, was a smooth step. In 1979, a thirty-member indirectly elected Pradesh Council was constituted by the promulgation of the Andaman and Nicobar (Administration) Regulation, 1979, whereby the earlier complaint that the Chief Commissioner, or for that matter, the Home Minister, called the Committees together infrequently was addressed effectively, and a formal procedure for the process of consulting the representative and experts of the territory was laid down. A Pradesh Council presided over by the Administrator, of twenty-four elected Pradhans of the various Gram Panchayats, the Member of Parliament and the senior Vice-Chairman of the Port Blair Municipal Board, three nominated tribal members, and, in case no woman found representation, a woman nominated for a term of four years, on the pattern obtaining in Arunachal Pradesh, was formed on 20 June, 1981. The Pradesh Council had Advisory functions to "discuss and make recommendations to the administration" on matters of administration relating to the Union Territory, involving general question, or policy and schemes of development in so far as they are related to matters enumerated in the State list or in the Concurrent list in the Seventh Schedule to the Constitution." This included the five year and annual plans, the revenue receipts and expenditure and matters of legislation for the union territory. The Regulation also provided for the nomination by the Administrator from among the Pradesh Council of five full-time Councillors, who were accorded status within the union territory as given to ministers in a state or union territory with legislature except that the advice of the Councillors to the Administrator on matters in the State or the Concurrent Lists was not binding.

The changed arrangement also affected the post of the Administrator. From 1982, it was upgraded to that of Lieutenant Governor, making available the services of a more experienced administrator than hitherto to the Island. The first Lieutenant Governor was M.L. Kampani (1982-85).

The Pradesh Council was endured for several years and further decentralization was introduced only in the 1990s, by the seventy-third and seventy-fourth amendments to the Constitution, which applied to the Andaman and Nicobar Island as much as they did to the rest of the country, but held deeper implications. In 1994, the Municipal Regulations of 1957 and the Panchayat Regulation of 1961 were repealed by the Andaman and Nicobar Island (Municipal) Regulation, 1994 and the Andaman and Nicobar (Panchayat) Act 1994, respectively, which were drafted to give effect to the greater autonomy and powers envisaged by the constitutional amendment, and to ensure that elections were held regularly for these bodies. The new municipality, with a total area of 16.64 sq.km and has eighteen wards, delimited afresh before election were held in 1995. The new Panchayat arrangement is a three-tiered one, with sixty-seven Gram Panchayat at village level, seven *Panchayat Samitis* at block level, and one *Zilla Parishad* at district level (Now two Zilla Parisad). While the Gram Panchayat members and their Pradhan and Up-Pradhan are directly elected, the Panchayat Samitis are constituted by indirect election, one member being sent up by each Gram Panchayat by election from amongst its members, and one-third of the Gram Pradhans being allowed into the Samiti every twenty months on a rotational basis. The Zilla Parishad's memberships comprised thirty representatives directly elected to that body, and seven *Pramukhs* or head of Panchayat Samitis, along with the Member of Parliament of the bodies are so constituted that one-third of the members of each at any given time are women, and the Chairperson of each, by rotation, a woman for at least one year of its five-year term.

The new Panchayat Act has the same jurisdiction as the repealed Panchayat Regulation, and is confined to the district of Andaman excluding the area occupied by the Great Andamanese, Onges, Sentinelese, and the Jarawas, but including the whole of the non-tribal Campbell Bay area. The Nicobar district is outside its purview. The blocks of Campbell Bay are included in the Zilla Parishad constituted for the Union Territory so that the District body also functions as a state-level body for all except the tribal areas.

The Nicobar District has been allowed to continue with its traditional system of government of a Chief, Second and Third Captain for each village; an Island Council comprissing all the village Captains and a Chief Captain they choose for themselves for each of the twelve inhabited Islands. An Island Council for each group of Island comprising the Captains of all the villages within its territorial jurisdiction. Modernity has inserted itself within this management in that the village Captains, since 1978, are elected every four years, by votes cast by all person more than 15 years of age; but tradition continues its hold through the practice that limits the contest for captaincy to five persons, nominated by the village leadership from among the village head, and disallows canvassing for vote.

The Zilla Parishad now being duly elected body, armed with power that extend into actual decision making and control of finances, the earlier Advisory Pradesh Council with the same jurisdiction, has been repealed as superfluous. This has led, not unexpectedly, to a demand for statehood from some quarters but regarding which the tribal have misgivings on account of their small proportion in the total population. Considering that the state election system has not been introduced into the Nicobar except for the choice of the member of Parliament for the Island, any state-level body to be put in place, would need to ensure that it does not force an abrupt change in the internal systems of government of the Nicobar or down out their voice by the sheer weight of numbers.

From the above mentioned developments it seems that slowly and gradually the islands are progressing in all the spheres including political autonomy. The demand for a legislature is genuine as it has been granted by the Central Government to Delhi and Puducherry. The inordinate delay for conceding such demand may be due to the peculiar economic and strategic considerations. Alternative models have been suggested from time to time in place of assembly but this is not acceptable to major political parties to carry out their programmes for all round development.

To conclude I would like to state that:

- Under these circumstances the need for state autonomy will definitely give greater participation for the people and lead to prosperity which is inevitable.
- The most accurate model for Andaman and Nicobar will be the Pondicherry Model.
- Regarding the financial crunch the solution will be in the respect of Mizoram, Manipur and Arunanchal Pradesh.
- The tribals of Nicobar may be induced to follow the same procedure like MP election or MLA election in their area without compromising the detribalization aspect.

- Above all there should not be any laxity for security or strategic importance.

As the topic of the Conference is poised with three critical angles such as strategic importance, political autonomy and sustainable development, much mind blowing debate, discussions and acceptance of past experiences should be taken into considerations before reaching a concrete conclusion for complete autonomy, now or after or never.

BIBLIOGRAPHY

Das, H.H. and Rath, R.N. (1989): *The Land of Coral Beds: Andaman and Nicobar Islands*. Berhampur: Kiran Publications.

Das, H.H. and Rath, R.N. (1991): *The Tribals of Andaman and Nicobar Islands*. New Delhi: Ashish Publishing House.

Dhingra, Kiran (2005): *The Andaman Nicobar Islands in Twentieth Century: A Gazetteer*. New Delhi: Oxford University Press.

Majumdar, R.C. (1975): *Penal Settlement in Andamans*, Delhi: Ministry of Education.

Mathur, L.P. (1968): *History of the Andaman and Nicobar Islands*. New Delhi: Sterling Publishers (P) Ltd.

Three-Tier Panchayati Raj (1992): 73rd and 74th Amendments to the Constitution of India.

Rath, Nirupama, (2006): *Education for Modernizing Tribals*, New Delhi: Deep & Deep Publications Pvt. Ltd.

The Andaman and Nicobar Gazetteer, 1901-1902.

10

Political State of Affairs *vis-à-vis* Political Autonomy for the Islands

Basudev Dass and Govind Ram

Prologue

Theoretically, politics is nothing but the way of life the peopie lead in a country by way of being governed by any specific system of governance. It includes its origin, ethnic, social pattern and economic development for, of, and by the people, especially in a democratic country like India. Politics also involves the subjects related to the boundaries of a State or area and its impact on its people and their cultural heritage.

Geographically, the islands of Andaman and Nicobar spread in an area of 8243 sq. km. in the Bay of Bengal consists of more than 550 islands (including very small rocky islets), of which only [illegible] are inhabited as on date. The entire island system is one of the most fascinating regions with a high degree of bio-diversity. Equally fascinating is its social ecology consisting of the tribal population as primitive and unique as the hunting, gathering groups as well as settled horticulturists, added by a wide range of immigrant population and though resettled at different points of time in history as the local, the post partition refugees, forest labourers, plantation workers, war veterans, government employees and businessmen.

The islands are divided into three districts, viz. South Andaman, Middle and North Andaman and Nicobar with Port Blair as its capital. The capital is situated in South Andaman District which has a sea distance of 1255 km. from Port of Kolkata and 1190 km. from Port of Chennai. Politically, the Island that forms a Union Territory, is administered directly by the Central Government through a Lt. Governor appointed under Article 238 of the Constitution of India and a group of his Secretaries and officials led by the Chief Secretary of the Administration. Located at the far South-Eastern side of the Indian mainland, these Islands are virtually much closer to some of the South-East Asian nations and practically a continuation of Malay Archipelago. Located in a high earthquake prone zone (Seismic Zone V), the region has two Islands of volcanic origin, viz. Barren and Narcondum, the former still live.

History

Any account of Andaman prior to 1789 may at best be termed as travelogues, some of them vague imagination, of course, interesting reading material. The first ever reliable history of Andaman dates back to 1789 when Lt. Archibald Blair, a hydrographer of the British Navy came to the archipelago to execute a brief of the Governor General of India, Lord Cornwallis, to survey the land, raise the British flag and set up a safe harbour for the refuge of ships in times of war or distress. Lt. Blair successfully executed the orders of the Government and established a colony selecting the Chatham Island in South Andaman in September, 1789, naming the place as Port Cornwallis. But on the recommendation of Commodore Cornwallis, younger brother of Lord Cornwallis, this small colony was shifted to North Andaman Island, in the year 1792. This new colony was again given the same name 'Port Cornwallis' and the earlier place of South Andaman was called the 'Old Harbour'. But, due to marshy and unhygienic land and inclement weather coupled with the resultant epidemic of malaria large number of casualties occurred in the colony and ultimately when the only British surgeon of the free settlement also expired, the small colony was closed and abandoned in May 1796.

Free settlers numbering 550 were shifted to Calcutta and 270 convicts brought for labouring were transferred to Penang. Besides this initially successful but ultimately unsuccessful British attempt of colonization, some other countries and ambitious travellers also attempted to explore feasibility of settlement or exploitation of natural wealth in Andamans. While the Danes made as many as four attempts to establish their occupation on Nicobars, in particular Nancowry between the period from the year 1756 to 1845, Austrians also made a single brief expedition to the Great Nicobar Island in 1868. But, obviously due to inclement weather coupled with lack of infrastructure, all such attempts miserably failed. This clearly proves that even before 1857 many big powers had their eyes on these small islands. But, as the British Empire already possessed its stronghold in the region including India, Burma and Indonesia, it is sure that even if not for penal settlement, some day or the other, British would have occupied Andamans as one of their colonies with safe harbour.

Due to increase in traffic in the Bay of Bengal, thereby requiring a safe harbour for refuge to the vessels in unfair weather, and above all the need of a safe and isolated place for incarceration of the freedom fighters of the first war of independence of India in 1857, the British, after an impasse of about sixty two years, for the second time occupied the Andamans in January 1858.

The Penal Settlement commenced from 10th March, 1858 when Captain J.P. Walker arrived on board the steam frigate *Semiramis* with 200 convicts, one overseer, two doctors and fifty naval personnel. The site chosen was the old harbour, naming it as "Port Blair" in recognition of the services rendered by Lt. Archibald Blair. Ross Island, situated at the entrance of the harbour became the headquarters of the penal settlement and remained so till 1942.

Before the establishments of the islands by the British in 1858 it had only the tribes from Mongoloid and Negrito origin. Mainly of the hunter gatherer type the Negrito group remained in the Andamans and included the Andamanese, Onges, Jarawas and the Sentinelese. Until 1858, their population was estimated to be over 5000 which drastically came down to a few hundreds. It was British to contact the Great Andamanese first in 1858 to face a strong resistance which was suppressed eventually by force. Perhaps this can go to the history of Andamans as the first Political battle on the land of the islands. The other two tribal groups stayed in the Nicobar District, viz. the Shompens and the Nicobarese. The Nicobarese, however, are now a civilized group and many among them now work within the ambit of bureaucracy, medicos, police, education, defence and private business establishments.

After the establishment of a British colony in Andaman Island in 1858, the Andaman and Nicobar Islands became the first penal settlement of the country. Bunch of freedom fighters as well as hard core criminals from mainland were transported to these Islands who cleared the forests around Port Blair and Chatham Island to create a settlement. Convicts continued to be brought to the Islands till 1942, when Japanese forces occupied the Islands. The whole-hearted co-operation of the islanders comprising convicts as well as their off-springs known as 'Local Borns' was, while on one hand, due to their high hopes of liberation from the British, on the other hand, to a greater extent it was under compulsion before the Japanese army. When the islands were re-occupied by the British in October 1945 the penal settlement was abolished. Along with the convicts and specifically after the construction of the infamous Cellular Jail, political prisoners too were brought in to isolate them from their contacts and activities in the mainland. Almost all the political prisoners were deported back to mainland while the other freed convicts and their descendents who did not, rather could not return to their homes, got settled in the Islands, on the meagre area of land provided to them for their sustenance.

The Non-Indigenous Population

By the turn of the twentieth century, these islands were inhabited more by the 'mainlanders' than the aboriginals. By the 1920s communities that were brought in included the Moplahs, Karens, Bhantus, Burmese and the Ranchis. Of these, the Moplahs were brought in from the coastal Malabar region of Kerala to contain the rebellion there; the Karens were brought from specific pockets in South Burma to work as labourers; the Bhantus—a group of denotified tribe, were brought mainly from the Etawah region in Uttar Pradesh, the Burmese came in as labourers as well as to work in petty services, and the Ranchis (including the Oraon, Kharia, Cheek, Munda and others) were brought in from the Chotanagpur belt to work as labourers, especially to clear the forests for settlements and plantations. The first group of the Ranchi workers came in 1918 with batches following through the years. Together they were around 34,000 heads by the beginning of 1950.

Post-Independence migration to the Andamans followed a pattern much different from the pre, 1947 movements of convicts, political prisoners, labourers and few select communities from different parts of the Indian sub continent. Refugee families from the East Pakistan were brought to be resettled. And with the beginning of First Five

Year Plan in 1951, rehabilitation packages were defined and given. Each refugee family from the erstwhile East Pakistan (now Bangladesh) was given five acres of paddy land, five acres of hilly land and one acre of homestead land with a support of milching and plough animals. The package was much generous compared to what was given to the settling convicts before 1947, which were given only three acres of land especially in the peripheral areas of Port Blair including Sippighat, Ferrargunj and Bimblitan. And this has been a bone of contention between the groups since then. The process of rehabilitation had indeed continued till 1971 with the last batch of the Bengali population settled in the Neil Island near Havelock and parts of Little Andaman Island.

In addition to the refugees settled, mainly from 1949 to 1956 and some up to early seventies, there was a large influx of people from Tamil Nadu from its specific districts. Though a small group of the Tamilians had already come during the early fifties and established shops and petty business, their influx began by the 1970s. And by 1990, the Tamil population had reached to the second dominating position followed by the Bengalis in the entire islands and the largest group in the South Andaman group having most of them making their encroachment-hamlets in and around Port Blair. It is also strongly believed that a sizable population of illegal migrants from Bangladesh and Sri Lanka has entered these islands especially during the last three decades. Apparently, such entries have been mutely accepted by the political groups and bureaucrats with vested interests.

Evidently, the Bengali speaking population from the erstwhile East Pakistan and the Tamil speaking population from Tamil Nadu helped such sneaky entries. Many among these entrants besides grabbing revenue land, have encroached upon large pockets of forest lands also, particularly in the North and the Middle Andaman. Such encroachments made up to 31st December, 1978, have now been regularized by issuing licences to the encroachers. Since the mid-eighties, there have been further encroachments, albeit protected by vested interests and political groups as vote banks, which now seems to be a never ending process mutely accepted by the administration.

Of the South Indian states from which a good deal of people moved to the islands especially since late sixties, the most prominent is Tamil Nadu, followed by Andhra Pradesh and Kerala. Significantly, an earlier batch of the Andhra fishermen were brought to the Andamans during late fifties and another group that came around the same time, had found employment especially in the jobs related to road and building construction undertaken by Public Works Department. Migration from Kerala became more conspicuous since the early sixties and a large number of such migrants who were unable to find employment in their native districts, were able to join the lower rungs of the bureaucracy in the islands easily, to a great extent due to their efficiency in ministerial jobs.

As per the 2011 Census, these Islands have a total population of 3.79 lakh. Over the decades, the highest growth has been during the 1951-1961 inter-census period followed by the next decade. Significantly, much of the rising decennial growth has remained concentrated in the Andaman group. In fact, a little more than 88 per cent of the total population in these islands, lives in the Andamans. The much curtailed movements of people to the Nicobar group of islands are primarily due to serious restrictions on non-tribal people to move and settle in these areas as imposed under the Andaman and Nicobar Islands (Protection of Aboriginal Tribes) Regulation, 1956.

The Bengalis, most among whom are descendents of refugees, and also those who have surreptitiously entered from Bangladesh, mainly belong to the lower and the middle rung. The refugees brought in even phases since 1949 through the fifties and then in 1964 and finally in 1971 were mainly settled in Diglipur (North Andaman), Rangat (Middle Andaman), in and around Port Blair (South Andaman) and the islands of Havelock, Neil and Little Andaman. The refugees from East Pakistan had mainly been agriculturists and most among the earlier batches took to cultivation. However, at a later stage, the second and third generation of the Bengali settlers gradually took to government and other petty jobs. Some of the later settlers, who came after 1964, got into growing vegetables especially in the islands of Neil, Havelock and Little Andaman.

The Tamil migration began during the fifties, a large number of them started entering the islands after 1970. With local support and chain like Kith-Kin-Peer migration, they began to dominate the services and the petty trade, business and the sales sector. In addition, they also work as subordinate agents and middlemen, and have encroached upon government land in the peripheral pockets around Port Blair as well as locations within its vicinity. Their presence is particularly overwhelming in the inter-islands vegetable trade, the transport sector, roadside vending, food joints, *pan-beedi* and cigarette kiosks and petty business in electronic and household goods. A small but muscular and labourious group of them is involved in sand extraction and selling at exorbitant prices.

A large section of the Hindi speaking population belongs to the 'local born' category, a term given to the descendents of Penal Settlers transported by the British. A majority of them belongs to lower and middle rung groups and depends generally on cultivation, petty services and government jobs. The Bhantus and the Moplahs initially started with cultivation and low paid jobs as well as activities related to running of petty food joints, but have gradually joined the main strata.

The Telugu speaking population mainly belongs to the scheduled castes and work as construction and road side labourers, as fishermen as well as low paid jobs in the service sector. Among the Malayalam speaking population while a section remains engaged in jobs in the lower bureaucracy and petty sales, there is another group working as cultivators and workers in farms and forests.

Among rest of the communities, it is the Ranchiwalas who have remained as one of the most deprived and marginalized lots till date. They were brought particularly as labourers to work towards clear felling of forests to create space for newer settlements, extraction of timber, a wide range of earth excavations, digging as well as construction works. Indeed the post-Independence 'development works' saw a large number of the second and third generations of the Ranchiwalas to be included in the labour force of the Andaman Public Works Department (APWD). Though they belong to different tribal groups such as the Oraon, Kharia, Munda, Mahli, Turi, Ghasi, Chik and the Dom, they are collectively labelled as the 'Ranchis'. The members of the Ranchi community though accorded a tribal status in the mainland, have never enjoyed any such status in the islands as this status has been reserved only for the aboriginal tribes in the Andaman and Nicobar islands. This community has never been an active beneficiary of government aided settlement packages and development schemes. It may not be out of place to state here that the other tribes, including that of the Nicobarese who have done reasonably well, enjoy several benefits and schemes of the government. The Ranchiwalahs seem to have been a neglected lot.

Mini India Becomes Part of India

In spite of a free pardon and an offer of repatriation granted to the convicts as well as ex-convicts at government expense, in 1946, a population of 14,000 preferred to remain in Andaman.

Notwithstanding the fact that the heroes of India's freedom struggle incarcerated in Andamans during the penal settlement, suffered many inhuman and intolerable brutalities at the hands of the British, the free colony which existed in Andamans on the eve of India's Independence on 15th August,1947 solely comprised the so called criminal convicts and their descendants.

In the post-war period, the Andaman and Nicobar Islands assumed greater importance for British, as in case of their withdrawal from India, which was almost evident after the war; these islands offered the only outlet to them for keeping their hold on Burma and Malaya. Within three months of re-occupation of the Andaman and Nicobar Islands, Lord Wavell started advocating the retention of the islands by the British government on account of their strategic value. With a deep foresight he argued, "We should not give up the Andaman and Nicobar Islands but should hold and develop them as outpost to Burma and Malaya." There is another important fact that just before India's independence on 15th August, 1947 many neighbouring countries like Burma, Indonesia and Australia had staked their claim for annexation of Andaman and Nicobar Islands to them, and on the ground of geographical proximity the claim of Burma was the strongest.

It is also little known that Bishop John Richardson of Car Nicobar inspired the tribes of Nicobar to petition to the British Parliament praying that since geographically and ethnically, the Nicobarese had nothing in common with India, the Nicobars be declared a separate British Colony. Surprisingly Indian leader like Krishna Menon was also not opposed to India's foregoing claim over the islands in lieu of settlement of its Sterling balance. Perhaps encouraged by such attitude the British India office excluded altogether any mention of the Andaman and Nicobar Islands in the Draft Bill which was prepared for the transfer of power to India and Pakistan after partition of the country. But, since the islands had long been administered as Indian Territory, fortunately any proposal to alienate them could not materialize.

The fact that between all this scramble the option as to which country they would like to be annexed to was given to the people of Andaman and Nicobar Islands, is perhaps never recorded anywhere in the history of these islands. But, such an option was given and some of the eminent citizens like Rathnam, R.C. Das *alias* Komi

Babu and Francis Lobo, all residents of Aberdeen, Saidu Moulvi of Phoenix Bay, Durga Prasad of Haddo, Lakshman Raju of Pahargoan, Kormayya of Birchgunj and Uma Prasad of Prathrapur, all of them since deceased, were invited to Delhi for a discussion and decision on this issue. It was the display of sheer patriotism on the part of these representatives of the people of Andamans towards their motherland India, wherefrom their predecessors were transported nearly a century ago that they unanimously opted for the annexation of Andaman Nicobar Islands to India thereby gifting the Mini India to Mother India. For the islanders this was the milestone on the path to become Indian to be governed by its own political leaders.

Post-Independence Colonization Settlement of Bengali refugees from erstwhile East Pakistan (now Bangladesh) in Andamans, aiming at food self-sufficiency through agriculture, proved a miserable failure as vast majority of the settlers had no knowledge or experience of agriculture or horticulture at all. Of course, a little more positive, farsighted and balanced approach would not have let the population of these islands to increase from a paltry figure of 30,971 in 1951 to 3,79,944 in 2011 Census.

Political History Through Peoples' Representation for the Socio-Economic Development of the Islands

With the declaration of Republic, the Islands were given the status of a Part 'D' State which was later changed to that of a Union Territory with the 7th Amendment Act, 1956 to the Constitution. Chief Commissioner was designated as the Administrator to work on behalf of the President of India *vide* Article 239 of the Constitution. An Advisory Council in the name of Chief Commissioner's Advisory Council, with four people's representatives was constituted in the year 1948 to advise the Chief Commissioner in framing of policies by representing the public opinion. The number of members was raised to five in 1948 and the Chief Commissioner's Advisory Council then comprised the nominated MP Mr. Lachman Singh, Mr. K.R. Ganesh, Mr. Rajani Ranjan Sarkar, Hajee Subhan Ali and Bishop John Richardson. In 1961 another body with six members was constituted to advise the Home Minister in the Centre with three *ex officio* members, viz. the MP, the Chief Commissioner, and the Sr. Vice Chairman of Port Blair Municipal Board and three non-official people's representatives. The Body was christened as the Home Minister's Advisory Council (HMAC). The advices is listed as:

(i) General questions of policy relating to the administration of the territory in the state field;
(ii) All legislative proposals concerning the territory in regard to matters in the state list;
(iii) Such matters relating to the annual financial statement of the Union in so far as it concerns the territory and such other financial questions as may be specified in the rules prescribed by the President; and
(iv) Any other matter on which it may be considered necessary or desirable by the Minister of Home Affairs that the Advisory Council should be consulted.

At a later stage the CCAC was given more importance due to the fact that the local views were needed to be taken into account more frequently. It was changed into a Committee instead of Council. The number of members were enhanced from 6 to 12 and then to 18 by 1973. Of the 18 members 15 were indirectly elected—2 persons from Municipal Board from among its elected members, 5 Pradhans from South Andaman and 5 from Middle and North Andaman, 1 captain from Nancowry and 2 captains from Car Nicobar. The HMAC was also included in the system of indirect election process. The HMAC then had 10 members and seven of them were elected by the members of the CCAC from amongst themselves. In 1977, the CCAC was further expanded with the inclusion of one each member to represent the three tribal communities, namely, the Onges, Andamanese and the Shompens, a non-tribal member from Campbell Bay and a woman member.

Meanwhile, through the promulgation of the Andaman and Nicobar Islands (Municipal Boards) Regulation, 1957, the Municipal Board came into existence in 1958 in Port Blair town with a population of 14,000 in nine wards. Of thirteen members, nine were elected and four were nominated by the Chief Commissioner. The Deputy Commissioner functioned as the *ex-officio* Chairman of the Board.

The islands outside the purview of the Town were brought under Andaman Nicobar Gram Panchayat Regulation 1961. This, however, did not include the tribes in Nicobar group of islands and other areas. This brought in popular representation and a growing say to the people in conducting the day-to-day developmental affairs in respective areas.

This created a concrete base and resulted formation of a Territorial Council for the Islands. With the promulgation of the Andaman and Nicobar (Administration) Regulation, 1979, the Pradesh Council was formed on June 20, 1981 with a term of 4 years each. Though 'Advisory' in nature it had functions to:

> "discuss and make recommendation to the Administration on matters of administration relating to the Union Territory, involving general questions, or policy and schemes of development in the matters enumerated in the state list or in the concurrent list in the 7th Schedule to the Constitution. This included the Five Year and Annual Plans, the revenue receipts and expenditure, and matters of legislation for the Union Territory."

The Regulation also provided for the nomination by The Administrator from amongst the Pradesh Council Members a five full time Counsellors, who were accorded status within the Union Territory as given to the Ministers in a State or UT with Legislature, except that the advice of the Counsellor to the Administrators on matters in the state or the concurrent list was not binding. The changed arrangement also affected upgrading the post of the Administrator from that of the Chief Commissioner to the Lt. Governor.

The Pradesh Council lasted for several years and did a lot good for the people of the islands. Though Advisory in nature, the Counsellors due to their personal spotless moral fibre, to-do attitude and personal relation, enjoyed much more autonomy and power then what was bestowed to them through the constitutional write-ups. They had zeal to work for and with the people. They not only made themselves accountable for every failure and success but also ensured the bureaucrats to share the flowers and brick-bats of the public. It can candidly be said in a Union Territory without Legislative Assembly that was an arrangement with perfect equilibrium of bureaucratic power and political democracy prevailed to a great extent.

But consequent to the 72nd Amendment to the Constitution of India the amended Andaman and Nicobar (Gram Panchayat) Regulation, 1994 was introduced and the Pradesh Council had to die untimely death to pave the way for three tier Panchayati Raj system with the formation of Zila Parishad in 1995. Sixty seven Gram Panchayats, seven Panchayat Samitis and two Zilla Parishads were created and later the bifurcation of the Andaman District into two, viz. South Andaman District and Middle and North Andaman District. Second Zilla Parishad also came into existence in the year 2008.

The Scheduled Tribe population of the Nicobar District and other areas has not been brought under the umbrella of Panchayati Raj system, but have been allowed to practice their traditional method. Of the six tribes, only the Nicobarese, by virtue of their larger population size and long years of contact with outside world through traders and missionaries are well educated, well settled, and are a part of mainstream who play the pivotal role in the islands' politics, but, only during the election for the lone Member of Lok Sabha. The tribes with the exception of the Jarwas and the Sentinelese, can also vote in the Parliamentary election alone.

The Nicobarese have their system of electing 1st, 2nd and Chief Captain at village and island level to run their administrative system, and the Government of India has an un-written nod to their Tribal Council which is yet to acquire a legal entity. Shan the Port Blair Municipal area, the rural area stands with a ratio of one elected representative per 130 voters. If the town is also included the ratio goes to 1: 200 voters. This is according to the 2009 voters' list available with the authorities.

History of Election in A & N Islands

The Andaman and Nicobar Islands consist of a single Parliamentary Constituency. It returns one Member to the Lower House. There is no Legislative Assembly. In this Union Territory, the first General Election to Lok Sabha was held on 18th February, 1967. Prior to this, during three terms of Lok Sabha, i.e. 1952, 1957 and 1962, Member of Lok Sabha from this Union Territory was nominated by the Administration and not elected by the people. The first of them was the leader of the Nicobarese, popularly known as the 'Father of Nicobars', Bishop John Richardson (1952-1957) followed by Babu Lachman Singh (1957-1962) and Lala Niranjan Lall (1962-1967), both from Port Blair. During 1967, there were 47,064 voters, comprising 32,386 male and 14,678 female. 36,732 voters out of the above used their franchise. Six candidates contested the Election in that term.

Table 10.1 shows the total number of electorates, vote polled and percentage of votes polled in the Election from 1967 to 2009.

Table 10.1: Total Member of Electorates of the Elections from 1967 to 2009

Year of General Election	*Electorate*	*Votes Polled*	*%age of Votes polled*
1967	47,064	36,732	78.04
1971	63,122	44,531	70.55
1977	85,308	60,692	74.14
1980	97,084	81,146	84.45
1984	1,15,534	91,077	78.83
1989	1,60,940	1,15,409	71.71
1991	1,69,120	1,08,822	64.35
1996	2,11,226	1,30,918	61.98
1998	2,32,013	1,47,698	63.66
1999	2,47,384	1,47,102	59.46
2004	2,41,353	1,53,825	63.73
2009	2,65,036	1,70,103	64.18

Source: Andaman and Nicobar Administration: Booklet published by Election Department.

Comments

This is an undeniable fact that the politics in a democratic system in a country like India is a politics of "Number" even today. The unprivileged, less or underprivileged, poor and suppressed people are the only tangible voters who decide the fate of the candidates.

General Findings

Being located far from the main part of the Mother India but due to its strategic location in the Bay of Bengal, the Andaman Nicobar Islands are directly under the Central Government. The lone Parliamentary seat in the Lok Sabha is more or less an expression of the community centred 'Vote Bank'. The situation has led to a near delinking of the issues facing the islands and the Parliament at distant New Delhi. And within such a scenario, it is the "Central" bureaucrats who hold, yield and articulate power through various central schemes and programmes.

Even the then Member of Parliament Mr. Manoranjan Bhakta was compelled to write and publish in the official media '*The Daily Telegrams*' once (August 1997): "Andaman and Nicobar Islands is placed in a unique position. Being Union Territory, it is directly administered by the Union Government. When the Country is committed for democratic polity, the people in the Union Territory are treated as a second class citizen. We do not have right to involve in the administration of the Union Territory. One man administration is the fact of life. He can do and undo anything he likes. The hopes and aspirations of the people in the Union Territory are crying in the wilderness. Those people who are coming from outside to these islands are deciding the fate of the islanders. A very suffocative situation which injures the pride and prestige of the common islander! In this UT, we the general public is captive in the hands of bureaucratic red-tapism, whimsical approach and attitude." *(The MP then was a Congress candidate and enjoyed the patronage of the Ruling Government in the Centre with a Congress nominated Administrator in the Islands).*

Political Findings

The Islands have indigenous population comprising tribes who are the original and real landlords of the islands plus the 'Local born' descendents of Penal Settlers who actually sowed, of course, under compelling circumstances, the seeds for evolution of a new civilization in these islands on one hand and the non-indigenous people who have come from 'Mainland India' at a much later stage when the islands got quite developed and fit for living and enjoying. The people were first brought by British under Penal Settlement and then by the Government of India under various settlement and rehabilitation schemes. The third section of people is encroachers, job seekers and businessmen, their foot-holds and real stake permanently fastened to the mainland India.

It was the people in the mainland India who brought the freedom for the country. When the question of retention of the islands arose, the representatives of the islands wanted to be a part of India alone. And they all had a sure inclination towards the Congress Party. Analogous was the situation with the settlers, who were the 'dream-Bengalis' of the then Chief Minister of West Bengal Dr. B.C. Roy of Congress, who wanted the Bengalis to prove their mettle in the islands by creating a smaller India here. And naturally the elections for Lok Sabha on a Congress ticket was a cake walk for any candidate. Till 1999 the Congress represented the islands in all sectors of elected body in the islands. It witnessed almost a feeble resistance from CPI(M) and others. It also had coalition with parties when failed to have absolute majority in Pradesh Council or Municipality a few times. It was the turn of Bharatiya Janta Party in 1999 and again in 2009.

The Political institutions in the Islands started with the Port Blair Municipal Board, Chief Commissioner's Advisory Council/ Committee, Home Minister's Advisory Council/Committee, upgraded Port Blair Municipal Council, Pradesh Council, Zilla Parishads and the lonc seat of Member of Parliament (Lok Sabha). With the defunct CCAC and HMAC, annihilated Pradesh Council and PBMB becoming PBMC, the three-tier ZP system, the PBMC and the institution of Member of Parliament remains in vogue.

The two other institutions are highly interested in public affairs if only those are related to construction activities. These are the activities which fetch the public representatives, right from village level to Zilla Parishad and Port Blair Municipal Council, the maximum returns which they would spent to win an election, the present and the next. The position and opposition goes with the wind soon the election results are declared, the appointments of Chairpersons and others are over and the committees are formed.

Political Autonomy: A Suggestion

Undoubtedly, the 'real' political representation alone can result the required change in a democratic country. We have the set-up which is malfunctioning, The Zilla Parishads blame of not being provided with needed fund. The departments transferred are either coming back to the administration or are of no delivery. In fact at present, there exist no political strength which can claim of doing well to their voters and fighting for the cause of the islanders as a whole.

At this juncture and proven political immaturity of the larger chunk of the leaders, it will be another blunder to offer an Assembly as vehemently demanded by many political as well as non-political groups. We had committed a blunder by scrapping the 'Pradesh Council' system where both, the politicians and bureaucrats were answerable and accountable in an Open House. Though advisory in nature, the politically elected members and Counsellors exhibited their zeal to serve the people as people had a forum available to them to question their representatives. Had the system been allowed to continue, the leaders would have become matured enough by now to ask for an Assembly and handle the needs of the islands and the islanders in a better way if not the best.

It is not that an error cannot be set right. A Pradesh Council or some analogous Institution is a correct answer with certain more powers and autonomy to the members and the Counsellors at this juncture. The planning and execution should go to them while the financial portion should be dealt jointly by the bureaucrats and the Institution. The representatives of the people need to be given more political autonomy with much financial restrictions.

And, at the same time the people/voters should also have the 'Right to Recall'. This is a system where and when the Peoples' elected representatives fail to deliver, the voters enjoy a 'Right' to 'Recall' them back through a signature campaign of majority voters of the particular Constituency or area as the case may be or in a manner whatsoever could be prescribed. This will force the elected representatives to work for the well-being of the society and the people who have voted them to the seats of power.

It is they who would then decide the requirements of the people and plan from and for the grassroots and not the bureaucrats. A separate Civil Service cadre for Andaman and Nicobar Islands is also the need of the hour. This will pave the way for both, the elected representatives and selected bureaucrats of the place who certainly have their attachment with the islands and the islanders to manage and deliver to the cause of the people of the islands.

BIBLIOGRAPHY

Andaman-Nicobar Administration (2010): *Election Department Booklet.*

Andaman and Nicobar (Administration) Regulation, 1979, for formation of Pradesh Council.

Bhakta, M.R. (1997): *The Daily Telegrams—Special Supplement 15-8-1997*, Andaman-Nicobar Administration.

Dhingra, Kiran (2005): *The Andaman and Nicobar Islands in Twentieth Century, A Gazetteer*, New Delhi: Oxford University Press.

Mazumdar, R.C. (1975): *Penal Settlement in Andamans*, New Delhi: Ministry of Culture, Government of India.

Part-IV

Developmental Process in Andaman and Nicobar Islands

11

Socio-Cultural Fusion and Sustainable Development in Andaman and Nicobar Islands

Nirupama Rath

"Sustainable development is development that meets the needs of the present without compromising the ability of future generations to meet their own needs. It contains within it two key concepts:

- *the concept of* ***needs****, in particular the essential needs of the world's poor, to which overriding priority should be given; and*
- *the idea of* ***limitations*** *imposed by the state of technology and social organization on the environment's ability to meet present and future needs*" (Brundtland Commission Report, 1987).

The concept of sustainable development is rooted in this sort of systems thinking *is based on* environmental, economic and social well-being for today and tomorrow. It helps us understand ourselves and our world. The problems we face are complex and serious and we can not address them in the same way we created them.

Cultural fusion in A & N Islands is one of the special features inherent in the society since the beginning of the settlement and occupation of the Europeans and the Asians. Intergroup solidarities are temporary bonds that already exist between groups but need to be brought to consciousness through a 'fusion of horizons'.

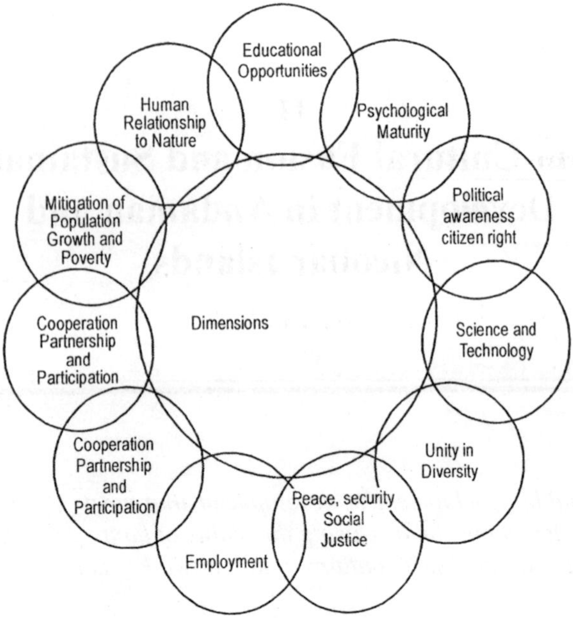

Fig. 11.1: Dimensions of Social Sustainability

Cooperation, Partnership and Participation

All governments must accept their responsibilities by introducing economic growth policies and programmes compatible with the protection of their own environment and that of others. They must ensure the protection of ecosystems of particular importance for agriculture and the way of life of the populations that depend on it. Furthermore, they must facilitate the participation of non-governmental organizations and decentralized or local communities to ensure that they can play a greater role in all development and environment related activities.

Mitigation of Population Growth and Poverty

A major hurdle to achieve sustainability is the alleviation of poverty. It has been widely acknowledged that poverty is one of the sources of environmental degradation. As population growth continues to increase, increasing pressure is being placed on the local ecosystem to provide basic essentials. According to the UN Population Fund, high fertility and poverty have been strongly correlated, and the world's poorest countries also have the highest fertility and population growth rates.

Table 11.1: Population Trend in A & N Islands, 1971-2011

Population	*1971*	*1981*	*1991*	*2001*	*2011*
Male	70027	107261	154369	192972	202330
Female	45106	81480	126292	163180	177614
Total	115133	188741	280661	356152	379944

Source: Census Report of Andaman and Nicobar Islands, 2011.

Table 11.1 depicts that within 10 years the male population has increased to 9358, Female population 14434 and total population 23792. It shows that the people are more conscious about the population growth which is a good sign of development.

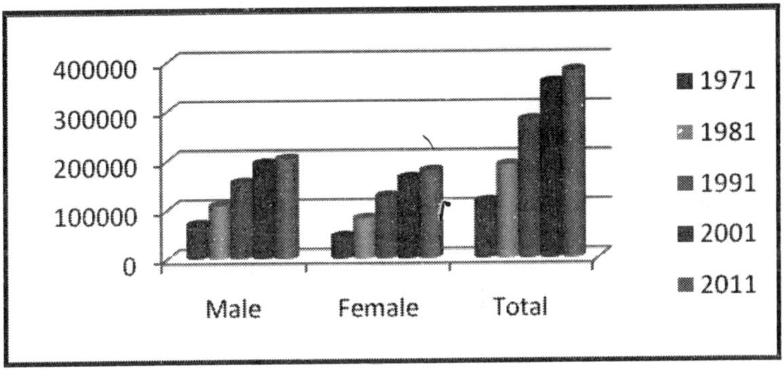

Graph 11.1: Population Trend 1971-2011

Table 11.2: Literacy Rate and Sex-Ratio in A & N Islands

	2001	*2011*
Literacy Rate	81.30%	86.27%
Sex Ratio	846	878

* Provisional Population Totals of 2011 Census of A & N Islands.

Source: *The Daily Telegrams*, 31st March, 2011.

A & N Islands now ranks 10th in the country so far as rate of literacy is concerned. The gap between the male and female literacy narrowed down from 11 per cent in 2010 to 8.27 in 2011 (*The Daily Telegrams*, 15.8. 2011).

Human Relationship to Nature

Forest and tribals have symbiotic relationship. The tribal people continue to live in the forest areas, although in isolation, but in harmony with nature. Recognizing this dependency, the National Forest Policy of 1988 stipulated that all agencies responsible for forest management, should ensure that the tribal people are closely associated with the regeneration, plantation, development and harvesting of forests so as to provide them gainful employment. Forests cover about 84 per cent of the islands' geographical area. Declining sources of sustenance have left them more vulnerable to food insecurity, malnutrition and ill-health. The cultural gap between the primitive tribal groups and the non-tribal societies is wide.

Extinction of Tribal Culture: As pronounced by the GOI, Welfare Programmes of Scheduled Tribes have to be based on respect and understanding of their culture and traditions and an appreciation of the social, psychological and economic problems with which they are faced. Therefore, along with various developmental policies and programmes initiated to improve the socio-economic conditions of the tribal people, there is also an urgent need to preserve and promote various aspects of the tribal culture and heritage, including their values of cooperation, community feeling, music, dance, literature, language, festivals/religion, knowledge and indigenous technology, skills, arts and handicrafts etc. The uniqueness of the tribal cultures which enriches the country's cultural mosaic, is fast disappearing and even getting distorted under powerful influences of the dominant culture (Table 11.3 and Graph 11.2).

Special facilities are provided in different fields through different policies and plans like National Policy for Empowering Tribals (NPET), National Resettlement and Rehabilitation Policy (R & R), Personnel Policy, A National Plan of Action for PTGs, Special Strategies, Special Central Assistance (SCA), Health Care, Food and Nutrition, Education, Basic Minimum Services, Employment and Income Generation, Agriculture and Shifting Cultivation, Forestry Development. Effective measures should be taken to improve the lot of the tribal women, Effective measures should be taken to improve the lot of the tribal youth, the tribal children and the tribal girl-children.

Table 11.3: Dwindling Tribes in A & N Islands Population Trend of PTGS during Last 10 years

Sl. No.	*Name of the Tribes*	*Population Trend*									
		2001	2002	2003	2004	2005	2006	2007	2008	2009	2010
1.	Shompens	389	389	389	389	389	389	389	389	389	389
2.	Ongese	96	95	96	94	97	97	97	97	96	101
3.	Great Andamanese	44	49	49	47	54	54	54	54	54	55
4.	Jarawa	240	266	266	300	300	309	307	309	351	365
5.	Sentinelese	39	39	39	39	39	39	39	39	39	39
	TOTAL	**816**	**838**	**839**	**869**	**879**	**888**	**886**	**888**	**929**	**949**

Source: Records from Department of Tribal Welfare.

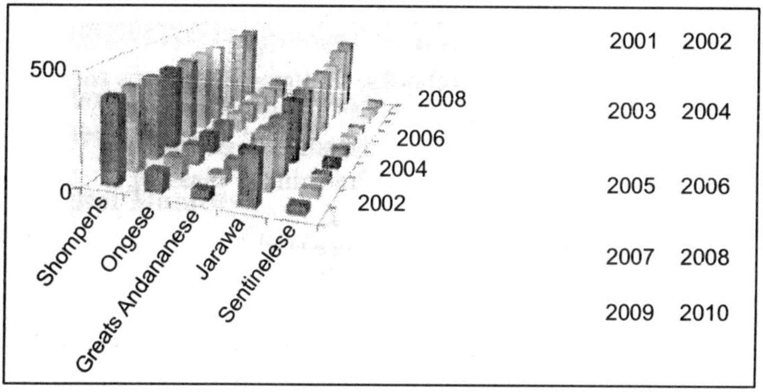

Graph 11.2: Dwindling Tribes in A & N Islands: Population Trend of PTGS during last 10 years

Educational Opportunities

The paramount importance of education in affecting social change is recognized. Mainstream education must now be realigned to promote awareness, attitudes, concerns and skills that will lead to sustainable development. Basic education which promotes functional literacy, livelihood skills, understanding of the immediate environment and values of responsible citizenship is a precondition for sustainable development. Such education must be available to every child as a fundamental right, without discrimination on the basis of economic class, geographical location or cultural identity.

Adequate resources and support for education for sustainable development are essential. An understanding must be promoted among key decision makers of the potential of education to promote sustainability, reduce poverty, train people for sustainable livelihoods and catalyze necessary public support for sustainable development initiatives. The empowerment of women and girls must be supported by actions to improve their access to basic and higher education, training and capacity building. The emphasis should be on gender mainstreaming.

The National policy on Education aims at ensuring free and compulsory education of satisfactory quality to all children up to 14 years of age. Keeping this as the main thrust area, the objective of the department of education is to provide primary school within 1.0 km. of every habitation with a population of 150 or above. Non-Formal Education Centres have been provided in remote habitations where primary schools are not available.

Following incentives are provided to all the tribal students and students belonging to BPL families:

- Free textbooks, notebooks, stationery, uniforms and school bags.
- Cooked mid-day meal to the students of classes I-VIII.
- Snacks to the students of Pre-Primary classes.
- Hostel stipends to hostellers.
- Free travel concession to those students who attend schools situated at a distance of 4 km. from their residence.
- Reservation of seats in professional/higher courses in various institutions of Mainland.
- Post Matric scholarship for tribal students studying in Mainland.
- Post Matric scholarship for class XI to XII to tribal students.
- Scholarship and financial assistance to pursue higher studies on mainland.
- Concession to the students in air and ship for studying in mainland.

Source: Directorate of Education, Andaman and Nicobar Administration.

There are 396 schools in A & N Islands spread over 36 Islands. Of these, 306 are managed by the Department of Education. The teacher pupil ratio is 1:16 against, all India average of 1:40 (*The Daily Telegrams*, 15th August, 2011, p. 12). The Administration is making all out efforts to increase enrolment and retention at school.

Table 11.4: Outlay and Expenditure of Annual Plans of 10th and 11th Five Year Plan in Educations.

Five year plan		*Annual plan*	*Outlay (Approved) in lakhs*	*Expenditure in lakhs*
10th Five Year Plan	1	2002-03	4650.00	4866.00 (Actual)
	2	2003-04	5100.00	4744.95 (Actual)
	3	2004-05	4877.00	4682.64 (Actual)
	4	2005-06	6012.00	5007.47 (Actual)
	5	2006-07	5500.00	5942.55 (Actual)
Total			**28344.00**	25243.61 (Actual)
11th Five Year Plan	1	2007-08	5990.00	
	2	2008-09	6600.00	
	3	2009-10	9837.00	
	4	2010-11	7259.00	
	5	20011-12	5479.00	
Total			**35165.00**	Continuing

Source: 11th Five Year Plan, Volume III-P: Z-1.

Table 11.4 shows expenditure on education which is not always in the increasing trend.

Psychological Maturity

Social sustainability focuses on individuals' behaviours, attitude and actions. The way of living towards a socially sustainable way may not necessarily provide a promotion of luxury and wealth, but rather, the development of reverse-consumerism. The ideal sustainable life style is not to end consumption but understanding the minimalistic requirement of it. Going back to the traditional source of behavioural teachings, parenting, the value of indirect education allows individuals to develop social awareness at a younger age.

Needs to develop:

- A positive attitude towards radical change.
- High aspiration.
- Vocational Guidance programmes.
- Aptitude based selection instead of category based selection.
- Organized systematic continuous counseling for the teachers, students, parents.
- Self-motivation to achieve the goal.

Political Awareness/Citizen Rights

The community provides democratic processes and open and accountable governance structures. In keeping with the objectives of the National Voters Day, a countrywide special campaign was taken up to reach out to the newly eligible (18 +) electors. As a result of these efforts, 51.65 lakh youths in the 18-19 age groups have been enrolled. The scenario in A & N islands is comparatively very low as regards to youth involvement connecting to age group of 18 +.

Table 11.5: National Population Register Data of A & N Islands as 2011 Regarding Youth Below 30 years.

Total/agewise population	*Population as per NPR*	*Eligible voters*	*Registered voters*	*Electors to population ratio*
Total population	386106	270623	264906	97.88%
18-19 years	–	14323	1123	7.82%
20-29 years	–	83344	78393	93.99 %

Source: National Population Registrar.

As per NPR (National Population Register 2009-10) figures there are 14,323 persons in these Islands in the age group of 18-19 years.

- As per Electoral Rolls, 2011, there are only 1120 persons of this age group, registered as voters, i.e. only 7.82 per cent of the eligible citizens are of this age group.
- It certainly implies that the students (18+) in colleges, ITIs, other Institutions have not shown enough interest to become an elector.
- This age group has to be tapped for ensuring their participation in the Electoral process.

Reasons for Low Registration for 18 + in A & N Islands:

- Migration for higher studies: For higher studies in mainland colleges after +2 the children of 18+ age group have no alternative but to go to mainland India. It is estimated that around 4000 students are admitted in different colleges, general, professional and technical institutions in Port Blair.

- Apathy, indifference towards election and election procedure. Apathy and lack of belief in politics as a medium for bringing about change. This manifests itself in several reasons that are normally cited for lack of participation such as "I don't have enough time", "How does a single vote matter", "There is no real leader" etc.
- Absence of effective and efficient political leadership.
- Lack of interest and initiative in grassroots level.
- Lack of belief in politics as a medium for bringing about change.
- Lack of awareness on voting rules and procedures among the rural youth of this age group.
- Ineffective functioning of community action groups, municipal agencies, voluntary organizations etc.
- Least involvement of educational institutions in the election process.

Table 11.6: Voters Turnout % in A & N Islands Parliamentary Constituency Polling Year: 2009

Tehsil	*Total Electors*	*Total Votes Polled*	*Percentage*
Diglipur	27,121	20,342	75.00
Mayabunder	17,083	11,867	69.47
Rangat	27,117	17,860	65.86
Ferrargunj	34,303	23,000	67.05
Port Blair	95,377	52,213	54.74
Little Andaman	12,449	8,610	69.16
Car Nicobar	13,730	10,143	73.87
Nancowry Group of Islands	9,160	6,626	72.34
Great Nicobar	5,013	3,324	66.39
Total	2,41,353	1,53,989	63.80

Source: Election Department, A & N Islands.

Table 11.6 shows that the total per cent of polling is 63.80 per cent. It denotes that the people of these islands are not so politically conscious. The table also depicts that the per cent of voting in Port Blair is 54.74 per cent. The polling in rural areas is better than urban area. It denotes the indifference of urban voter towards their voting rights.

Graph 11.3: Voter Turnout (in %) in A & N Islands Parliamentary Constituency. (Polling Year: 2009)

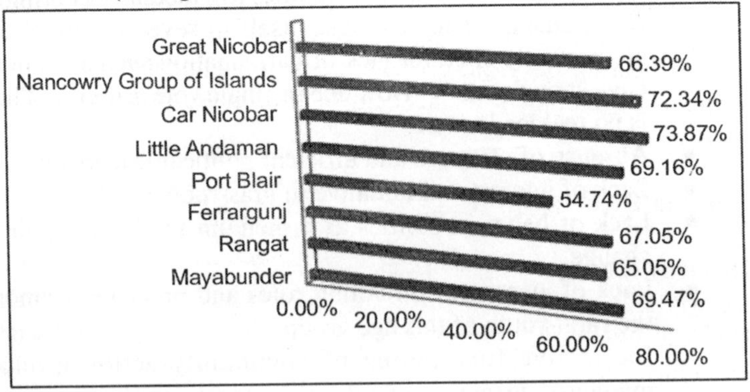

Source: Election Department, A & N Islands. (See Table 11.6)

Science and Technology

Science and technology is fast changing area which needs always to be updated. In this technocratic world everybody should be acquainted with modern technologies to peep the world. As it is far distant place it becomes difficult on the part of administration as well as people. For the better participation in all fields there is the need of strong and effective mass media which is to some extent, not up to satisfaction.

Developing countries need not follow the conventional path to development with regard to technologies but must use to their advantage the cutting edge technology options now available. Mechanisms must be put in place to make available to developing countries the latest technologies at reasonable cost. Technology transfer must be informed by an understanding of its implications in the social, economic and environmental contexts of the receiving societies.

Technologies must be usable by and beneficial to local people. Where possible, existing local technologies must be upgraded and adapted to make them more efficient and useful. Such local adaptations should also lead to the upgradation of local technical skills.

Within five years there is a fast change in the IT sector in these islands. Still it is lagging behind which needs more attention. The precautions are taken and facilities are provided. The Department of

Science and Technology is to act as catalyst, facilitator and enabler to promote scientific and technological capabilities. The Department intends to plan and co-ordinate various research projects which have special bearing on socio-economic development of these islands. There is development in the field of Information technology and E-Governance.

Unity in Diversity

Diversity encompasses visible and non-visible individual differences. It can be seen in the makeup of your workforce in terms of Race, Culture, National origin, Region, Gender, Age, Politics, Religion, Ethnicity, Disability, Socio-economic differences, Family structure, Health, Values etc. During British Occupation, the Penal authorities issued notice to the term convicts to call their families and provided them a piece of land and other life support items. To add some more women folk to the settlement the Imperial government instituted a committee to investigate the increasing mortality rate among the convicts at Port Blair.

Apart from the efforts by the state, the settlement was also offered and encouraged the convicts to bring their families from mainland India. There were nearly two hundred convicts who were willing to take a chance and made such applications. 266 letters were dispatched to kin and family members of the convicts. Out of 266 letters in only two cases women travelled to Port Blair. Later the officials confirmed that the families of convicts were reluctant principally on account of caste taboos.

Government of India, sent Alfred Swain Lethbridge, the Inspector General of Prison in Bengal with Lyall, who visited Port Blair in January 1890. Their extensive report in the month of April 1890 observed, "Provision of more women as wives for self-supporters is one of the chief needs of the settlement."

Table 11.7: Year-wise Convict Deportation to Andamans (1874-1901)

Year	*1-16*	*17-40*	*41-60*	*Over 60*
1874	20	4,582	1,991	476
1881		8,730	2,180	542
1891		8,815	2,421	502
1901		7,264	3,945	635

Source: Census Report 1901, Andaman and Nicobar Islands.

Table 11.7 denotes that maximum were in the age groups of 17-40 and 41-60 which were the cause of sex related crimes.

Table 11.8: Convict Population (Adults) during 1881-1905

Year.	*Convict population (Adults)*			*% of Females*
	Male	*Female*	*Total*	
1874	7,654	907	8561	10.60
1881	11,766	1,329	13,095	10.14
1891	12,532	1,439	13,971	10.29
1901	13,235	1,477	14,712	10.03
1905-06	16,070	1,494	17,564	8.49

Source: Imperial Gazetteer of India, Provincial Series, A & N Islands, p. 64.

Table 11.8 depicts the deportation of women convicts in the settlement. It shows that per cent age of female convicts were mostly within 10-11 per cent whereas in 1905-06 it was 8.49 per cent.

The political prisoners deported to the settlement were Bengali, Punjabi, Sindhi, Telugu, Malayalam, and Hindi speaking people.

The convicts were encouraged to call their wives and children from India. 468 members of the family of the Moplahs convicts joined them in the Andamans by 1926. Similarly, the Bhantus, the Sikhs and the Burman convicts were allowed to call their families.

It is worth citing here that as soon as the news of the Japanese occupation reached Car Nicobar in 1942 (Richardson, 1947), the traders were compelled to leave after the war. The Muslim traders from the island of Minicoy in the Lakshadweep came to be the dominant group among all in Nicobar (Richardson, 1947). According to the survey in 1931, of the 3,632 Nicobarese in Car Nicobar, 559 could converse in Hindi and 157 of them in Burmese. The situation in the central and southern islands was different. These had more intercourse with Malays and hence of the 2,531 Nicobarese there, 793 spoke Malay (Bonnington, 1931). Most of the traders got married in Nicobar; but when they are tired of them, they abandoned them and their children. Someone will marry the divorced, once again. In this way half castes children were born; left behind and uncared for. Because their religion forbids them to live with none other than Muslim religion relatives, they became vagabonds. Moreover they look down on their fellow Nicobarese.

There were marriages between the people of different religion, region, language which in course of time became a practice, and this was the cause of cultural fusion where there was no stink towards others.

In the Andaman and Nicobar Islands, where the Hindus and the Sikhs celebrate Eid and Christmas, the Muslims and the Christians celebrate Diwali and Baisaakhi lighting up *diyaas* (lamps), bursting crackers and offering prayers at Gurudwara alike, and thus share outstandingly inspiring message of *"Sarva dharma samabhava"*, *"Vasudhaiva Kutumbakam"* (Universal Brotherhood).

Peace, Justice and Security

Social disruptions like *war*, *crime* and *corruption* divert resources from areas of greatest human need, damage the capacity of societies to plan for the future, and generally threaten human well-being and the environment. Broad-based strategies for more sustainable social systems include: improved education and the political empowerment of the people.

Graph 11.4: Crime Statement of A & N Islands (2007-2011)

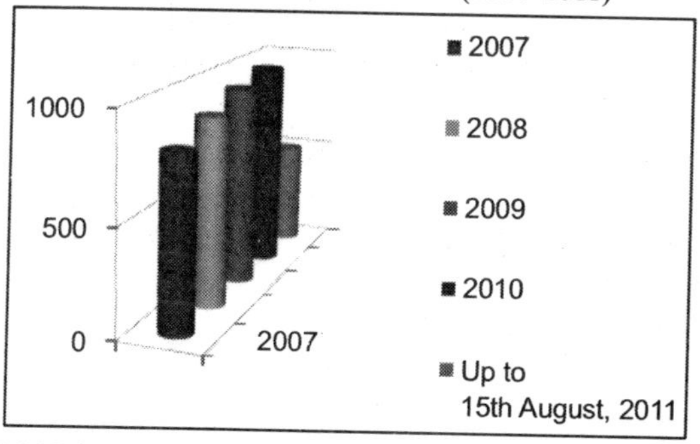

Source: A & N Island Police, Crime Branch.

It was a peaceful and crime free society though the settlement started with convicts, criminals and political prisoners. There was hardly a report of crime, corruption, malpractice etc. Efforts are on to curve if there are any.

In the aftermath of the Kargil operation, the importance of unified operations under a central command was felt necessary to handle present day conflicts, more so in the A & N regions and as a result of the Kargil Review Committee and on the recommendation of the Group of Ministers, the Andaman & Nicobar Command (ANC) was commissioned in 2000. It was formed on 8th October, 2001 as the country's first unified command comprising of Army, Navy, Air Force and Coast Guard as its four integral components. The primary role of the ANC is safety and security in the Andaman sea region (*The Daily Telegrams*, 15.8.2011).

Employment

Employment facility is a symbol of sustainable development. Up to last part of 1985 there was no unemployment problem and so there was no competition. After the completion of the different course there is no job opportunity in these islands which leads to frustration among the youths. Despite a large number of educated youth, there is a shortage of skilled manpower. This is the dilemma.

The problem lies in the education system. The Indian education system has a mismatch with the requirements. Institutes teach whatever they want. Institutes do not teach what is required. Country does not require what institutes teach. The syllabus committees have not been interfacing with the requirements. Many big industries have set-up their own in house training programme to fight with the problem. Most of the newly employed youths are compulsorily undergone employers own training programme. This enhances cost of employers enormously. It also wastes time.

Table 11.9: Total No. of Applicants Registered and per cent of Placement

	Total No. of Applicants Registered			*Placement*		
	Male	*Female*	*Total*	*Male*	*Female*	*Total*
As on 31.3.2011	26583	14239	40822	154 (0.579%)	137 (0.962%)	291 (0.713%)

Source: Employment Exchange (as on 31.03.2011).

Table 11.9 reveals that the placement for males is 0.579 per cent, for female 0.962 per cent and total 0.713 per cent in Government sector. There is no avenue for the employment in these islands as there are neither big industries nor companies. Only in the Government sector very few can be accommodated. Now the youths have started self-help groups with the bank loans and other plans/provisions suit to them.

Conclusions

The Universal Declaration on Cultural Diversity (UNESCO), 2001 elaborates the concept by stating that "cultural diversity is as necessary for humankind as biodiversity is for nature"; it becomes "one of the roots of development understood not simply in terms of *economic growth*, but also as a means to achieve a more satisfactory intellectual, emotional, moral and spiritual existence." In this vision, cultural diversity is the fourth policy area of sustainable development.

Though some of the points which are the symbol of sustainability, are attained but not up to the mark, socio-cultural fusion creates a mixed culture mingled in such a way that it is difficult to find out the traditional culture. For the better planning of sustainable development this aspect has to be taken into consideration. Social, cultural and educational development is the strong base of sustainability. The following suggestions are to be taken into consideration for sustainable development in A & N Islands.

- Precautions are to be taken to avoid the fissiparous tendencies like sectionalism, regionalism, lingualism, parochialism which may be impediment to such a harmonious society.
- For this broad outlook there is the need of community participation.
- IT sector development.
- Access to Mass media should reach the unreached.
- Employment-oriented education and diversified vocational training, which has been recognized as the need of the day, should be given top priority.
- Special efforts should be made to vocational education both at the middle/high school levels, depending upon the need and demand.
- Quality education.
- Tribal empowerment.
- PRI's are provided power but needs training how to implement the ideas and procure national values, develop leadership qualities and how to reach the unreached.
- The students (18+0 age group) have to be tapped for ensuring their participation in the Electoral process.
- For the better planning of sustainable development this aspect has to be taken into consideration. Job-oriented courses

should be accorded priority to extend functionally viable and productive education in tribal areas.

- A better governance regime is required to ensure cooperation and compliance. People of A & N Islands with Administration should plan and implement progressively for better sustainable development where everybody's suggestions, active participation, and, cooperation are required.
- It is incumbent upon the states, parliamentarians and local populations to work together, by cooperating and forming partnerships, to establish the basis for sustainable development.

BIBLIOGRAPHY

A & N Islands.11th Five Year Plan. Volume III.

Administration Report of the Andaman and Nicobar Islands, 1895.

Administration Report of the Andaman and Nicobar Islands, 1894.

Administration Report of the Andaman and Nicobar Islands, 1896-97.

Bonnington, M.C.C., 1932. *Census of India-1931 Andaman and Nicobar Islands*. Calcutta: Superintendent, Government Printing Press.

Brundtland Commission Report, 1987), *World Commission on Environment and Development 1987*. Towards 'Sustainable Development', *Science Age*, 1987.

Census Report 1901, *Andaman and Nicobar Islands*.

Election Department, A & N Islands. National Population Register Data of A & N Islands as on 05.01.2011.

Election Department, A & N Islands. Voter Turnout Percentage In Andaman & Nicobar Islands Parliamentary Constituency Polling Year: 2009.

Employment Exchange, A & N Islands, 2011 *Imperial Gazetteer of India Provincial Series A & N Islands*. 1994. New Delhi: Asian Educational Services.

Provisional Census Report 1911, Andaman and Nicobar Islands.

Records from Department of Tribal Welfare.

Records from Police Department of A & N Administration.

The Daily Telegrams, Special Supplement, 15th August, 2011.

The Universal Declaration on Cultural Diversity (UNESCO, 2001).

12
Sustainability in Agriculture in Andaman and Nicobar Islands

Pearl Devdas

Introduction

Sustainable development is a term that was first brought into common use by the World Commission on Environment and Development, a group appointed by the United Nations. The Commission made sustainable development the theme of its final report, *Our Common Future*, published in 1987. They defined the term as a form of development or progress that "meets the needs of the present without compromising the ability of future generations to meet their own needs." The transition to a sustainable civilization is hard to picture at present. Nevertheless, like justice, equity and freedom, it is important to uphold sustainable development as an ideal, a goal towards which all human societies need to be moving. To achieve it will take a radical shift in our societies, involving deeply held ideologies both of nature and human relationships with the new technologies ushering in. It is more relevant in case of small Islands like Andaman and Nicobar where the nature itself is more fragile and delicate to handle with. Future growth in agriculture would have to necessarily come from increased productivity from a shrinking natural resource base through efficient management. Agriculture growth and development can become sustainable only if we judiciously use our costly and limited water and land resources with the help of modern science and technology. Better agricultural practice will promote conservation of agriculture, organic farming which will help in sustainable production in agriculture. Such practices will no doubt bring about sustainable growth in agricultural sector in the long run in Andaman and Nicobar Islands.

Development is at crossroads with enormous consequences. Never before has humanity faced an array of problems as critical as the ones now faced. As forbidding and portentous as it may sound, what is at stake is nothing less than the survival of mankind itself particularly in small Island Nations around the world.

Where once nature seemed for ever the dominant force on earth, evidence is rapidly accumulating that human influence over nature has reached a point where natural forces may soon be besieged. The humanity on earth began to appreciate the depth of the potential danger of the so called development and its impact on our planet and our civilization.

The first major manifestation of the popularisation of sustainable development occurred at the *United Nations Conference for Environment and Development (UNCED)* in 1992 at Rio De-Janeiro, Brazil, (the Earth Summit) from 3rd to 14th June, 1992. As per the Agenda 21, the Rio Declaration on Environment and Development, the Statement of principles for the Sustainable Management of Forests were adopted by more than 178 Governments.

Agenda 21 is not a static document. It is a plan of action and meant to be hands on instrument to guide the development of the earth in a sustainable manner. It is based on the premise that sustainable development of the earth is not simply an option: It is a requirement. Agenda 21 is also based on the premise that sustainable development of the earth is entirely feasible. The bold goal of Agenda 21 is to halt and reverse the environmental damage to our planet and to promote environmentally sound and sustainable development in all countries on earth. It is a blueprint for action in all areas relating to the sustainable development of our planet into the 21st century.

Sustainability

Sustainable development is a term that was first brought into common use by the World Commission on Environment and Development, a group appointed by the United Nations. However, sustainable development means different to different people.

A Sociologist focuses on human needs and concepts like equity, empowerment, social cohesion, and cultural identity. The Economists are mainly concerned with growth, efficiency and maximum use of resources. An Ecologist and a Geographer show their greatest concern for preserving the integrity of natural systems, for living within the carrying capacity of the environment and for dealing effectively with pollution. Yes, it is true that there are many dimensions to sustainable development:

- Environmental,
- Social,
- Economic,
- Political, and
- Technological.

The transition to a sustainable civilization is hard to picture at present. Nevertheless, like justice, equity and freedom, it is important to uphold sustainable development as an ideal, a goal towards which all human societies need to be moving. To achieve it will take a radical shift in our societies, involving deeply held ideologies both of nature and human relationships with the new technologies ushering in. It is more relevant in case of small islands like Andaman and Nicobar where the nature itself is more fragile and delicate to handle with.

Andaman and Nicobar Islands

The Andaman and Nicobar Islands are an archipelago consisting of a group of 572 islands, islets and rocks with a total area of 8249 sq. km., located in the Bay of Bengal. The islands form an arc spreading over 740 km. The Andaman and the Nicobar group of islands are separated by the Ten Degree Channel. The official population count as per the 2011 Census was 3,79,944 spread over the three districts— The North and Middle Andaman, The South Andaman and the Nicobar.

The Andaman and Nicobar group of islands holds special interest for bio-geographers, ecologists, economists, anthropologists, sociologists and oceanographers for its diverse ecosystem. Anthropogenic factors responsible for the regression of ecological growth and the degradation of species diversity as well as the natural deleterious processes like cyclone, erosion, siltation, disease, pests (Boring sponges and bivalves), algal blooms, indiscriminate exploitation of environment, dredging, reclamation and pollution have definitely intimidated the islands ecosystem.

Therefore, there is undoubtedly a need to focus our attention towards a sustainable island ecosystem. Some broad areas where sustainable development can work effectively in safe guarding these islands' environment are:

- Agriculture,
- Tourism,
- Fisheries,
- Forest, and
- Industries.

Sustainable Agriculture

Green revolution in agriculture has made a significant contribution on aggregate supply of food grains, ensuring food security to the growing population. Now, agricultural growth faces a serious challenge in terms of sustainability of resources, indiscriminate use of chemical fertilizers and pesticides. Consequently, it has led to an increasing awareness and a need to move away from input intensive agriculture to sustainable farming practices worldover. Excessive use of chemical fertilizers, chemical pesticides and chemical herbicides has long lasting and hazardous effects on:

- Soil,
- Quality of agricultural produce,
- Health of farm workers,
- Consumers of the agriculture produce, and
- Terrestrial and aquatic life and environment.

Better agricultural practices are those which are safe to the environment, human beings and all living things on earth and also enhance the agricultural productivity. In India, we did practice these methods of farming in traditional agriculture since long. Now, these practices have once again entered our agricultural sector. These farming systems are:

- Sustainable Agriculture,
- Alternative Agriculture,
- Conservation Agriculture, and
- Organic Farming.

Sustainable agricultural practices should be economically, environmentally, and socially viable and also contribute positively to local livelihood. It is based on long term goals but not a specific set of farming practices. It is usually accompanied by a reduction of purchased inputs in favour of managing on-farm recources (Desai & Pujari, 2007).

Alternative agriculture encompasses a vast array of practices and enterprises, all of which are considered different from the prevailing or conventional agricultural activities for example the non-traditional crops, other farm products (Aquaculture) and other enterprises based on farm and natural resources like food processing and direct marketing etc.

Conservation agricultural practices includes minimum or zero tillage, letting crop residues get back into the soil instead of burning, immaculate land leveling to ensure the even spread of water, applying only need-based fertilizers and water to crops. The benefits of such practices are manifold. It helps in enhancing soil fertility, prevents environmental pollution caused by burning of crop residues, saves labour and energy required for repeated land tilling, and also reduces the use of water in agriculture, sparing it for other purposes.

The greatest advantage of conservation agriculture is that by letting biological residues get back into the soil, it transforms agriculture from a carbon emitter to a virtual carbon sequester by converting crop land into carbon sinks. Conservation agriculture is estimated to have spread globally to over 100 million hectares. In India, it is now practiced on about 2 million hectares (Goutam and Bhardwaj, 2011).

Organic manure production as well as organic cultivation of spices/paddy/pulses/vegetables is taken up through High Value Agriculture Programme/Rashtriya Krishi Vikas Yojana and is proposed to cover 10,000 farmers. About 948 vermi/organic compost units have been constructed. For regular supply of earthworms to the farmers 31 vermi-hatcheries have been established. About 9028 hectares of land in Car Nicobar district is planned to bring under this programme.

Thus, better agricultural practices should focus on sustainability in agriculture by adopting:

- Agricultural practices with reduced use of off-farm inputs with less harm to the environment as well as the consumers. Use of bio-fertilizers and bio-pesticide should be encouraged.
- Efforts should be made for better cropping patterns keeping in view the physical capacity of land.
- Improved methods of soil conservation, water, energy and biological resources as excessive use of chemical has resulted in degradation of our soil eco-system.
- Water is a crucial component of agriculture growth. Better water management by adopting such irrigation practices like drip and sprinkler irrigation which reduces the wastage of water. Rain water harvesting to increase water availability as well as recharge our ground water aquifers.

Future growth in agriculture would have to necessarily come from increased productivity from a shrinking natural resource base through efficient management. Simultaneously, conservation of natural resources must receive sustained attention. Agricultural growth and development can become sustainable only if we judiciously use our costly and limited water and land resources with the help of modern science and technology. With all these efforts, combined with the efforts of the farmers it is hoped that the agriculture sector will soon have total transformation in these islands. Better agricultural practice will promote conservation of agriculture, organic farming which will help in sustainable production in agriculture. All the inputs required for these farming systems will have to be produced locally which will thereby create more rural employment in agriculture, lower the cost of production as well. Such practices will no doubt bring about sustainable growth in agricultural sector in the long run in the Andaman and Nicobar Islands.

Organic farming or rather natural farming is the need of the day not just for the islands' farmers but for the entire country and world as well. The situation of the islands is different from mainland in preserving the biodiversity when compared to rest of the world. Organic farming is promoted in these islands in a mission mode. These islands are blessed with natural resources and also have all the qualities to go for complete organic farming. The entire islands cannot be changed into organic farming at one go, so to start with a small area can be taken up for organic agriculture and once the result is convinced by the farmers, the entire land could be converted to organic. Tamil Nadu Agriculture University, Coimbatore is providing all kinds of assistance as well as technical know-how to the farmers of these islands for taking up organic farming.

Organic farming is being taken up in a big way in these islands. As a part of it "Promotion of Organic Vegetable Cultivation" in Mission mode was launched in Neil Island on 1st February, 2015. Administration is promoting organic farming in the Islands and trying to declare the Andaman and Nicobar Islands as Organic Islands by 2018. 75 per cent subsidy is being extended for the organic inputs from 2016-17. The concept of "Kisan Mandi" will be introduced soon in Port Blair for facilitating direct marketing by farmers so as to avoid middlemen. "Brand Andaman" in vegetable, species and honey will be made and efforts are on to get certification for "Brand Andaman" so that our organic products can compete in the national and international market. The soil in these islands is fertile and provides ample scope for organic farming in these islands. Organic produce has a good national and international market and we can market our produce in Thailand as well.

The concept of organic farming is very much native to these island. Agricultural operations in these islands were carried out under rainfed conditions and thus have wide opportunities for implementing organic farming practices. This opens the door to immense possibilities for improving the soil health and overall environment and providing sustainable livelihoods in these Islands by updating the age old systems with modern research and techniques. The soil in this system is a living entity and the soil's living population of microbes and other organisms are significant contributors to its fertility on a sustained basis and must be protected and nurtured at all cost. Organic farming system relies on crop rotation, crop residues, animal manures, legumes, green manures, safe off-farm organic waste and aspects of biological pest control to maintain soil productivity and tilt to supply plant nutrients and to control insect, weeds and other pests.

The islands are very rich in biodiversity, and the agro climatic conditions are very much congenial for the organic cultivation of crops. Organic farming technologies need to be modified to further enhance the yields. It is desirable to invest in organic farming particularly in paddy, coconut and species in order to improve and develop the organic system in the Andaman and Nicobar Islands. The first tool to adopt organic farming is to enrich the soil not the crop. In A & N Islands, only about 5-7 per cent of total area is under agriculture and vertical growth of productivity is the only option. Challenges of biotic and abiotic stresses are more in the islands. "Organic agriculture" is perceived as the effective approach towards protecting the sensitive marine and terrestrial environment, high yielding, stress tolerant and good quality varieties can play an important role in enhancing and sustaining crop productivity.

About 30 varieties of field and horticultural crops mostly derived from the locally adapted germplasm which are safe to use and environment friendly, have been developed by CIARI, Port Blair. The varieties developed from the local germplasm showed better yield and adaptability and hence farmers can adopt it easily. The farmers can come forward for seed multiplication and even private firm can be contacted for seed multiplication. Seeds and planting material production in these islands will reduce cost and reduce chances of introduction of new diseases/pests through seed and planting material consignments from mainland.

In organic farming, farm wastes play an important role. Even a single blade of grass should not go out of the farm. It can be converted to compost. Every farm can have at least one cow for dung and urine collection. Vermi-composting of coconut palm wastes by using locally available earthworms is widely adopted by the farmers of these islands. The vermicompost and vermiwash can be utilized in augmenting vegetable production and floriculture in A & N Islands. Organic farming technologies involve growing cover crops and green manure crops. To enrich the soil biomass, yield and nutrient, contribution of Glyricidia alley cropping in coconut garden can be augmented in these islands.

In the Andaman and Nicobar Islands, more than 50 per cent of cultivable area is under coconut but the yield per palm is less as compared to other states and therefore, we should go for value addition of coconut which will fetch better price for the produce. Before adopting organic farming preliminary planning is required for growing such crops so that the farmer can get income on daily, weekly, monthly and annual basis.

Organic farming is an integrated approach where in all aspects of farming systems are interlinked and work with each other. The success of organic farming depends on climate, soil, agricultural biodiversity, socio-economic condition and market opportunity. As our islands receive rainfall from May to December, so during these months vegetables may be taken in low cost poly-house. Farmers may concentrate more on plantation crops. To take up organic farming the criteria to be kept in mind are:

- Identification of plantation areas.
- Surrounding land cover to be used for organic conversion in a phased manner.
- Quantifying the organic residue production at farm level.
- Its nutrient content.
- Suitable decomposing methods and value addition.
- Assessing the crop requirement and nutrient supplying capacity of the soil.
- Developing a nutrient supply model through organic matter within the farm to meet the crop requirement.
- Identifying measures to supplement the gap through external organic sources.
- For organic farming water harvesting is must. Farmers with their initiative and hard work can produce organic spices and give a brand name which will fetch a good price.

High value crops including vegetables and plantation crops can be brought under organic cultivation. The efforts towards organic cultivation has been a gradual process since many years. On 23rd October, 2003, the soil cultivation-*cum*-demonstration farm at Sippighat was declared organic and renamed "Organic Horticulture Farm."

Under UT plan, High Value Agriculture Programme and RKVY the Agriculture Department made concerted efforts for promoting organic cultivation to bring changes in the conventional agriculture of these islands. In Nicobar Islands, traditional natural farming system is practiced since centuries. Nicobar District except Campbell Bay, by default is practicing natural farming. To boost the effort towards organic and to increase the productivity of coconut, Car Nicobar Coconut Mission was launched on 28th January, 2009. Seeing the success of Car Nicobar Coconut Mission, Teressa Coconut Mission was launched during December 2011. As a result significant increase in productivity has been observed in both the Islands. Only organic techniques are being promoted in some of the Panchayats (Ferrargunj Panchayat in South Andaman District, Ramnagar Panchayat in N & M Andaman District and Kinyuka Village in Car Nicobar in Nicobar District) adopted under the Saansad Adarsh Gram Yojana. In order to demonstrate organic practices to the farmers efforts are taken to convert the Progeny Farm, Jirkatang and the Multipurpose Farm, Kerelapuram into organic farms. "Promotion of Organic Vegetable Cultivation" at Neil Islands in Mission mode was launched on 1st February, 2015 to promote organic farming in Neil Island, the vegetable bowl of South Andaman District.

Conclusions

1. There is scope of growth of organic farming in these Islands in a phased manner, subject to the availability and proper mobilization of organic inputs and technical support.
2. Rainfed regions of A & N Islands undoubtedly offer good scope for organic production of crops, for which research and development, capacity building through trainings both to farming community and field level functionaries are very much needed on different aspects of organic production like cultivation, harvesting, certification and marketing.
3. An Integrated Organic Farming System model have to be developed island-wise/soil category-wise to demonstrate various components of organic farming such as soil health care, soil and water conservation, solar energy harvesting, organic input preparation, renewable energy use, mixed farming, mulching, cultural and mechanical means of wed, insect and disease management, biodiversity conservation, seed sovereignty etc.
4. The entire Nicobar group of Islands offers scope for organic cultivation of coconut and other plantation crops whereas Andaman is highly suitable for organic spices, and after soil organic carbon improvement and amelioration of acid sulphate soils to considerable extent of area can be taken under paddy, sugarcane and in arable lands under vegetables.
5. Already a policy "Mission Organic" (MORGAN) is in place and need to be systematic and implementable as it possesses greater practical value.

6. A & N Islands are rich in biodiversity and the agro climate conditions are very much congenial for the organic cultivation of niche crops. However, organic farming technologies need to be fine tuned and updated to further enhance the yield of species, coconut, tropical fruits, high value vegetables and to some extent fine quality rich varieties in a cropping system mode.
7. Organic production in rainfed areas of A & N Islands not only boost the economy of this region but also sustain the productivity of natural resources and encourage eco-tourism.
8. For income generation the existing plantations can be developed into Agri-tourism model wherein the tourists can visit the farm and enjoy the farming activities by doing themselves and in return the tourists will pay to the farmer.
9. Multiple cropping should be followed by the Island farmers so that if one crop fails, another will come up and thus the farmer will not bear the total loss.

BIBLIOGRAPHY

Connel, O. (1992), Sustainable Agriculture—A Valid Alternative. *Outlook on Agriculture* 21(1).

Desai, B.K. and Pujari, B.T. (2007), *Sustainable Agriculture: A Vision for Future.* New India Publishing Agency, New Delhi.

Goutam, H.R. and Bhardwaj, M.L. (2011), Better Practices for Sustainable Agricultural Production and Better Environment in *Kurukshetra.*

Gautam, RK (2016). "Improved varieties of Horticulture crops for organic farming in Andaman and Nicobar Islands." Proceedings of State Level Seminar on Promotion of Organic Agriculture for Sustainable Development in Andaman and Nicobar Islands, Port Blair.

Jeykumar, S. (2011). Sustainable Agriculture in India—An Overview, in *Kurukshetra.*

Nadkarni, M.V. (1996), Forest, People and Economics, *Indian Journal of Agriculture Economics*, Vol. 51, Nos. 1(2).

Nebel, B.J. and Wright, R.T. (2000), *Environmental Science*, Prentice Hall.

Rodal, K. (1983), Breaking in Ground: The Search for a Sustainable Agriculture, *The Futurist* 1 (1).

Sharma, T.V.R.S. (2016). "Technologies involved in recycling Farm wastes in Plantation crops." Proceedings of State Level Seminar on Promotion of Organic Agriculture for Sustainable Development in Andaman and Nicobar Islands, Port Blair.

Somasundaram, E. (2016). "Organic Agriculture Development and promotion in A & N Islands." Proceedings of State Level Seminar on Promotion of Organic Agriculture for Sustainable Development in Andaman and Nicobar Islands, Port Blair.

13
Renewable Energy Options for Power Generation in Andaman and Nicobar Islands

Manohar Singh

Introduction

The Andaman and Nicobar Islands have a total area of 8249 sq. km. out of which 7171 sq. km., i.e. 87 per cent is forest cover. These islands are situated in the tropical zone with bright sunshine and are blessed with evergreen thick dense tropical natural rainforest; and the normal growth rate of trees is higher than that in the mainland.

Electric Power: Present Scenario

Due to geographical and topographical peculiarities of these islands, including separation of the islands by sea over a great distance, there is no single power grid for all the electrified islands and instcad a power house caters independently to the power requirement of an area/island, through a dedicated T & D systems.

During 2010-11 around 240 MU were generated and peak demand of 46 MW was met at a per capita consumption of 515 kWh against a national average of around 800 kWh. There are no power storages in the Andaman and Nicobar Islands.

Nearly 93.4 per cent of 81.2 MW installed generating capacity in the Andaman and Nicobar Islands is Diesel Based and 6.6 per cent capacity is from Hydro (5.25 MW) and Solar (100 kW); The renewable resources generate around 4.1 per cent of total energy.

Around 87 per cent of households are electrified. Around 75 per cent of energy is consumed by the domestic and commercial sectors and only around 5 per cent by industries.

Diesel Generating Capacity: Present Status

The energy generation and peak demand of the island grid of some major islands of Andaman and Nicobar during 2010-11 are as given below:

Table 13.1: Demand of Energy Capacity

Sl. No.	*Island*	*Installed Capacity (MW)*	*Energy Generation (MU)*	*Peak Demand (MW)*
1.	North Andaman	6.60*	10.33 @	2.80
2.	Middle Andaman	11.60	22.30	4.80
3.	Long	0.39	0.51	0.12
4.	Havelock	1.33	3.64	0.79
5.	Niel	0.56	1.05	0.27
6.	South Andman	41.64	179.60	32.00
7.	Little Andaman	6.47	8.28	1.80

Sl. No.	*Island*	*Installed Capacity (MW)*	*Energy Generation (MU)*	*Peak Demand (MW)*
1.	Car Nicobar	6.52	6.92	1.60
2.	Teressa and Chowra	0.67	0.82	0.25
3.	Katchal	1.27	1.13	0.26
4.	Nancowry and Kamorta	1.10	2.36	0.44
5.	Great Nicobar	2.71	4.22	0.80
6.	Other Islands	0.33	0.22	0.07

Source: Electricity Department, A & N Islands.

Note: Renewable Energy—* 5.35 MW (6.6%); @9.88 MU (4.1%).

Future Power Requirements

The Energy and Peak load requirements have increased by around 8 per cent and 7 per cent respectively during last decade.

According to 17th Electric Power Survey (EPS) of India, conducted by the CEA, energy and peak load requirements for the

A & N Islands are projected to be 344 MU and 77 MW by 2011-12. These are likely to double within a span of next ten years, to 779 MU and 132 MW respectively by 2021-22. However, these are likely to be much less as per past trends and present generation.

Additional generating capacity would need to be established so as to meet the energy demand in the coming years, which is most likely by establishing new Diesel Generating sets.

Diesel Power Generation: Constraints

Transportation of Diesel from Port Blair to various islands poses various difficulties due to rough seas and stormy weather specially during monsoons, which results in non-availability of fuel and curtailment of power supply in remote islands.

During last year around 45,000 tons of Diesel Oil costing around Rs. 200 crore were burnt for generating 240 MU of power which produced 1,68,000 tons of CO_2, a greenhouse gas, as per CEA base line data of 0.70 kg/kWh. of CO_2 emission by diesel engines. The cost of generation in A & N Islands is clearly the highest in the country (around Rs. 11.50/kWh) due to high cost of diesel oil. Electric power is highly subsidized to the extent of around 77 per cent. The actual cost of power generation would further increase to around Rs. 14.00/ kWh. if the existing subsidy on diesel of Rs. 6.0/lit and transportation cost from mainland (Haldia) to Port Blair of Rs. 3.00/lit is considered and added to the present HSD Oil cost of Rs. 38.15/lit. as per D.G.S. & D. rate contract.

Demand Side Management: Use of CFLs

Good quality CFL are to be made available to consumers at a meagre cost of Rs. 10-15, comparable to that of incandescent bulbs, so that high initial cost of CFLs is not a constraint in its penetration specially to rural poor households.

A study was done for providing 4/5 numbers of 15/25 watts CFLs in place of 60/100 watt GLS, to each of the 60,550 households in 11 islands. The cost of providing 2,80,000 CFLs was Rs. 4.12 crore. This replacement of GLS by CFLs would result in yearly reduction of:

(i) Energy requirement by 9.6 MU and peak demand by 5.5 MW;

(ii) Diesel consumption by 2690 KL costing Rs. 10.2 crore;
(iii) CO_2 emission of 6720 tons earning carbon credits of Rs. 53 lakhs; and
(iv) New capacity addition of 8 MW costing Rs. 28 crore.

The payback period on initial investment is less than 6 months, due to high cost of diesel generation.

Renewable Energy for Sustainable Development

The State Development Report 2006 on A & N Islands finalized by Planning Commission, calls for tapping of non-conventional energy sources instead of the high cost diesel power generation. It suggests studies to design suitable projects. Installations of wind farm at Car Nicobar, OTEC plants at South Andaman and exploitation of sea tide energy sources have been suggested.

Establishment of renewable energy system will supplement and reduce dependence on the diesel based power generation, and will be sustainable in long run, as these offer multiple advantages:

- They are environmentally sustainable and economically viable.
- Decentralized power generation to suit local needs.
- Viable solution for energy problem in remote islands.
- Rural socio-economic growth.
- Raising forest in the form of energy plantation.

Ocean Energy: Studies

OTEC

As per preliminary study by IIT, Chennai during 1984, four sites in South Andaman were found to have potential to install OTEC plants. However, there are no operational plants in the world and OTEC is in technology development stage.

Tidal Power

A CEA team visited few creeks in South Andaman during 1992 and identified some locations for further study. However, the average tidal variation in Andaman and Nicobar Islands is less than 2 m, which is very low as compared to other locations in the country at Cambay, Kachchh and Sunderbans which have 5-6 m of tidal variation. Hence tidal power generation in Andaman and Nicobar Islands, would not be techno economically viable at present.

Wave Energy

A 150 KW wave power plant was established by IIT, Chennai at Vizhinjam, Kerala as a pilot project, during 1991-92, but this plant got damaged within one year due to cyclonic waves. There are no operational plants in the world and this technology is under development.

Wind Energy: Assessment

The Andaman and Nicobar Islands are generally hilly and are characterized by low ranges of hills and valleys, and some islands are flat.

The MNRE had conducted wind resource assessment programme at 10 locations in these islands since mid 1990s, for identification of high wind prone sites with an annual mean wind speed of 18 km/hr and above.

Only one location at Car Nicobar was found to have an annual average wind speed of around 18 km/hr., and wind power density of 174 Watts./m^2, which is lower than the requirement. No other location was having even this wind potential.

Wind farms would require around 10 Ha/MW of plain land, free from obstructions, to maintain required distance between the turbines. Considering the topography and around 90 per cent forest cover of these islands, sufficient land would not be available for large wind farms in Andaman and Nicobar Islands.

Access to windy locations at hilltops for movement of cranes for erection of higher capacity turbine rotors on towers of around 50 m height would also pose problems.

Hydro Energy: Status

A 5.25 MW Hydro Electric Station at Kalpong, the largest river in North Andaman, was established 10 yrs. back at a cost of around Rs. 65 crore.

This plant till date has generated around 89 MU of electricity saving around 25,000 KL of HSD costing Rs. 70 crore and reducing 62,300 tonnes of CO_2 emission.

There are no other large rivers of sufficient head and discharge in these islands. Two/Three small rivers and streams could be harvested which have small power potential of around 100-500 KW.

Solar Energy: Performance

As per ground solar radiation data of IMD Station, Port Blair, the average annual solar radiation available for SPV modules, at optimum collector tilt angle of 35°, is 4.8 kWh/m^2/day (1750 kWh/m^2/year), which is lesser than the national average of 5.5 kWh/m^2/day. One 50 kWp grid connected SPV Power Plant was established each at Neil Island and Havelock Island during 2002-04, with Battery backup, and were feeding power to the island diesel grid.

Havelock SPV Plant

It was 7 km. away from diesel power house and at the tail end of 11 KV feeder. It developed problems of component corrosion failures and battery and is non-functional since 8/08. This plant had not performed satisfactorily and electricity generation per day per kWp. was below 3.4 kWh.

Niel SPV Plant

It was connected the busbars of nearby diesel power house, and also developed problems of component corrosion failures and battery and is non-functional since 10/10. This plant had better performance but the electricity generation per kWp per day was also below 3.4 Kwh.

5 MW SPV Power Plant at South Andaman—Proposed

A 5 MW SPV Power Plant, having mono crystalline Modules, to be connected to a 33 KV sub-station 800 m away, is being established by NTPC at Port Blair at a cost of Rs. 81 crore as an IPP. This plant will, on an average, feed 6.24 MU of electricity per year, at a capacity utilization factor of 14.2 per cent and generation of 3.4 kWh/kW/ day, at a tariff of Rs. 17.91/kWh, for 25 years. It is estimated that PV cell degradation etc. will reduce the plant output to 80 per cent in the 25th year. 5MW capacity has been felt appropriate for grid stability, due to intermittency associated with Wind & SPV power outputs, as the day time peak demand is around 20 MW.

During 25 years lifetime, it is estimated that this plant would generate 156 MU of electricity saving 41260 KL HSD Oil costing Rs. 157 crore at present market rate. It would reduce CO_2 emission by 1,09,300 ton as CERs and earn Rs. 7.90 crore by Carbon trading at the rate of 11 Euros. The A & N Administration would be paying Rs. 279.60 crores to NTPC for this purchase of solar energy in 25 years.

Bio Mass Based Power Generation

The following technologies are technically and commercially viable and proven and could be established at different islands for base load power generation, to replace the diesel generation.

(i) Gasifier with 100 per cent Gas Engines.
(ii) Combustion based power generation.

The successful operation of Bio-Mass based power generation system would require abundant and continuous supply of biomass resources. These could be coconut fronds, shells and husk; Arecanut fronds and husk; Red Oil Palm Fronds, Empty fruit bunches, and fibre; old coconut, arecanut, ROP and Rubber trees, lops and tops during forestry operations etc. and fuel wood from energy plantations. The various Electricity Regulatory Commissions in the country have fixed the tariff for sale of electricity produced from Biomass power projects to state grid which is ranging between Rs. 3.50-5.00 per kWh, with 3-5 per cent annual escalation.

Gasifier with 100 per cent Gas Engines

Systems up to 500 kW capacity of proven technology are available and functioning at different locations in the country since last few years.

Combustion Based Power Generation

Biomass in direct combustion method is used as fuel in the steam boiler to produce high pressure steam, which is expanded in turbine generators to produce electric power.

This technology is very reliable as the various components of the system are being used for different applications for a long time now. Such combustion based power plants of 2 MW and above capacity, mostly in 5 MW range, are operating at many locations in the country, utilizing bagasse and biomass as fuel, since many years.

12 MW, Energy Plantation Based Biomass Power Plant at Tamil Nadu

A 12 MW IPP which would utilize 1 lakh tonnes of casuarina and other biomass per year from private energy plantations, is coming up at Villupuram, Tamil Nadu; having an annual rainfall of 1020 mm; to feed 84 MU of power to TNEB Grid.

20 MW, Biomass Based Power Plant at Kaui Island, Hawai, West Pacific, USA

Kaui Island in the Hawaiian Archipelago has an area of 1456 sq. km. with a population of 67,000 at density of 46 persons per sq. km. Around 15 lakh tourists visit this island every year and the electric power requirement is 80 MW, which is presently met by Diesel Generation.

A 20 MW biomass based power plant, the biggest in the world, is being set-up in this island which will generate 25 per cent of the islands electricity needs. The fuel will be grown in the island in different energy plantations and private farmers will cultivate biomass crops so that the Kaui island becomes energy self sufficient. This plant will result in decrease of more than 350,000 barrels (56,000 KL) of petroleum import to Kaui and retention of around $ 30 million (Rs. 140 crore) in local economy.

Little Andaman Island: Proposed Biomass Based Power Generation

Little Andaman is the 4th largest Island of Andaman Group having an area of 732 sq. km. with 90 per cent forest cover and population of 18,800. The Andaman and Nicobar Forest Plantation Development

Corporation (ANFPDC) has established a Red Oil Palm Plantation in 1593 Hect. and local farmers have cultivated coconut and arecanut in 1582 Hectares. The fronds, empty fruit bunches, fibre, shell and old trees of ROP plantation and coconut and arecanut fronds generate agro residue which can be used as fuel for biomass based power generation.

The Andaman and Nicobar Forest Plantation Development Corporation (ANFPDC) initiated a proposal for establishing a 1.5 MW Biomass based power generation capacity in the island, which would need 15,000 tonnes of biomass per year, though the surplus agro residue available was estimated at around 40,000 tonnes/year.

Energy Plantations

Select species of trees and shrubs are grown and, once they attain a specific height and growth in a shorter time, are cyclically harvested and are cropped or coppiced periodically for their biomass to be used as fuel wood, so as to satisfy local energy needs in a decentralized manner as inexhaustible and sustainable renewable energy source.

The tree/shrub species for energy plantation are *Acacia, Prosopis juliflora, Eucalyptus, Subabul, Casurina equistifolia, Bambusa balcooa* (Bema Bamboo), *Melia dubia, Paulownia* etc.

When fossil fuels such as coal, oil, gas etc. are burnt, they release CO_2 to atmosphere, which is the main GHG that contributes to global warming. Bio Mass absorbs CO_2 and emits O_2 while growing as energy plantation during photosynthesis under sunlight; which is balanced when the biomass is burned. If biomass resource is used sustainably, there are no net carbon emissions over the time frame of a cycle of biomass production.

The attractive features of energy plantations are:

(i) Heat content of wood is similar to that of Indian coal.
(ii) Wood is low in Sulphur and hence less polluting.
(iii) Ash from burnt wood is a valuable fertilizer.
(iv) Reduces soil erosion and regenerates soil.
(v) Purchase of fuel from rural families generates rural jobs and rural prosperity, rather than expenditure of foreign exchange for import of diesel oil.
(vi) The local power plants will provide assured market for fuel wood from energy plantation of local farmers, at pre-

negotiated prices and avoid cost of transportation of diesel from Port Blair to Islands.

Casuarina as Energy Plantation

Casuarina is a large evergreen tree, with straight slender long stem (32 m) with angled branchlets, minute and scale like leaves, which survives up to 40-50 years and the wood is very hard. Casuarina is raised as an agro-forestry crop in the country in TamilNadu, Karnataka, Kerala, Maharashtra and Gujarat and is used as timber, poles, scafolds, rafter and fuel. Casuarina tree also protects soil erosion, stabilizes loose soil and sand dunes, conserves environment and functions as a wind breaker.

In the Kachchh district of Gujarat, which has an annual rainfall of 250 mm, energy plantation in 1000 hect., waste land was initiated in 1990 and a 500 kW grid connected biomass gasifier system was established during 1998.

The IFGTB, Coimbatore, along with Forest Department, Port Blair took up a project during 2005 for eco-restoration of tsunami devastated coastline of Andaman Group of Islands, by planting Casuarina, which have shown very fast growth at Little Andaman, South Andaman etc. Casuarina grows as a natural forest in many part of A & N Islands and is also planted during *Van Mahotsavas.*

Beema Bamboo: High Yielding Energy Plantations

Beema Bamboo, which is a clone of *Bambusa balcooa* bamboo found in Assam and N.E. India, is multiplied by tissue culture. Beema Bamboo plantations have been established in many parts of the country and also by Hemarus Technologies Ltd., Belgaum, Karnataka; Agrigold Ltd., Andhra Pradesh and Suryasharkra Power Corporation Ltd., Hyderabad.

Some private farmers in Gujarat, Tamil Nadu and Karnataka have also established such plantations. National Mission on Bamboo Applications (NMBA) is also encouraging large scale plantation of suitable varieties of bamboo, all over the country.

The growth of Beema Bamboo planted by Forest Department at Nayashahar, South Andaman has also been encouraging, and are suitable for tropical climate of these islands for production of biomass and poles.

MNRE Report on "Dedicated Energy Plantations and Forest Residues"

MNRE prepared a detailed report during August 2011 on "Dedicated Energy Plantations and Forest Residues", which mentions that "7000-8000 tonnes of solid biomass (small chips, twigs, branches) are required annually to generate 1 MW at 70-75 per cent PLF, with calorific value of 3500-4000 kcal/kg." Casuarina plantations are able to generate 20-25 tonnes/hect./year of biomass, in 4-6 year rotation, having a net calorific value of 3500 kcal/kg, which is suitable both for gasification and combustion. Beema bamboo plantations are able to generate 30-40 tonnes/hect./year of biomass per year in 3-4 years rotation.

Beema bamboo has been tested for fuel characteristics and found to be very ideal for generation of electricity either by gasification or combustion; and has a calorific value of 4000 kcal/kg. Such energy plantation in around 300 hectares of degraded/marginal forest and non forest land; as per draft document on "National Mission for Greening India" by MOEF; could provide sustainable supply feed stock for one megawatt power plant. Such plantations would require around 100 man days per hectare.

The States are to take initiative for promoting dedicated energy plantations linked with biomass power projects in Forest/Non-Forest and degraded lands in association with Forest Departments; and on lands available with Forest Corporations.

The States to formulate simple guidelines for developing energy plantations linked with biomass power generation as announced by Government of Rajasthan.

Sustainable biomass projects would be promoted to be implemented on PPP mode.

MNRE has provided around Rs. 225 crore during the 12th Plan for resource assesment surveys and establishing plantation projects of minimum 100 Acres size.

Conclusions and Recommendations

(i) With 94 per cent diesel based generation, costing more than Rs. 14.0/kWh. and difficulties in transportation of Diesel to distant islands, whose consumption will increase in future, diesel based development would be non-sustainable.

(ii) The Planning Commission, MNRE and State Development Report 2006 are emphasizing for utilizing all Renewable Energy Resources.

(iii) In the tropical climate of ANIs having very high rainfall and sunshine, scientifically managed energy plantations would produce large quantity of biomass and generate rural employment.

(iv) Around 400 hectares of Casuarina and Beema Bamboo plantation, yielding around 20-25 tonnes/ha./year, on 4-5 years rotation, would produce around 8,000-10,000 tonnes of Biomass. This would be sufficient to operate one megawatt plant producing 6.5 MU of electricity and also generate employment for 200 persons around the year.

(v) Energy Plantation in 1593 Ha. of Forest Corporation's ROP area at Little Andaman would sustain 4 MW Power Generation.

(vi) 600 Ha. of Forest Corporation's 40 years old Rubber Plantation at Katchal would sustain 1.5 MW Power Generation.

(vii) Kamorta, Nancowry and Teressa Islands have large grassy lands. Assuming that 10 per cent of total area of these islands (356 sq.km.) being usable grassy area for growing suitable species of energy plantations, the biomass would sustain 9 MW Power Generation and employment for 1800 local persons would be generated.

(viii) The Energy Plantation in these islands, i.e. Little Andaman, Teressa, Katchal, Nancowry and Kamorta could be established and maintained on PPP mode, and the Biomass Production could be locally utilized.

(ix) Gasifiers with 100 per cent Gas engines in modular form, could be operated on PPP mode at all these islands for power generation.

(x) Combustion based power generation systems of capacity 2 MW and above, can be operated at Little Andaman and Car Nicobar on PPP mode for power generation.

(xi) Good quality CFLs to be made available at very nominal cost, for replacement of all incandescent bulbs in all households, for reducing energy requirement, peak demand and diesel consumption; as the payback period will be only 6 months due to diesel generation.

14
Sustainable Tourism Development in Andaman and Nicobar Islands

Hema Bannerjee

Introduction

Sustainable development is defined as a pattern of social and structured economic transformation (i.e. development), which optimizes the economic and social benefits available in the present without jeopardizing the likely potential for similar benefits in the future. A primary goal of sustainable development is to achieve a reasonable and equitable distributed level of economic well-being that can be perpetuated continually for many human generation. In recent times, the term sustainable development has become a new catch phrase. It has become a common parlance for all concerned, from every country up to the level of UNO. The term was used by the Brundtland Commission which coined, what has become the most oft-quoted definition of sustainable development as "development that meets the needs of the present without compromising the ability of future generations to meet their own needs, improved living standard for all better protected and managed ecosystem and a safer, more prosperous future" (Brundtland, 1987). Thus sustainability is a paradigm for thinking about a future in which environmental, societal and economic considerations are balanced in the pursuit of development and improved quality of life. Sustainable tourism development envisages:

1. Operating within natural capacities for regeneration and future productivity of natural resources.
2. Recognizing contribution that people, communities, customs and lifestyle make to tourism experience.
3. Providing these resources with equitable share in the economic benefits of tourism.

Concept of Sustainability

Sustainable development, therefore, is the development that takes the impact on the environment into account and tries to minimize environmental damage to the maximum possible extent. Sustainable development is generally thought to have three components: environment, society and economy. The well-being of these three areas is intertwined not separate. The sustainability paradigm rejects the contention that casualties in the environmental and social realms are inevitable and acceptable consequences of economic development. To be precise, sustainable development is a process in which economics, trade, energy, finance, agriculture, industry and all other decisions are implemented in such a manner so that it becomes an important tool to usher into a society which is economically, socially and environmentally sustainable in all respects. Therefore, the prime objective of sustainable development is to meet the needs of the present without compromising the ability of the future generations to meet their needs by properly maintaining the balance (Chakroborty, 2009).

Tourism related Developments

The hubs identified as principal excursion points for development are Diglipur, Mayabunder, Rangat, Port Blair, Havelock, Neil island, Little Andaman, Katchal and Great Nicobar. Thirty six beach sites spread over 15 Islands will be appropriately showcased to attract tourism investments. The Andaman and Nicobar Administration has initiated steps to develop tourist cottages, tourist vehicles, water transports, and entertainment facilities in various tourist destinations. Forest Department, Forest Corporation as well as Andaman and Nicobar Islands Integrated Development Corporation have participated in the development of tourist spots and facilities in the respective areas. Private guest houses, hotels have come up in suitable places along with restaurants bar and other comforts. There has been an increase in the number of tour operators in these Islands. In the recent times, there has been an increase in the availability of number of products and informative materials for the tourists in the local market. Sales- *cum*-exhibition centres have been opened by the Anthropological Survey of India museum, Forest Emporium, Fisheries Department Aquarium, Naval Sea Coral Emporium, Khadi Gramodyog Sales Emporium and District Cottage Industries Sales Emporium. A group of professional and non-professional guides have been engaged to help the tourists regarding their programmes and stay in these Islands.

Future Prospects

To attract more and more tourists from the mainland as well as abroad, tourism infrastructure needs tc be upgraded to cater to the demands of the high end tourists. House boats can be introduced in the creeks of these islands for the nature loving tourists to have a better view of the nature. Instead of organizing annual Islands Tourism Festival, exhibition, food festival and cultural festivals need to be organized to attract domestic as well as international tourists. Tourism circuits need to be established to have perfect inter-islands connectivity. In recent years, one thing that has been noticed, is that lots of tourists are not able to visit other islands due to non-availability tickets.

The Andaman and Nicobar Islands society is virgin and an unpolluted heaven for islanders as well as tourists. The Andaman is an upcoming tourist destination. The natural greenery and deep blue sea water along with silver clean sandy beaches welcome the travellers from various parts of India and abroad. It is a paradise known for its peaceful social life and hospitality of local people. These small islands are enriched with the past history of the British untold stories of torture, inhumane treatment of Indian convicted prisoners and killing of thousands of innocent unarmed aboriginal tribes. Both the British as well as the Japanese cruelty is still alive in and around Port Blair. Cellular Jail, Ross Island, Viper Island and Humphrygunj martyrdom are some of the historic places attracting the tourists, academicians, historians and research scholars. As these islands are far away from mainland India and surrounded by sea water, the frequent communication is an all time problem for government. The air fare is very high.

Vision of Tourism in the Islands

To promote tourism industry by exploiting its bio-diversity and enriched forest, sea and coastal beauty, the Directorate of Tourism have encouraged the private parties to come up with tourism development as an alternative source of income and employment. Department has identified and developed few tourist destinations in and around Port Blair and other Islands. The vision of the administration was to develop an unmarked island destination for eco-tourism without disturbing its natural beauty and its sustainability, especially to protect the aboriginal tribal heritage and their free movements. A new tourism policy was formed in 2009 by the local administration to meet the upcoming demands of tourist destination. Tourism is increasingly considered to be the emerging lifeline of these islands. There are only 13 islands available for tourism development. The policy identified 36 beaches spread over 15 islands which will be appropriately showcased to attract tourism investment (Bannerjee, 2012).

Focus on Tourism Developments

The Andaman and Nicobar Administration have decided to play a key role in the achieving the objectives of sustainable tourism developments for the islands economy.

(a) Augmenting infrastructural facilities.
(b) Providing the required support facilities and incentives to investors to encourage private investment in the tourism sector.
(c) Facilitating availability of trained manpower by providing training and exposure to local youth.
(d) Prepare master plans and strategies.
(e) Providing faster mode and adequate transport facilities for connectivity.
(f) Ensuring adequate safety and security for tourists.
(g) Encouraging public-private partnership.

Table 14.1: Arrival of Tourists in Andaman and Nicobar Islands from 1991-2013

Year	*Domestic Tourists*	*Foreign Tourists*	*Total Tourists*	*% in tourist increased*
1991	32242	2248	34490	—
1992	35817	2435	38252	9.76
1993	35000	1771	36771	–4.02
1994	50737	3798	54535	32.57
1995	64490	3839	68339	20.19
1996	67958	5796	73754	7.34
1997	73558	4724	78082	5.54
1998	74732	4915	79647	1.96
1999	77448	6035	83483	4.81
2000	81432	4634	86066	3.00
2001	85866	5249	91115	5.54
2002	90629	4707	95336	4.42
2003	93899	4281	98180	2.90
2004	105004	4578	109582	10.40
2005	30225	2164	32389	–238.34
2006	118580	9045	127625	74.62
2007	136015	10975	146990	13.17
2008	124439	12512	136951	7.33
2009	142045	13692	155737	12.06
2010	180781	14615	195396	20.25
2011	202221	15814	218035	10.38
2012	230732	14981	245714	11.26
2013	240607	17811	258418	4.91

Sources: Directorate of Information and Tourism (2014): Port Blair.

The arrival of tourists in the new millennium in these islands has increased remarkably except in 2005. The sudden decline in tourist traffic to Andaman was due to high density earth quake followed by the killer Tsunami in December 2004 which hit the Bay Islands and claimed thousands of lives. The volume of foreign tourists has increased since then. To revive the lost tourism sector due to earth quake and tsunami in 2004, Union government had instructed the employees of Central Government Organizations to avail LTC to Andaman. According to, Mr. G. Dinakaran, the then President of Andaman and Nicobar Tourism Guild, LTC tourism is killing the industry. The unscrupulous traders and travel agencies in mainland are benefiting from tourists coming to Andaman. Andaman is the only destination in the world where the tourists make money. With the help of fake bills, both the tourists and agencies earn approximately Rs. 25000 from each tourist for a trip to Port Blair (*The Light of Andaman.2007*). Around more than one lakh tourists arrive in

Andaman yearly out of which 90 per cent visit Havelock. A group of agencies are engaged in selling the tickets in black, of ferry boats and other entry points and charging extra from the tourists. The cost of food in the hotel is very high at Port Blair.

A number of job opportunities have started with the development of tourism industry. Tour permitted vehicles ferry, auto/taxi, luxury cars, buses are operated by hotel owners and tour operators. Ticket agencies, Package Tour Companies have developed a good network with mainland cities. Many local people have started tourism related activities like opening tourist cottage, vehicles, restaurant-*cum*-bars, hotels etc. Bars have been opened indiscriminately in and around city areas and tourist places. There is no doubt that many people have benefited who are attached in many ways to tourism business.

Problems Associated with the Development of Tourist Spots in Various Parts of the Islands

Social security and cultural integrity are inevitable aspects which cannot be ignored while defining the term 'Sustainable development'. Hence in the areas where tourism industry is developing, all these sensitive issues should be taken into account. The spots identified are mostly settlement areas where the Bengali and other community people, uprooted and migrated from their ancestral places, were rehabilitated. These rehabilitated families have managed to reorganize their socio-cultural lives. The new generations have gone through a transitional stage. The entry of thousands of tourists and increase in the tourist activities have not only changed the mode of developmental aspects of these areas but has also resulted in creating an alien socio-cultural atmosphere which has brought about a vast change in their lifestyle.

Havelock is a role model of the tourism development in Andamans with the increase in the pace of the development, the related infrastructure has also grown. People have become business oriented. The price of land has become so costly that it is beyond the reach of the common people. The lands are being sold out to hoteliers from mainland at an exorbitant rate. There has been an increase in the number of middlemen in this process. The cost of living has risen. Education has been affected due to high concentration of tourists. In spite of increase in the frequency of water vessels, the local passengers are unable to get tickets at reasonable rates. The employment opportunity has increased both in the case of skilled as well as unskilled labourers. But the jobs in the skilled sector are being availed by the mainlanders. There has been an increase in the number of family litigations in the recent times. There has been disintegration in the family/community relationship. More people have started consuming liquor especially the younger generation as a result of which there has been erosion of values among them. Disputes have become a common feature between the land owners who have leased out their lands and hoteliers when the latter refuse to leave the land even after the expiry of their lease. There has been an increase in the encroachment of undemarcated forest land as well as revenue land. There has been an increase in the illegal construction of buildings by violating the coastal regulation. Moreover, the frequent movement of tourist vehicles in the Jarawa territory has not only disturbed and limited the free movement of the Jarawa tribal people but also has resulted in bringing about an imbalance in the fragile ecology of this area. There has been instances of tour operators charging extra from the tourists by promising them a view of the indigenous tribal people of Andamans.

Neil Island, a tourist spot having three thousand populations at present, is facing acute problem. A very few tourists are reported to visit these island but in the name of tourist development, at least five bar-*cum*-restaurants have been opened attracting lots of local people. The consumption of liquor has increased to a very great extent and has affected the younger generation very badly.

Within a decade, the tourism activities has developed manifold. As a result, all the local as well as mainland investors have started taking interest in purchasing land preferably in tourist spots, in seabeach line, market place etc. Hence, the cost of land in such areas is exorbitantly high. The agricultural land, plantations and hilly lands are being sold out by the local cultivators. Within a couple of years, the cost of land has increased hundred times. The spots identified for tourism development are mostly settlement areas, where Bengali and other community people have been rehabilitated by the Government of India as cultivators. The settlers are now selling out their land at higher rates to business people. The unscrupulous middlemen actively negotiate with the parties. In many of the cases, the middlemen cheat the innocent villagers at the time of agreement and sale of lands.

With the increase in the sale of land in the recent times, there has been an increase in the number of middlemen. There has been lot of instances where there has been increase in the disputes between the owners and the hoteliers. Due to frequent movement of vehicles in the Jarawa territory, the free movement of aborigines has not only been limited but has also created an imbalance in the fragile economy due to the promotion of the tribal tourism by the stake holders of tourism sector. There is a need for a complete ban on child labour in the restaurants. Besides these, line permits need to be introduced for the domestic tourists to visit the islands. Tourists trade regulation needs to be introduced to have check on unauthorized tour operators.

BIBLIOGRAPHY

Andaman and Nicobar Administration: *Tourism Policy, 2009*, Port Blair.

Andaman and Nicobar Administration (2009): *Basic Statistic*, Andaman and Nicobar Islands.

Bannerjee Hema and Swapan K. Biswas (2012): Sustainable Tourism and its Impact in Islands Society: A Comprehensive Study In *International Journal of Trade in Services,* Vol. 4(2).

Brundtland Commission Report 1987: World Commission on Environment and Development 1987. Towards 'Sustainable Development', Science Age.

Chakroborty, Manas and Anindya Guha (2010): Sustainable Development In *South Asia Politics*, Vol. 9(5).

Das D., Basudev: *The Light of Andaman,* September 2007.

Department of Tourism (2014): Basic information on Tourists in Andaman, Andaman and Nicobar Administration.

Planning Commission (2005): State Development Reports, Andaman and Nicobar Islands, *India Today*, May, 2008.

15

Development *versus* Conservation of Little Andaman

An Approach Paper with Special Focus on Tourism

Sweta Banerjee

Introduction

Development is a commonly used phrase. Linguistically, development is the gradual growth of formation of something; more precisely it is the process by which a thing or a person matures, changes or advances to another stage to realize inherent potentials. The term can be used in many context, viz. Economic, Political, Environmental, Science and Technology etc. It is also defined as a process of expanding human choices, taking into account equity, sustainability and empowerment aspects. Now-a-days there is a word in circulation: Human development. The concept of development gained prominence in the post-Seoncd World War period. In fact, the nations started their economic growth in order to achieve the development in a greater way and fast. This has rationally increased the industrial growth in most of the developed and developing nations but it was realized by the end of 1960s that so called development did not bring the desired change in the standard of living in the majority of people living in the poorer countries. Rapid industrialization along with urbanization and modernization has resulted in the depletion of natural resources at a very fast pace without achieving development in the true sense. The United Nation's Conference on the Human Environment held in Stockholm in 1972 raised the first signal about the negative aspect of prevailing development strategies. The conference took the initiative to redefine 'development' and laid a political foundation for 'sustainable development'. 'Sustainable Development' is a very appealing phrase developed in the penultimate decade of twentieth century. The term came into focus in the 'World Conservation Strategy' published by the Bruntland Report in the year 1987. The principals regarding sustainable development received global acceptability after the United Nations Conference on Environment and Development (UNCED) was held in Rio de Janerio in June 1992. The earth summit initiated the thinking towards natural resource conservation and sustainable development on a global scale (Bebarta, 1992).

Definition and Approach

An **"environment"** is the whole of surrounding things. Surroundings are defined by a central entity. In ecology, environment refers to the surroundings of humankind. Generally, environment refers to the biological, physical and social things on the earth or in inhabitable space outside the earth's atmosphere.

The environment has two major components-physical and cultural. Physical components include geology, soil, climate, natural vegetation, landscape etc. and cultural components include forestry, agriculture, industry, the elements of land use and demography.

Ecology is the scientific study of the relations that living organisms have with respect to each other and their natural environment. Ecology is a sub-discipline of biology, the study of life. The word "ecology" was coined in 1866 by the German scientist Ernst Haeckel (1834-1919). The various components of the nature especially the interaction of living organisms with their biotic environment gives the importance upon ecology. Tansley (1935) stressed, "The term eco-system includes not only the organisms but also the whole complex of physical factors forming what we call the environment." E.P. Odum (1969) on ecological system rightly said "Any area of nature that includes living organisms and non-living substances interacting to produce an exchange of materials between the living and non-living parts, denote an ecological system or eco-system."

Recent awareness regarding environment, natural resources and its conservation reflects a growing concern. Due to population explosion and different developmental activities on this earth, there is an increasing pressure everywhere on the tropical evergreen rain forests, leading to their rapid destruction. Due to this, very limited patches of virgin tropical forests are now left all over the world, Little Andaman being one. The Island is endowed with a very rich variety of plant and animal life both on land and in sea, of which some are unique. But in recent years, with increasing human activities in the Island the natural ecosystem is getting increasingly disturbed. Previously isolation helped conserving different endemic plants and animals in Little Andaman. But later, developmental activities in this Island were mainly restricted to harvesting of forest resources with uncontrolled pollution of sea which may ultimately lead to the extinction of many marine fauna. The native tribal community of the Island, i.e. the Onge are also in the threshold of extinction because they are closely related with natural environment. The socio-economic development of the tribal people from mainland outlook has been taken into consideration without paying much attention to native cultural tradition and ecosystem. It is still noticed, even now, that the hunter-gatherer community protects and preserves their environment and have extensive knowledge about the plants and animals around them.

Since the Island is open for rehabilitation of displaced persons as a measure for the development of Island along with the activities by Forest Department and Forest Corporation and harbour activities for better communication facilities both by Andaman Harbour Works and Andaman Public Works Department (APWD), an influx of officials and Ranchi tribal people arrived in the Island. The outsiders treated forest as they treated it in the mainland and started clearing forest and burning it for settlement, agriculture and fuel apart from the allotment of land and timber given to them for building their houses.

The natural eco-system of the Andaman and Nicobar Islands including Little Andaman may be divided into three different ecosystems:

1. The Forest Ecosystem.
2. The Mangrove Ecosystem.
3. The Marine Ecosystem.

Each of the systems depends on one another to form a total ecosystem. Functionally each system differs from another, but in totality different functions of the systems help to form an ecosystem which consequently governs the entire environment of a particular place. The three natural ecosystems help to form the resource base for the Man-made Ecosystem—Forestry, Industry, Agriculture and Fisheries, as man and environment are an extremely complex interactive phenomenon. Ecologically Little Andaman has remained stable for a long period of time with a variety of flora and fauna and the hunter-gatherer tribe the Onge.

Little Andaman Island has an ecosystem that does not occur anywhere else in the Andaman or in Nicobar, mainly extensive fresh and saline water marshes and peat [report of the Task Force on islands, coral reefs, mangroves and wetland: Environment and Forests for the Eleventh Five Year Plan (Planning Commission, 2007)].

Wetlands provide sustenance and nurture biological diversity as is evident from the concentration of birds, especially water fowl, mammals, reptiles, amphibians, fish, invertebrates as well as countless plant species and their association with open landscape, wild life, local traditions etc.

Table 15.1: Some Forest Resources of Andaman

Type of Forest/Animals	*Name*	*Scientific Name*	*Description*
Tidal Swamp (about 1150 sq.km.)	*Mangroves*	Rhizophora mucronata, Bruguiera gymnorrhiza, Carapa oborata, Sonneratia acida, Nipa fruticans,	Nipa is the most important as a roofing material.
Littoral forests	*Bulletwood Thitpok Badam Karanj Poon*	Mimusops litoralis, Tetrameles nudiflora, Terminalia procera, Pongamia glabra,	Said to be of little economic importance, they are cyclone buffers and shoreline stabilizers
Andaman moist deciduous forests	*Paduk white chuglam white dhup papita kokko*	Pterocapus dalbergioides, Terminalia bialata, Canarium euphyllum, Pterocymbium tinctorium, Albizza lebbek,	Provide a number of valuable timber species. Grow mainly on lower hilly grounds below 100m elevation

(Contd.)

Type of Forest/Animals	Name	Scientific Name	Description
Andaman semi evergreen forests	*Gurjan* *Letkok* *Bombeza* *Didu* *Lakuch*	Dipterocarpus alatus, Pterygota alata, Albizzia chinesis, Bombax ceiba, Artocarpus lakoocha,	Mainly confined to well drained valleys, containing a mix of valuable deciduous and evergreen timber.
Bamboo brakes	*Bamboo*	Oxtrenanthea nigrociliata, Bambusa schizostachyoides,	Due to thin wall and small size of the common bamboo (Oxtrenanthea) it is of little commercial importance. MOST important for incent sticks.
Cane Brakes	*Cane*	Calamus palustries, Calamus congisetus,	Cane is very important as a construction material and also has been used in many areas for tying log rafts Various uses are documented.
Southern Hill Top tropical evergreen forests	*Gurjan* *Cangan* *Thingan* *Dhup*	Dipterocarpus retusas, Mesua ferrea. Hopea andamanica, Canarium manii, Euphorbia,	Stunted vegetation on steep slopes and subjected to high winds. Of little commercial value but of utmost value in preventing hillside erosion.
Andamans tropical evergreen forests	*Gurjan* *Taungpeinne* *Red Bombway* *Bakota* *Khataphal*	Dipterocarpus grandiflorus, Artocarpus chaplasa, Planchonia andamanica, Endospermum chinese, Baccaurea sapida,	Multi storeyed evergreen forest with numerous valuable trees. Throughout the islands as caps to the lower hills and gentler slopes
Giant evergreen forests	*Gurjan* *Gurjan* *Lakooda* *Laichini* *Thitkandu*	Dipterocarpus alatus, Dipterocarpus gracilis, Artocarpus Gomeciana, Amoora wallichii, Pometia pinnata,	This is the climax forest formation of the Andamans. It occurs along streams but has been largely cleared from these areas for agriculture.
Sea cucumbers	*Holothurians 40 species*	Wide distribution	Food

(*Contd.*)

Type of Forest/Animals	Name	Scientific Name	Description
	including commercial species		
Shells (molluscs)	*Many species including Trochus, Turbo*	Some abundant, most status unknown	For mother of pearl and fancy work (export)
Lobsters	*12 species*	Abundant	Food
Prawns	*12 species*	Abundant	Food
Crabs	*60 Species including 3 commercial species*	Abundant	Food
Oyster	*Blacklip pearl oyster*	Status unknown	For mother of pearl and fancy work (export)
Giant clam	*Tridacna spp.*	Common	Food
Fish	*Many species*	Most status unknown	Food, sport
Deer	*Axis axis, Muntiacus muntjak,*	Abundant in most areas but not in Little Andaman	Food, sport, skin, velvet (export)
Wild pig	*Sus andamanensis,*	Abundant in some areas of the islands	Food for tribals
Crocodile	*Crocodylus porosus,*	Unknown	Food, leather, medicine (export)
Sea turtles	*Four species*	Common	Food, leather, calipee (export)
Water Monitor Lizard	*Varanus Salvator*	Abundant in some areas	Food, Leather (export)
Venomous snakes	*6 species*	status unknown	Venom (export)
Orchids	*Many species*	Some species abundant on felled trees	Export market
Bee honey	*Several species*	seasonally abundant	Trade items for tribal
Butterflies, moths, others anthropods	*many species*	some species abundant most species status unknown	Export market
Swiftlet nests	*Collocalia*	Status unknown	Trade item for tribal

(*Contd.*)

Type of Forest/Animals	*Name*	*Scientific Name*	*Description*
Swiftlet nests	*Collocalia fuciphaga,*	Status unknown	Trade item for tribal (export)
Medicine herbs	*Many species*	status unknown	Medicines (export)

Source: Bhaskar, 1979; Whitaker and Whitaker, 1979.

Geographical Settings

Little Andaman is a flat Island with moderate elevation in the centre. The coast line of this Island is mostly flat and does not rise more than 15 metres from the sea level. The coral reefs encircle the Island. In the interior of the Island, the coast line gradually rises and attains the altitude above 200 metres in the central part. The Island is about 122 kms. way from Port Blair. The Island is situated between latitudes 10° 30′41″ N-10° 54′ N and between longitudes 92° 25′15″ E-92° 33′East (Tables 15.2a and 15.2b.).

The Andaman and Nicobar Islands lie close to a recognized sub-terranean line of weakness. However, earthquakes of great intensity have not been recorded. The reason for Andaman's escaping violent earthquakes may be that they are just off the line of Greatest Weakness, which runs from Sumatra through Great Nicobar, Car Nicobar, Barren and Narcondam to the Arakan-Yoma. The interactions of seismo-tectonic movements and sea level change in the eastern parts of the Bay of Bengal which have resulted in the occurrences of many complex phenomena in the landscape patterns of Little Andaman and its adjacent islands of the Andaman and Nicobar Islands.

At the south-west corner of the Hut Bay in the south-east part of the Island, occurrences of beds of recent coral rocks *in situ* are noted above the present sea level. On the other hand, the Archipelagic character of the present Arakan coast shows evidence of and also the presence of submarine ridge between Baranga Islands and Cheduba. We should keep in mind that the Andaman and Nicobar Islands were certainly at one point of time connected with the Arakan Yoma. In conformance with this deduction, the so called 'Sundashelf' which was found during Pleistocene times, is a tract of dry land connecting Java, Sumatra, and Borneo.

On 26th December, 2004, an earthquake, with the magnitude of 9.2 (Stein, and Okal, 2005) hit the islands, followed by a Tsunami.

Table 15.2a: Geographical Account of Little Andaman

Location	*10° 30′1″N–10° 54′N 92° 26′15″E–92° 33′E*	
Area	731.416 sq.km.	
Mean Annual Rainfall	3000 mm	
Temperature	25° C–30° C	
Population (2001)	16892	
	Onge	95 (2010)
	Nicobarese	1365
	Others	15432
Land Use (Revenue)	3435.96 hectares	
FOREST PLANTATION		
Natural regeneration area	154.7 hectares	
Red oil palms	1593.0 hectares	
Spices	21 hectares	
Reserved Forest (including tribal reserve of 52.296 hectares)	67091.0 hectares	

Source: Forest and Plantation Development Corporation (1989) and Field Survey (2010).

Table 15.2b: Profile of Andaman and Nicobar Islands

Area	*8249 sq.km*
Number of islands	572
Inhabited islands	38 (2001 Census)
Population	3,79,944 (2011 Census)
Estimated population-2009	4,65,000
Climate	TROPICAL
Area under forest cover	90%
Humidity	70-90%
Tribes	6
Endemic birds	39
Endemic plants/animals	150 SPECIES
Average annual rainfall	3200mm
Coast line	1912 km (1/4th of India's 7500 km)
Exclusive economic zone	6,00,000 sq.km (30% of India's EEZ OF 20,00,000 sq.km)
Natural hazard profile	Seismic Zone V
Tourist arrivals-2008	Domestic-123914 Foreign-12512 Total-136426

Source: Andaman and Nicobar Administration Directorate of Tourism, Port Blair.

The southern islands of the archipelago were the worst hit. Little Andaman was the only island affected in the Andaman group of islands. The natural world was damaged a lot. No human technology could ever minimize or prevent the damage. But nature works in strange ways. The mangrove forests along the coastal areas reduced the impact of the Tsunami. It is on record. Subsequently, the ecosystem has developed again and we are enjoying its many benefits.

Some Onge huts along the western coastal areas damaged due to the occurrences of a series of cyclonic storms. There was loss of lives and huts. The Onges have shifted from topographical sheets (1968), determining land use zone.

The climatological records indicate that the temperature varies between 21° C to 30° C in a year, without having any perceptible difference between daily maximum and minimum temperature. Actually January is the coolest month (20° C), and April is the hottest month (34° C). The South-West and North-East monsoon rainfall occurs here throughout the year, and the Equatorial type (i.e. convectional rainfall) occurs over the region during May to December (mean annual rainfall 3000 mm). April and May and November and December—these four months are subject to cyclonic disturbances. From several large uprooted trees and trunks along the eastern coast, as witnessed during fieldwork, the ravages of cyclonic storm originating from the North-East monsoon are clear and it is supported also by the old memories of the Onge tribal people.

It has direct impact on the development of not only agriculture and settlement growth, but also on the occurrences of soil formation, soil erosion and growth of natural vegetation, as well as on the total geomorphologic setting of this area. In the Andaman and Nicobar Islands including Little Andaman, agricultural activities, specially plantation agriculture depend largely on annual rainfall and temperature conditions. Two irrigation projects namely Krishna Nallah and Vishnu Nallah have not yet proved adequate in the field of water supply especially during dry months.

Definition and Present Trend in Tourism

Tourism is one of the fastest growing industries in the world today. The first known instance of travelling abroad for leisure as we know it, was that of Queen Sheba visiting King Solomon (Young, 1973). Since then travel for both pleasure and business has increased enormously.

At the international level, the World Tourism Organization (WTO), through its ten point global code of Ethics for tourism approved in 1999, focused on ecosystem and environmental threats, and gave attention to tourism. The major environmental threats to the tourism industry have been identified as:

1. Global warming,
2. Loss of Bio Diversity, and
3. Deterioration of a biotic environment (climate, soil, water and air), that nurture biotic component of ecosystem.

Tourism is the short-term movement of the people for recreation and leisure away from their usual residences, and it is not limited within own country. It is international in character. It may be indoor and outdoor in nature. In rural areas it is mainly outdoor recreation and in cities it is mainly indoor in nature. In rural areas especially in remote islands activities and development may affect the ecosystems within which the recreations operate.

Table 15.3: Outdoor Recreational Activities

Driving for pleasure	
Walking for pleasure	This is a useful distinction—the latter is the serious version.
Outdoor games	These should be of an informal nature, requiring little or no fixed equipment.
Swimming	Includes sub-aqua activities. It is implied that a 'natural looking' water body is involved, not a 'pool'. Surfing also included.
Bicycling	
Fishing	
Nature study, archaeology	
Nature walks	Includes both guided walks and self-guiding nature trails.
Boating/sailing	This category means motor boats on inland waters and sea.
Canoeing	Inland water and offshore.

(Contd.)

Sea sailing	Sail only.
Sightseeing	Of cultural interests rather than appreciation of views etc.
Caving	Restricted to limestone pothole country.
Horseback riding	Including pony trekking.
Camping	Including 'day-camping', not easily separable from picnicking; also caravanning: difficult to separate in North America.
Picnicking	
Ice skating	Outdoor only, on naturally frozen water.
Tobogganing	
Snow skiing	
Mountain climbing	Synonymous with rock climbing: fell-walking and scrambling under hiking.
Motor sports	Hill trials, motorcycle scrambles over informal courses.
Water skiing	
Wind-surfing	A surfboard with a sail.
Hand gliding	Powered hand gliders introduced in late 1970s.
Flying	Both powered and gliding.

Source: After I.G. Simmons, 1986.

In rural areas the manipulations of ecosystem is more apparent. Arable/Agricultural land may be taken to build tourist complexes or their product may be high priced for the hotels. Local people cannot afford—which is a serious problem in Seychelles. Buildings, roads, soil disturbance, water contamination, wildlife loss etc. may all be found and are specially serious in fragile areas such as high mountains and islands (UNESCO, 1973,1974b).

In a city, the impact of tourism on resources and environment is external—extra noise, congestion, extra traffic, parking problem etc. But, in rural areas this impact/effect is quite internal in nature. Expansion of tourism without well planned policy may affect the eco system.

Construction of hotels and associated activity related with development — along shoreline produce huge amount of silt offshore and sometimes killing coral reefs as in Fiji (Baines, 1977). At Sousse, in Tunisia, hotels have been built in dune slacks. The slacks are converted to gardens but the pumping of water has lowered the sub-regional water table below the reach of small farmers. Tourists walking across the dunes to the sea erode the vegetation, and so the sand blows into the hotels. Waste/sewage water always pumps into the sea untreated and wind and ocean currents always bring them back. The untreated sewage may cause cholera and other water-borne diseases to the host country.

Present Trend of Tourism in Andaman Islands with Focus on Little Andaman on the Basis of Sustainability

Tourism in the Andaman and Nicobar Islands can be developed if proper steps are taken into consideration. The diverse effects of it will have on the island, like its fragile ecology and environment and other aspects (which will face diverse affects). The opinion of the islanders' should also be taken into account while integrated planning is taking place.

In fact, the National Action Plan for tourism published by the Ministry of Civil Aviation and Tourism in 1992 together with the UNDP drafted a development strategy for environmentally sustainable tourism in the islands.

Table 15.4: Benchmarking of Andaman and Nicobar Islands with Other Islands

Name of Island/Island Nation	*Area (sq.km)*	*Population in Lakh 2001-2005*	*Density of Population (net Density of Population)*	*Per Capita Income 2005 in $*	*Area Under Forest (%)*	*Area Under Agriculture*	*Tourist Arrivals in Lakh 2005*
A & N ISLANDS	8249	3.56	43 (431)	637	90	2.3	0.56
SOLOMON ISLANDS	28896	5.81	20 (180)	1900	88.8	0.03	0.09
FIJI	18274	9.18	50(91)	4100	44.6	35	5.50

Source: Andaman and Nicobar Administration, Directorate of Tourism, Port Blair.

Table 15.4 (*Contd.*): Area under Agri (in 2005)

Name of island/ Island nation	Area (SQ.KM)	Population in Lakh 2001-2005	Density of Population (Net Density of population)	Per Capita Income 2005 in $	Area Under Forest (%)	Tourist Arrivals in Lakh 2005
MALDIVES	300	3.86	1287 (1331)	4600	3.3	3.95
SEYCHELLS	451	0.82	182 (546)	16600	66.7	1.29
SINGAPORE	707.1	46.08	6517 (6739)	49990	3.3	89.43

Source: Andaman and Nicobar Administration, Directorate of Tourism, Port Blair.

In the Pacific Ocean, the Galapagos Island (Ecuador) is the perfect example of how tourism and conservation can benefit each other. Ecuador's commitment to the protection of the Galapagos Island and its biota led to the establishment of the Galapagos National park in 1959. Tourist activity within the park, which comprises 90-95 per cent of the archipelago's land area, is strongly regulated by the park authority through licensed guides. Damage to the environment is kept to a minimum by restricting visitors to well-marked paths. Majority of tourists have accommodation on houseboats which keeps the destruction of the forest and land environment to a minimum.

Encroachment has been a regular feature of the island. The mainlanders exploited the forest goods for commercial and industrial purposes. The natives of the island, the Onge, were cornered. The guests grew at an alarming rate. Soon, there were more outsiders than natives. There were only about 95 odd Onge. After the Tsunami, they left the south bay settlement and moved to Dugong Creek.

In the Union Territory of the Andaman and Nicobar islands, Little Andaman is the southernmost island of the Andaman Archipelago. It is located 48 km. south of Rutland Island. Little Andaman falls under the jurisdiction of the South Andaman sub-division. Its maximum length from north to south is about 40 km. The breadth from west to east is about 24 km. The total area of the Island is 731.60 sq. km. (according to FPDC it is 731.416 sq. km.). Human activities arc creating pressure/placing burden on the natural resources of the coastal zone beyond their carrying capacity. Human society is presently using resources and reducing it at a rate which is not sustainable. The growth of the human population, combined with the consistent urge to outdo and create more and better things for life is threatening the very existence of a healthy aesthetical and productive zone in a challenging state. The presence of human beings has been a major factor in most environmental issues, hence, the solutions under CRZ regulation may provide realistic solutions. We need to change our attitude and behavioural approach. The right approach and attitude may result in innovative solutions to the world's overall environmental problems. Accepted definition of sustainable definition has emerged from the report for our common future, published by the World Commission on Environment and Development (commonly referred to as the Brundtland report): sustainable development is "development that meets the needs of the present without compromising the ability of future generations to meet their own needs". The Brundtland Report elaborates on its definition by stating that sustainable development is not a fixed state of harmony, but rather a process of change in which the exploitation of resources, the direction of investments, the orientation of technological root practices, are important to protect and preserve the environment. Sustainable tourism development involving the community can contribute to the promotion of knowledge on environmental awareness, management of resources etc. which are the common properties of the people and act as pressure groups, contributing to a positive change in the lifestyle of the islanders. They need to become active participants in the policy making processes, making their opinions heard on growth, development and conservation measures. They are capable of engaging the islanders in efficient resource management, reversing the degradation of natural resources and implementing strategies for the development and institutional change are made consistence with future as well as present needs.

Sustainable development does not mean growth by any means; it does not mean absolute prevention of resource usage, sustainable development demand a change in the content of growth, to make it less material and energy intensive. Sustainable development emphasize that a greater knowledge and appreciation of, as well as, respect for the natural world is essential. To achieve this aim education and consciousness growing about our environment is the first priority including awareness about over-consumptive lifestyle.

Participation in grassroots organization like CBO (community based organization, e.g. sustainable coastal community) and SHG (self help group) sustainable tourism development community (STDC) — are increasingly contributing towards sustainable development through participation of masses, advocating demonstration/pilot projects, monitoring and research of projects, as well as co-operation and networking within different CBO, SHG and government departments.

The women, indigenous people and the youth should work together for sustainable use of land, biological and genetic resources and energy. They also work for reducing waste generation, recycling wastes into productive activities and finding ways of disposing wastes, creating a healthy habitat, preventing waste of resources and pollution and taking measures to restrict polluters.

The 1912 km. coastline of the Andaman and Nicobar Islands offers good scope for the sustainable development of coastal communities and sustainable tourism. Sustainability and sustainable development have created a balance between development and conservation. They have become the set goals for environmentalists around the world. The pressure that people put on the natural resources of costal zones is beyond their capacity to absorb impact causing adverse effects. We need to change the way we think—We do not sustain the environment, the environment sustains us. We are only a tiny part of the environment, not its master.

Suggested Tourism for Little Andaman

To keep in line with sustainable development proposition, Little Andaman can offer:

(1) Safe and unexplored white sandy beach, mangrove creek, green virgin forest and diverse Bio kingdom, Red oil palm plantation, whisper and other waterfalls, Elephant safari, elephant training programme, Krishna nala and Vishnu nala water dam sites.

(2) Excellent coral reefs.

(3) Tourist friendly population line with complete communal harmony represent mini India and always ready with helping attitude and in pleasant mood.

(4) Ample scope for adventure tourism such as;
   (a) Coastal trekking
   (b) Jungle trekking
   (c) Leisure tourism
   (d) Fishing
   (e) Medical/health tourism
   (f) Creek tourism using local country boat/engine boat.
   (g) Cruise tourism can offer quality tourists and minimum damage to fragile eco-system

(h) Honeymoon package can be offered.

Help of trained and licensed guides will minimize the damage to natural resources—forest, mangrove and marine ecosystem. Restrictions in the Tribal reserve areas are already in force. In addition to this if required, preventive measures should be enforced to unauthorized exploitation of endangered flora and fauna including smuggling. Setting up of interpretation/multi-media centre at Hut Bay with maps and other basic information about the archipelago is required in the present scenario. This can be operated by the Tourist agents with the technical assistance of the Governments. The marketing of Island tourism can be done through International tourism bodies by networking them with south-east Asia tour package etc. whose main attraction could be—***green environment with eco-shelter***—for the accommodation purpose.

Some Recommendations for Sustainable Tourism Development

Role of knowledge development is absolutely necessary for the sustainable development of the island as indigenous knowledge of the aboriginal inhabitants, the Onges and other settlers (Nicobari, Bengali and Tamil settlers) should be utilized.

There is a need for Forest Information System to create knowledge bank about the forest resources of the total island for better natural resource management and to achieve the aim of SFM (Sustainable Forest Management). A & N Medicinal Plant Board should develop information system and give local settlers proper training and skill development. They can use the Onge's ethno botanical knowledge (before it is lost for ever) and should maintain strict vigilance, and the harvesting of both medicinal and aromatic plants should be done in sustainable manner. Local women can participate for setting up of nursery of both types of plants. This will attract the tourists as well.

In addition the following measures are likely to promote sustainable tourism and economy of the island:

1. Research work should be encouraged on a controlled basis. The authority should consider suggestions of long-term basis researches as well, keeping the future in perspective.
2. Nomination of this unique island for the UNESCO Natural Heritage Site category, which is a necessary step for the

preservation of the bio-diversity of the Andaman and Nicobar islands. It would also be beneficial for the islanders and create interest in them to keep their surroundings intact, thus the damage done by the settlers and tourists can be checked.

3. Declaring South Western part from South Bay, beyond Nicobaree settlement areas, through West bay, up to Dugong Creek as a biosphere reserve. The proposal must be presented before the Central Government for approval—In this connection, it may be mentioned that the whole of Little Andaman Island is already declared as the Reserved Forest area including the tribal reserve areas.
4. Mangrove swamp may be declared as the Ramsar Wetland to preserve the unique swamp diversity of the island as swamp areas are the next main target of the poachers after forest.
5. Development of Intellectual tourism—People may be encouraged to visit places of the island and arrangements can be made for seminars, symposium, workshop etc.
6. Special Development of Red Palm Area ***for pleasure drive, since good roads already exist.*** We need to establish Nature interpretation centres and international standard washrooms with maintenance.
7. Attention to proper sanitation, medical facility, restroom facility, supply of clean water to the visitors as per international standard, to promote growth of tourism, boating, swimming, fishing at tsunami affected fishermen settlement can be introduced (now in abandoned condition), fishermen use the area for anchoring their boats and associated work. In this regard it would be important to take precautions in buoy anchorage for boat and ferries to save the coral.
8. Interest need to be grown amongst the local people towards orchids and its conservation. Setting up of an Orchid Sanctuary may be a good start.
9. Utmost care and strict vigil are needed for saving the islands resources from the hand of greedy people who do not hesitate to follow illegal methods. **Encroachment should be strictly dealt with.**
10. Eco-shelter with local available materials may be set up at the Netajinagar area as it is nearby village from Butler bay where tree houses and camping can be reintroduced. Proper care should be taken to preserve the marine resources

especially corals. Museum on tribal lifestyle and culture (Onge and Nicobari) and souvenir shop (with miniature form handicrafts would be available) can be set up at Hut Bay adjacent to suggested information centre/interpretation centre/multi-media centre.

11. At present Little Andaman produce sufficient vegetables and is the vegetable bowl for the Nicrobar Group of Island. Hence a vermi-composting unit may be set up at Ramkrishnapur village so that people get chemical free food or Organic foods (it will enhance the long-term production capacity of land). The Agriculture Department should train the farmers about the use of natural pesticide.
12. Human Resource development-training and capacity building in both conservation and eco tourism can be introduced in Polytechnic in Port Blair. Participation of local people should be on the priority basis.
13. These measures would also generate employment scopes for the islanders.

The above measures would make the tourists feel the bonding with nature in the island and they should be encouraged to leave it as they found it originally. At the same time length of stay of the tourists in the islands should be restricted to save the natural resources of the island.

Complaints regarding exploitation and harassment received from the tourists should be treated on priority basis. Evaluation sheet can be taken from the tourists regarding their experience in the island and their suggestion and feedback can be considered for future improvement in tourism sector in the island. This feedback form should be available at eco-shelter, Forest guest-house, PWD guest house and at information centres. Proper documentation of available resources and the Onge knowledge is urgently needed. Mapping of the island in details is required.

Approach for Development

The sustainable development could be even more accelerated in the non-governmental outfits and can be integrated in the development process through:

- Involvement and participation of CBO in the island's governance

- Integration of transportation and land-use (bicycle and walking route).
- Uplifting human spirit, especially for the Onges.
- Reduction of waste generation and consumption of non-renewable resources, respecting the earth's ecological capital, through training/workshops.
- Expansion the knowledge of ecological interest and make people understand and live within the natural ecological carrying capacity of the island.
- Eradication of poverty and ensure a dignified life by providing employment, housing and medical facilities. People of all communities can feel safe, and enjoy diverse cultural life.
- Infusion of the traditional knowledge of the Onges with today's scientific knowledge.
- Active participation in security and safety of the island as it is strategically important for reporting about foreign and inland poaching to administration.
- Arranging Nicobaree tribal dance and on the special occasion 'Onge' tribal dance — it would be a memorable experience for the tourists. Settlers can also participate in this type of cultural events.

Conclusion

Nature has given us a lot. And those gifts were meant for everyone on the earth. All creatures have the right to enjoy those gifts.

- We, the civilized human beings, perhaps the first creature of its kind, in the present scenario, initiated to act against the dictum of the Supreme Being. Our actions for so many centuries have brought this planet today at a very fragile condition in order to establish ourselves supreme of all creatures. In order to achieve that, to our ignorance, we have completely damaged or destroyed the habitat of many species which are now irreparable. Our many acts have extinct many species from this earth and many are in the verge of extinction or under the process of further adaptability. And all these we have done in the name of development.
- This word itself carries a distinct mark of superiority and ego. Do we really need to be so?

- We have at last realized that pace of development has to be linked with conservation of all natural resources available with us in order to achieve the future living strategy.
- The emission of Green House Gases (GHG) and its terrible and horrible effects have shattered us all and left us panicked. We all know Carbon (C) is the element which is available in almost 90 per cent of the known substances. And this is the element, if allowed uncontrolled to mix freely in the atmosphere, will cause increase of atmospheric temperature thereby creating all imbalances in the nature's condition. We are now talking about Carbon Sequestration to find an instant solution to the Climate change scenario. In fact this will further our interests in more developments. Already Clean Development Mechanism (CDM) has been introduce under Kyoto protocol by the Regulating Authority of the module and India is one of its signatory. This is a mechanism where plantation of different forest species are to be taken in the waste land or degraded land to sequestrate the atmospheric carbon and lock it inside the green trees hereby creating a carbon sink for which monetary benefits will be given.

The ocean is the biggest carbon sink of the nature followed by forests. Therefore, there is an urgent need to protect the available forests covers throughout the planet. If we able to do so, we may be able to conserve the left out biodiversity. This should be mandatory for all the nations and countries. Only about 10 per cent of forest cover is available in the globe today. Less than 9 per cent may prove fatal for survival of life on this planet. This is equally applicable to Andaman and Nicobar Islands. Though the island's forest cover is about 86 per cent and possesses ¼ of the country's coastal line, utmost dedication is required for conserving the natural beauty. Tourism is one of the areas which can play a vital role in generating and adopting strategies for sustainable developments which will ultimately result in responsible Tourism.

The extent, to which the island ecosystem would be able to accept the change caused by tourists, should be kept in mind. We should analyze the benefits not only in monetary terms but also under sustainable development strategies and policies.

Finally, conservation of all natural resources and utilizing them in a scientific manner may lead to a stage of sustainable all-round development where tourism can play the vital role.

BIBLIOGRAPHY

Andaman and Nicobar Administration, Directorate of Tourism, Port Blair (2010).

Baines, G.B.K. (1977): The Environmental demands of Tourism in coastal Fiji in J. Winstow (ed.) *The Melanesian Environment*. Canberra: ANU Press.

Bandhopadhyay, Sweta (2002): *Environment of Little Andaman: A Geographical Appraisal*, Ph.D. Thesis.

Beatley, Timothy; Brown, J. David and Schwab; K. Anna (1994): *An Introduction to Coastal zone Management,* Island Press, Washington D.C.

Berbeta, Kailash Chandra (2004) *Forest Resources and Sustainable Development: Principles, Perspective and Practices*. ISBN—81-8069-095-4.

Bhaskar, Satish (1979): *Sea Turtles in the South Andaman Islands—Hamadryad*, Vol. 4 No. 1, January.

Odum, E.P. and Odum, H.T. (1969): The Strategy of Ecosystem Development, *Science*, 164.

Report of the Task Force on Islands Coral Reefs, Mangroves and Wetlands in Environments and Forests—For the Eleventh Five-Year Plan. 2007-08 (Government of India, 2007).

Saldanha, C.J.: (1989): *The Andaman and Nicobar Lakshadweep — An Environmental Impact Assessment*, New Delhi: Oxford and IBHN.

New Simmons, I.G. (1986): *The Ecology of Natural Resources*, Edward Arnold.

Stein, S. and Okal, E.A. (2005): Speed and Size of the Sumatra Earthquake, *Nature*, 434.

Tahsil Office (1994, 2010): *Tahsildar's records Hutbay Little Andaman.*

UNESCO (1973): *Ecology and Rational use of Island Ecosystem.* Paris: UNESCO Man and the Biosphere Programme (MAB), Report series No. 11.

UNESCO (1974b): *Impact of Human Activities on Mountain and Tundra Ecosystems*. Paris: UNESCO Man and the Biosphere programme (MAB) Report series No. 14.

UNESCO (1973): *Conservation of Natural areas and of the Genetic material they contain*. Paris: UNESCO Man and the Biosphere Programme (MAB) Report series No. 12.

Whitaker, Romulus (1985): *Endangered Andamans, Environmental Service Groups*, World Wild Life Funds India & MAB India, Department of Environment.

Young, G. (1973): *Tourism: Blessings or blight*? Harmandsworth: Penguin.

Part-V

Other Issues

16
Penal Settlement in Andamans

Niranjan Das

The Andaman and Nicobar Group of Islands, also known as the Bay Islands, lies in the southern part of the Bay of Bengal. An archipelago of 572 islands, islets and rocks, it once formed part of a continuous mountain range, stretching from Cape Negrais in Myanmar to Achin Head in Sumarta. Cape Negrais was an extension of the Arakan Hills range. one of the ranges that run down the Eastern Himalayas. Port Blair, the capital of the Andaman and Nicobar Islands is 192 km. from Cape Negrais in Myanmar, 1230 km. from Kolkata 1190 km. from Chennai and 1278 km. from Vizag.

This group of islands covers an area of 8249 sq.km.–2672 sq.km. of South Andaman District, 3763 sq.km. of North and Middle Andaman District and 1841 sq.km. of Nicobar District. The Andaman group of islands is spread over 467 km. in length and the maximum width is 52 km. The length and breadth of Nicobar group of islands is 259 km. in length and 58 km. in width. The most important island in the Andaman Group are North, Middle and South Andaman—popularly known as Great Andaman. Out of 572 islands, only 38 Islands are inhabited. Port Blair is connected either by road or by sea to all these 38 Islands. Great Nicobar is the Southernmost islands which is about 540 km. from Port Blair. Indira Point in the Great Nicobar Island is the last point of the Indian territory. Over 80 per cent of the islands are covered with dense evergreen tropical forests. The original natives who are the earliest migrants, consist of both Negritos and Mangoloids, living in these islands in their respective area since time immemorial and in total isolation till recently. The total population of the islands was about 380581 according to 2011 Census.

I

Historical Background

The Andamans have been surrounded in mystery for centuries due to their inaccessibility and hostile tribes. There is no authentic account as to how these islands came to be known as the Andaman and Nicobar Islands. Legends have it that the name of Andaman owes its origin to the Malayas, who have known the islands from time immemorial. The Malayas used to sail across the seas, capture some of the aborigines and give them away as slaves in trade. The Malayas called them the islands of *Handuman* because that is how they pronounced the name Hanuman of the Ramayana, and *Handuman* eventually became Andaman. Claudius Ptolemaeus, popularly known as Ptolemy, the great geographer of the Roman Empire, located these islands in his maps in the second century B.C. He described these islands as islands of the cannibals. Reference of these islands as *Andaban* is found in the wittings of I'Tsing, the Chinese traveller of the seventh century who also described the inhabitants as cannibals. Marco Polo, the explorer of Venice passed by these islands during the course of his travels in A.D. 1260. Sir Henry Yule, who wrote a commentary on Marco Polo, has suggested that *Angamanian*, the name Marco Polo used, is an Arabic dual indicating two Andamans—the Great one and the Little one. Some trace the origin of the word *Angaman* to Ptolemy who described them as "the islands of good fortune", and hence the forms of *Angaman, Agdaman* and ultimately Andaman.

Nicolo Conti, in an attempt to give the word Andaman a meaning, called it "the island of Gold", whereas in the great Tanjore inscriptions of A.D. 1050, the islands were mentioned under the translated name *Timaitture,* which means the islands of impurity—perhaps because they were considered the abode of cannibals. There is less mystery about the name Nicobar, because through the centuries Nicobar had often been referred to as the land of "the naked people." I'Tsing described them as *lojen-kue*, which means "Land of naked people."

The Arab travellers called them *Lakhabalus* or *Najabulus*, which was perhaps a mis-transcription of some form of Nicobar, because it also means land of the naked. In the Tanjore inscriptions they are mentioned as Nakkavaram, which translates as "land of the naked." Marco Polo's *Necuveran* (AD 1292), Rashiduddin's *Nakwararn* (AD 1300) and Friar Odoric's Nicoveran (AD 1322) are obviously the corrupted for 15th and 16th century Portugues' *Nacabar* and *Nicabar* and the modem Nicobar.

Before the discovery of the Cape of Good Hope, there does not appear to have been much contact between the European and the Nicobaris. But once the sea route was open, European expeditions to the Far East became quite frequent, and the Nicobar group of islands fell *en route*, as it were. In 1556 Captain Fredrick touched the shores of one of the Nicobar islands. Many years later, in 1601, during the reign of Queen Elizabeth I, Sir James Lancaster paid a visit to these islands while on his way to the spice islands. He was followed by a Spanish missionary Father Dominic Fernandes while on a voyage from Malacca to Madras.

II

New Settlement in the Andamans

In the late eighteenth and early nineteenth centuries Indian convicts were transported to Southeast Asian countries largely to meet labour requirements and to develop infrastructure to cater to the interests of the British Empire. A substitute for capital punishment, penal transportation was intended to impart a benign and merciful appearance to colonial authoritarianism and at the same time was used for dealing with problems of collective crime. This punishment was resurrected and deployed whenever the colonial order felt threatened by a popular upsurge or a collective resistance by the colonized people.

The penal transportation was extensively resorted to during the 1780s, 1820s and post-1857. These were also periods of the rise of banditry, *thuggee* and popular rebellions in the Indian mainland. Most of the convicts transported to these places were convicted of dacoity, murder and banditry. The character of colonies having convict stations or employing labour on a particular scale was different from that of settler colonies. It is really the use of a colony particularly for penal purposes, as a prison, which qualified it as a penal settlement. The colonization of most of the overseas and far-flung colonial began with the use of penal labour, because most of them required a certain amount of resources and labour input in order to make them habitable by European standards. The actual character of the settlement was decided only after they were developed, depending on the strategic, economic and political needs of the colonial state. As a result many colonies like Andamans became convict settlements.

The East India Company established its first penal settlement for the reception of Indian convicts at Fort Marlborough in Bengkulu or Bencoolen (1787-1825). It was situated in the Sumatra Island, almost on the western coast. Penal settlements were also established at other places like Penang otherwise known as Prince of Wales Island (1790-1860), Malacca and Singapore (1825-60) and the Burmese provinces of Arakan and Tenasserim (1828-62). Transportation of Indian prisoners to overseas penal settlements started in 1787 emptied over-crowded mainland prisons and assured new company settlements a supply of cheap labour. In fact the convict workforce was vital to the development of early colonial infrastructure.

A large number of Bengal prisoners convicted for various crimes were sent to Benkoelen penal settlement in Sumatra. Later on prisoners from Madras and other provinces were also sent often to establish a settlement. According to Sir Thomas Stamford Raffles, Governor of Sumatra, the object of transporting convicts to a far off place was to reclaim them from bad habits but he pointed out in a letter written to the Government of India that in the system prevailing in the penal settlement at the time the above objectives were not achieved. In his opinion even these prisoners who expressed an inclination to reform themselves, were not given sufficient encouragement. In fact, the authorities mainly employed the convicts in the tasks of clearing forests, making roads and for developing the settlement at Singapore, Penang, Malacca, Tennaserim and Aracan and the Andamans.

Lord Cornwallis, the Governor-General of India, was very much interested to establish a colony in the Andaman Islands. John Ritchie being assigned the task of conducting a survey of the islands of the Bay of Bengal, visited the islands in 1777 and submitted a report to Warren Hastings, the then Governor-General, explaining the potentiality of this archipelago. In 1788, Capt. Buchanan after visiting the coasts of the Andamans convinced the Governor-General to conduct a survey of these Islands. In 1788, Lord Cornwallis asked Lieutenant (later Captain) Archibald Blair, one of the early distinguished hydrographers of the East India Company and

Lieutenant Robert Hyde Colebrooke, the Surveyor General of India to survey the Andaman Islands.

In a letter dated December 19, 1788, Blair was clearly instructed about the purpose of the survey. "The material object of the survey is to ascertain in which part of the island there are good harbours and which it would be most suitable for the Company's advantage to project one."

He was further instructed to ascertain about natural and vegetable production, reigning winds arid currents, rise and set of tides, variation in atmosphere, changes in climate due to stormy weather, availability of fish, wood, water, clay, lime and stone. Commercial possibilities of timber and sea-shells available in large quantities in the Andamans were also to be determined. As regards the aborigines, Blair was advised to follow a conciliatory policy to win their confidence by means of "persuasion, presents and other allurements but not by force or deceit."

With the task to do the survey in and around the coast of the Andamans, Lt. Blair left Calcutta on 20 December, 1788 and reached Interview Island on 29 December. After spending several months in the Andamans to complete the survey, Blair returned to Calcutta in the first week of June and submitted his report to Lord Cornwallis on 9 June, 1789. Lord Cornwallis was very much impressed for the clarity of the report containing valuable information about the land, vegetation, flora and fauna, winds, tides, climate etc. supported by charts and maps whenever necessary.

The Governor-General in Council, in its meeting on 12 June, 1789 decided to take possession of islands for the purpose of establishing a safe harbour for the British fleet in the event of war and of providing shelter to the vessels of the East India company to escape the fury of monsoons, Besides, in order to prevent the predatory activities of the Malay and Chinese pirates and to exercise the hegemony of the British Government, it was felt necessary to establish a colony, not a penal colony in the islands. Captain Blair's report was so strong and encouraging that the uphill task of establishment of the first settlement on the islands was assigned to him. Dr. Moutat, however, believed that Blair was entrusted to establish the first convict settlement in the Andamans.

Captain Blair sailed for Andaman on 17 September, 1789 with some artificers, labourers and a few soldiers and reached on 28 September. He accomplished this responsibility by setting up a small settlement on Chatham Island on the Southern Bay which was named Port Cornwallis, now called Port Blair, in the Great Andaman. Thus the first ever attempt to establish a settlement in the Andamans was made in October 1789. This was the beginning of the ingress of the non-aboriginals into the tribal territory.

For the first time convicts from British India were deported there to help in its development. Within a few days, with the help of the convict labourers, Blair was able to clear some area and makes a redoubt on which the Union Jack was hoisted to proclaim its Official possession by the British.

By August 1790, the settlers numbering one hundred and nineteen had cleared the greater portion of the site in Chatham Island and planted vegetables and fruit trees on it. Meanwhile, the settlers who had paid visits to Calcutta in batches for their persona! affairs were allowed to take their families to the new colony.

Earlier on 13 April, 1790, Blair had reported that north-east harbour in the North Andaman (now at Diglipur) deserved the attention of the Governor-General for its advantageous location to start settlement work. Consequently, in November 1790 Commodore Cornwallis, brother of the Governor-General, after visiting the site informed his brother, "I think north-east harbour is vastly superior for a fleet of Man-of-War to Port Cornwallis", and recommended to shift the colony from its present site in the southern harbour to the new harbour in the north-east islands.

On 16 October, 1792, the final order was issued for the shifting of the settlement to the new harbour for the purpose of developing a naval arsenal base there. The removal was ordered mainly on the following considerations:

"(1) the new harbour (North-East) was more capacious and commodious than the old harbour (South-East),
(2) the excellence of climate,
(3) the docility of the aborigine inhabitants, and the fertility of the soil.
(4) On 5 November, 1792, the Governor-General engaged Captain Alexander Kyd of the Bengal Engineers to be the Superintendent of the new settlement and advised Lt. Blair to effect the shifting of the colony."

Abandoning the old settlement at Port Cornwallis, Blair came to the new site in North Andaman with 360 settlers on 30 December, 1792 while Kyd took over the charge on 5th March, 1793.

Captain Kyd was very optimistic about the bright future of the new settlement and started with all enthusiasm to make it a success. But with the passage of time, the condition of the new settlement deteriorated because of insalubrious weather and increasing rate of mortality. Moreover, complete dependence on the government supply made the Settlement a constant burden. Extensive work for the Settlement was also too expensive as labourers were to be brought from India and other places only on higher pay. On 4 February, 1796, Kyd reported to the Secretary to the Governor-General about the high death rate of the settlers due to inclement weather and other administrative problems and proposed to abandon it. On 8 February, 1796, the Governor-General in Council decided to withdraw the Settlement "considering the great sickness and mortality... and the great expense and embarrassment to Government in maintaining it."

It was further decided that the withdrawal was to be completed before the onset of the monsoon. Finally, in May 1796, the first settlement in the Andamans was abandoned by bringing back 550 free Bengali settlers, men, women and children, the European artillery and Sepoy guards to Bengal but provisions and 270 convicts were sent to Penang.

Thus the first recorded attempt to establish a settlement in the Andamans proved futile and was abandoned after six and a half years. The islands went to its absolute isolation for the next sixty two years till it was reoccupied.

III

Penal Settlement

In 1824, Port Cornwallis was the rendezvous of the fleet carrying the Army to the First Burmese War. In the 1830s and 1840s, shipwrecked crews who landed on the Andamans were often attacked and killed by the natives. Reports on the outrages committed by the inhabitants of the Island on ship-wrecked seamen continued to disturb the British rulers and in a letter No. 4152 of 28th November, 1855 addressed to the Secretary to the Government of Bengal, the functioning Secretary to the Government of India enquired as to the measures proposed for the protection of British subjects as might unluckily be cast away on the Andamans.

The Government of Bengal asked Captain Hopkinson, the Commissioner of Arakan to submit a report. Hopkinson submitted his report on 8th February which was forwarded to the Government of India on 29th February, 1856. In his report, Hopkinson favoured the re-occupation of these Islands by establishing a penal settlement. While Captain Hopkinson's letter was with the Government of India, a report about the murder of some Chinese sailors at the Andamans was also received. Under these circumstances, the Court of Directors ordered in October 1856 that the Andaman Islands should be explored with a view to founding a settlement there. This exploration, however, could not be undertaken until the end of 1857. The idea of establishing a penal settlement in the Andamans was, therefore, already in the process of finalization when the First War of Independence broke out on 10th May, 1857.

An Andaman Committee presided over by Dr. F.J. Mouat, Inspector of Jails, Dr. G.R. Playfair, Assistant Surgeon and Lt. J.A. Hoothcote the Indian Navy was constituted by the Government of India on 20th November, 1857, "to examine the shores of the Andaman Group of Islands and select the best site there for the establishment of a penal settlement." On the recommendation of the Andaman Committee submitted on 1st January, 1858, the Governor-General-in-Council decided on 15th January, 1858 "to establish a penal settlement on the Andaman Islands for the reception, in the first instance, of convicts sentenced to imprisonment, and transportation, for the crimes of mutiny and rebellion and for other offences connected therewith, and eventually for the reception of all convicts under sentence of transportation when for any reason it may not be thought expedient to send to the Strait Settlement or to the Tenasserim Provinces."

The penal settlements centreed round the harbour of Port Blair, namely Ross, Chatham and Viper Islands and Port Blair. The remote islands were considered to be a suitable place to punish the freedom fighters. Not only were they isolated from the mainland, the overseas journey (*Kala Pani*) to the islands also threatened them with loss of caste, resulting in social exclusion.

Captain Henry Man, Executive Engineer and Superintendent of convicts at Moulmin was sent to reoccupy the islands formally for the establishment of the Penal Settlement at the old harbour which was to be identified by the name of Port Blair in honour of Captain Archibold Blair, who had discovered it about eighty years ago. Captain

Man had with all due ceremony raised the Union Jack at Port Blair on 22nd January, 1858, and thus formally annexed the Andaman Islands.

In the letter of C. Beadon, Secretary to the Government of India, Captain Man was instructed: "It may be assumed that the class of rebels and mutineers who are sentenced by the Civil and Military Tribunals to the secondary punishment of transportation or to imprisonment, will not include any of the worst offenders, and therefore, that the convicts with whom you will have to deal in the first instance will, for the most part, be men who have been led to the commission of crimes against the State by the example of others and not men of a desperate or unmanageable character." He was vested with frill judicial and executive authority over the whole of the Andamans.

Although Captain Man was sent to annex the Bay Islands, the responsibility of the new settlement was assigned to Dr. James Paffison Walker, who had a great deal of prior experience as a jail superintendent at Agra, and who was a nominee of Dr. Mouat, Chairman of the Andaman Committee. Shortly after the First War of Independence was suppressed, the British executed many rebels. Those who survived were exiled for life to the Andamans to prevent them from taking any active part in any upsurge against the British. Accompanied by two hundred freedom fighters, Lala Mathura Das, an Indian overseer, Nawab Khan and Kareen Baksh, two Indian doctors and a guard of 50 men of the old Naval Brigades under the Command of Lt. Templer, Dr. Walker along with jailor David Barry left Calcutta on 4th March, 1858 on board the company's steam frigate Semiramis and reached Port Blair on 10th March, 1858.

The Tenth of March, 1858, the 'Arrival Day' of the first batch of the 1857 heroes, thus marked the beginning of the history of the modem Andamans that gradually began to take shape with the passage of time. The 'Day' is now observed as 'Andaman Day' as an annual feature, mainly through the efforts of Madan Mohan Singh of Junglighat who happens to be the great grandson of Mangal Singh Dogra of the first batch of penal settlers that arrived here with Walker.

Another batch of 175 convicts arrived by transport ship "Roman Emperor" which had sailed earlier from Karachi on 27th February, 1858. Of these only 171 convicts disembarked, the remaining four having died on board the ship on the way due to the rigours of the long arduous voyage. On 29th March, 1858 by steam frigate "Pluto" came with fifty Burmese artificer convicts for erecting a wooden store house. The transportation of convicts mostly in batches of around 200 men mainly from Calcutta continued.

By 16th June, 1858, the number of convicts received in the Andamans was 773. It increased to 1330 by September 1858 and to 1949 by December 1858. It would be saddening to note that deaths and escapes of convicts at the settlement took a heavy toll as indicated in the year-wise break-up of their arrivals and disposals as at the end of the year 1860:

Arrivals		**Disposals**	
1858	1949	Died in Hospital	1710
1859	1813	Died outside	24
1860	733		1734
	4495		
		Executed	91
		Escaped	379
		Transferred & released	89
			2293
		No. at the end of 1860	2202
			4495

The pressure on Walker's administration could be understood by the fact that out of about 3700 convict-arrivals in the tenure of Walker during the one and a half years he was in command (10 March, 1858 to October 2, 1859) as many as 1700 convicts succumbed to death mostly due to malaria, dysentery and such other diseases.

During the initial period of the penal settlement in the Andamans, there was no rule and regulation for the administrators to be followed, and Dr. Walker, the Superintendent of the Settlement, exercised the enormous powers at his command according to his whims and caprices.

For proper and effective deployment of the convicts, Walker proposed to introduce cash payment and allow convicts to provision themselves from shops managed by convicts. Goods would be supplied from the Settlement stores at fixed prices and an account would be kept with the head convict shopkeeper of each division who would make weekly remittances. The arrangement, Walker argued, would greatly simplify the Settlement accounts, economies establishment, prevent wastage and offer an inducement for economical habits and provide an important step to self-management by the convicts. Walker claimed that his objective was to offer every inducement to habits of self-reliance and self-management by so arranging that good work would bring its own rewards and idleness its own punishment.

Walker had worked out that each convict would be paid 2 annas per day for the allotted work executed by him, and with extra work earlier or later than the working hours could even earn 3 annas per day. A section-gangman would be paid Rupees 4 per month and a sub-division gangman also at the same rate at Rupees 4 per month.

Walker's idea was that each convict for a fair day's labour would be allowed a fair day's wages out of which he must meet the expense of food, clothing, cooking utensils and working implements. Medicines and medical facilities would be the only necessaries provided free of cost by the Government. Walker had thus drawn up an elaborate programme for the reception and management of the convicts. He was, however, very harsh towards the prisoners. Convicts were handcuffed together in pairs and these handcuffs were never opened. During working hours the worst characters were taken to sea beach, and an iron bar being passed through the fetters of a number of them, they were thus fastened to the earth, and made to do what they could in a sitting posture.

The tortures imposed by Walker increased day by day. To incite a terror-phobia among the convicts, on 8 October, 1858 a small island named Viper Island about two and a half miles from Chatham and about five miles further into the harbour from Ross was formally occupied. It was developed for the accommodation of convicts. The jungle was almost entirely cleared by Walker. The top of the hill was cut off up to 16 feet to make a considerable level space for the construction of buildings. The earth thus excavated was used to reclaim the low-lying area on the eastern coast of the Island. The Viper Jail, the first-ever regular jail to be built in the Settlement was originally erected on the reclaimed land in 1864-65 and completed in 1867. It was later shifted to a better site higher up on the hill because of unhealthy condition at the former site. The jail building, surrounded by large boundary walls, was designed to accommodate about 2000 convicts. The buildings at Viper were made of *pucca* masonry unlike the wooden structures for the accommodation of convicts built elsewhere in the Settlement. Some of the remains of the brick masonry boundary walls could be seen even today. A hospital was first built on the reclaimed land and later another building higher up with hundred beds was also constructed with boarded floor. By the last decade of the century Viper Island Hospital was considered as one of the four major hospitals in the Settlement.

The hardcore criminals called 'Chain-gang' were mainly kept in this Island for undergoing punishment and rigorous labour. The prisoners who were sentenced to undergo this punishment by the Superintendent's Court, was chained together and locked up at night by a chain running through their legs through the coupling of irons. To infuse terror the first gallows was built there on a hilltop so that it could be seen from far off places.

Life of a prisoner in the beginning of the settlement was very miserable. They were transported to the penal settlement without any prior arrangements. Even the basic needs for the establishment of the settlement were received after ten days of their arrival. During the rainy season they had no place for a safe shelter other than staying in tents. The condition improved a little by November 1858, when accommodation for one thousand prisoners on Ross Island was provided. The prisoners were accommodated in barracks of a temporary nature with thatched roofs and mat walls which leaks continuously during rainy season.

The arrangements for food, clothing and shelter in the settlement were not adequate for human beings. The unhealthy climate and absence of adequate medical care and proper food made their life miserable and they began to die of minor diseases such as malaria, dysentery, pneumonia etc. The freedom fighters were ruthlessly punished for violation of jail rules and regulations. These heroes of the First War of Independence not only faced the inhuman treatment of the British authorities in the settlement but also had to suffer at the hands of aborigines of the Andaman Islands. From the very beginning of the settlement the aborigines attacked the working parties, as a result of which a large number of them were killed while at work in different convict's stations of the penal settlement.

Up to June 16, 1958, that is within just a little over three months of the establishment of Penal Settlement, the Settlement had received 773 convicts of whom 66 died due to diseases, 60 were under medical treatment in the hospital and as many as 228 had fled away of whom 88 were recaptured. Though two of them were forgiven, 86 were hanged in one day. This was the nature of torture and outrageous oppression meted out by Walker. For this sort of cruel treatment, he was under constant threat to his life. On 1 April, 1859, nearly 200 Punjabi convicts conspired to murder him and he had to run away to save his life. To tackle the problem Walker not only adopted more savage measures but also sought certain steps to keep him and other officers safe even by alluring the convicts to be dependent on the mercy of the British.

These circumstances encouraged frequent escapes from the settlement. At dead of night on 18th March, 1858, a group of twenty one convicts escaped from Ross Island in rafts, made ready for the purpose hidden in the jungles. On 23rd March another group of eleven convicts escaped from Ross Island in a similar way. The escape of convicts continued in spite of the risks involved in it.

On the night of 23rd April, 1858, a bigger group of 91 convicts escaped from Ross Island and crossed over to the other side. One of them was convict No. 276 Dudnath Tiwari, a sepoy in the 14th Bengal Native Infantry Regiment, sentenced to transportation for life for his role in the first War of Independence. He was miraculously saved from certain death at the hands of the Great Andamanese—one of the four Negrito tribes of the Andamans. He stayed with them in the jungles as one of them for about a year and moved with them from place to place. He married their two girls, namely Leepa and Jigah. During the period he also learnt their language. Around 10th May, 1859 he sensed that the aborigines were planning to attack the settlement. From Tarmugli alone about 300 Great Andamanese in 20 canoes set out towards Port Blair. On their way they were joined by another big group of aborigines accompanied by an escaped convict Sadloo and other groups coming from different camps all armed with bows and arrows. On 16th May they encamped at a place about two and a half miles from Port Blair. Dudhnath and Sadloo were asked to stay there in the camp with the children and the women.

At the dead of night when all others were asleep, Dudhnath stealthily left the camp and rushed to the convict station at Aberdeen. Walker, the Superintendent was apprised of the situation. He immediately made all arrangements by placing guards and police in their positions. But even before he could complete his plans, the attack of the Great Andamanese had already begun very early in the morning of 17th May, 1859. The convict barrack at Aberdeen were occupied and tools and implements were carried away. In this uneven battle of bows and arrows against guns and shells the aborigines were gunned down and ultimately forced to retreat into the forest leaving how many dead behind, 'nobody knows'.

This engagement afterwards came to be known in the history as the "Battle of Aberdeen." This may rightly be considered as the war of liberation launched by one of the four autochthon Negrito tribes of the islands to oust the foreign rulers of their homeland. The battle of Aberdeen fought by the aborigines to secure the liberation of their homeland also resulted in change of policy of the British administration towards the aborigines hoping to remove the scars of the battle with friendly gestures. This ultimately resulted in the foundation of "Andaman Home" with a view to civilizing the Great Andamanese. This habitation, set up at Ross Island, was a collection of huts with an enclosure surrounded on all sides by a bamboo fence, In 1863, Rev. Henry Corbyn, the Christian priest of Port Blair of the Bengal Ecclesiastical Establishment was made In-charge of the Home where twenty eight Great Andamanese lived. The Government of India sanctioned an allowance of Rupees 100 per month for its upkeep. The inmates of the Home were instructed in English with the object of acquiring means of mutual understanding with them to secure lasting benefit of the settlement.

Whatever the intention of the Britishers towards the Great Andamanese might be, this Home was also a repressive institution *albeit* disguised as a charitable one. The condition of the Home was pitiable. The only dwelling in the Home was a small cow-shed which the tribals shared with cattle. They did not relish the food, mainly coarse rice. They resented wearing clothes and living in dingy shed. Besides, they declined to yield to the civilizing processes and even would hate to learn English. Indeed, they were kept under strict surveillance at the Home and their movements were restricted. As a result, the Great Andamanese became acrimonious and resentful.

Consequently, defying the confinement with an urge for freedom, on the night of 1 March, 1864 a band of forty Great Andamanese inmates of the Home including women and children left Ross Island and fled to the jungle of South Andaman after crossing the channel. Major Ford who succeeded Col. Tytler as Superintendent of the Penal Settlement commented about the semi-captivity of the Great Andamanese thus: "It was impolitic to restrain them on Ross Island, they must be free to go and come amongst us."

Though Rev. Corbyn was officially placed in charge of the Home, the day-to-day management of the Home was entrusted to convicts. "The misconduct of the Naval Brigadesmen and the convicts who were associated with the Andamanese included in main the misconduct with the women inmates of the Home" as Portman had very mildly put it, and resulted in wide spread infection of venereal diseases within the entire Great Andamanese community including even those living in the far interior jungles.

The most catastrophic impact of the confinement on the Great Andamanese was the addiction to opium, tobacco and liquor, apart from sexual exploitation and the concomitant transmission of venereal disease on the other. As a result, epidemics like pneumonia (1868), syphilis, measles, influenza broke out that decimated them and their population came down harrowingly to 19 in 1961 from 624 in the 1901 Census. Though there has been a slight increase from 19 in 1961 to 43 in 2001, the most worrying fact is that the Andamanese males have lost their vitality and their females their fertility. The Great Andamanese are perhaps today the weakest ethnic community awaiting total extinction in the days to come.

It may be interesting to note that the Andaman Home at Ross Island was the first but not the last or the only 'Home' set-up by the British in the Andamans to bring the aborigines closer to civilization and establish friendly relations with them. A number of such Homes were also opened around Port Blair and also further interior such as Navy Bay near Port Blair, Viper Island, Haddo, Port Mouat, Lekra Barnga on the east coast of South Andaman, Chriya Tapu on Macpherson Strait at the southernmost tip of South Andaman Island, Kyd Island, Pirij, Gop-Paka-Bang, Brigade Creek and Dundas Point, all in the latter half of the nineteenth century. The experiment with the "Home" model proved to be deleterious. There the Andamanese learnt to smoke and chew tobacco, took to alcoholism, contacted diseases unknown to them, and were given new food to which they were not accustomed. Their customs and mode of life were greatly altered. All these had a devastating effect on their lifecycle. They lost the vitality which was wholly dependent on being remaining untouched. And in the process eight out of the ten steps of the Great Andamanese tribes were wiped out.

Today, a memorial has been raised for the "Battle of Aberdeen" in the newly constructed Water Sports Complex. It was inaugurated by Vakkam Purushotam, the then Lt. Governor of Andaman and Nicobar Islands on 15th August, 1994 with the following salutation: "This monument is built in the memory of those Andamanese Aborigines who bravely fought the "Battle of Aberdeen" in May 1859 against the oppressive and retaliatory policy of the British regime." It is made a part of the Aberdeen jetty.

Walker decided to set up the Headquarters of the settlement at Chatham Island. But due to scarcity of water sources in the Chatham Island, Walker had to change his decision and selected Ross Island, hardly two and a half miles away from Chatham for the establishment of the Headquarters of the penal settlement. Ross was called "Chang-Ekee-Bood" in the Andamanese dialect but was known to have been named by the British after the marine surveyor Daniel Ross who had earlier surveyed the Islands. Incidentally, 'Ross' was also the name given to a survey ship often used by Portman, Officer-in-charge of British Relations with the Aborigines in the last quarter of the nineteenth century.

The shifting of the Headquarters from Chatham to Ross Island was approved by the Government of India on 7th May, 1858. Since then, it remained the headquarters of the British Government till the occupation of the Islands by the Japanese Imperial Forces on 23rd March, 1942.

Overlooked by Mount Harriet (1196 ft), the third highest peak in the Islands, Ross is a small Island at the mouth of Port Blair harbour hardly 200 acres in area with the eastern slope rising rather steeply on to the ridge about 200 feet above the sea level at its north-eastern side while the western side of the Island gradually slopes down to the sea shore leaving a narrow strip of flat coastal belt along the western shore facing Aberdeen less than a mile away across the Sesotris Bay. Ross is about 4500 feet in length and about 2000 feet in width at the widest part, the contour of the hill top gradually lowering down, except for a little hump, from the north towards the south. The two small whitish sandy beaches at the northern and the western coasts together with the dotted black granite rocks surging their heads at both ends of the Island above the blue black waters add a natural beauty to Ross that stands like an eternal sentinel guarding the entrance of the harbour against the onrushing high waves from the open seas beyond. The building up of the Headquarters at Ross in those days was by itself an immense task. Skilled men, stores, materials and equipments were at first procured from Moulmein Port in Myanmar, but thereafter had to be procured from Calcutta regularly because of its highly superior markets. Calcutta being the seat of the Government then, it was all the more necessary for the Settlement Administration to keep regular and better contact with the Indian Capital for all official matters.

The magnitude of the task of clearing the jungles in any of the Andaman Islands could only be appreciated by those who have actually witnessed the nature of the vegetation in these Islands. In Ross Island the jungle was so dense and its entanglement by gigantic creepers so complete that it was almost impassable except along the narrow pathways used by the aborigines. The jungle at Ross Island was continuous and had no plains or clear land in between. It was so dense that trees when cut could not be felled without using great force to ground them, or brushwood when cut could not be removed easily owing to the intricate binding by century-old creepers. In this immense, arduous task of jungle clearing, the hands that once held rifles against the British rulers in India in 1857 were, as fate destined, holding axes and choppers to fell the huge trees and slash the creepers in the virgin prime forests. And in that act many of them perished.

The prisoners were put on the hardest labour in the settlement. They had to work about nine hours a day in the tropical climate and dense forest. They were engaged not only for clearing thick tropical jungles but also employed in digging wells, cutting earth, filling swamps, cooking and constructing huts. The 'hard labour' of chain gangs working under stern Jamadars and overseers quickly produced the necessary infrastructure. The forest was entirely cleared. Good teak was available in abundance which was used for the development of the Island. Ross Island started taking shape as the construction work was initiated in the cleared area. Palatial bungalows for the administrators and barracks for the prisoners, a jail and a formidable gallows for those who refused to reform sprung up on Ross and Viper. A sawmill on Chatham supplied the timber. Iron grills, chains, fetters, shackles, flogging stands, and oil mills came directly from England.

The Island was transformed into a comfortable place for the British who were posted there. The seventy acre Island was divided into halves by a wall running from the east to the west. The accommodation of the British officers and soldier's barracks remained in the north of the wall on the hilltop, while the convicts and the barracks of Indian soldiers were in the south.

Though the life of the prisoners in the Ross Island was a tale of torture and sufferings but the settlement officers did not leave a stone unturned to make the isolated Ross a paradise for them. Within a fairly reasonable period of time the little Island Capital had the imposing Chief Commissioner's Bungalow, British troops' barracks, armoury, official residences, printing press, bazar, clubs, dance hall, swimming pool, tennis courts, churches, Eurasian and European schools, a temple and a mosque, water reservoir, distilling water plant, hospital, bakery, ice plant and electricity as well. The inscription on the graves in the European Cemetery of the Ross Island, describes the mental status of the European officers. Set amidst an evergreen foliage, and with no dearth of convict labourers to keep the place spotlessly neat and clean, Ross Island acquired its own place of glory.

The Bazar at Ross Island was the hub of all activities during the end of nineteenth and beginning of twentieth century till the occupation of the Japanese. The ruins of Bazar still remind us the bygone era where European and Indian customers came for the purchase of their daily necessities.

On 26 June, 1941 at 5.21 PM local time, (IST 4.21 PM) an earthquake of greater magnitude rocked the Island. As a result of earthquake a crack developed in the whole Island from its central part of the road. A number of buildings on the Ross Island were damaged. The downfall of this "Paris of the East" began with the occupation of Andaman Islands by the Japanese Imperial Forces. As a result of the Japanese air raids the Chief Commissioner C.F. Waterfall shifted his residence and the seat of Administration to Aberdeen, Port Blair in January 1942. The Japanese forces occupied Andaman and Nicobar Islands on 23 March, 1942. After the reoccupation of the Islands by the Allied forces on 7 October, 1945, 87 years old Penal Settlement was finally abolished on 7 October, 1945. The allied forces of Rajputana Infantry planted a victorious War memorial at Ross Island during 1945.

The Supreme Commander of INA and Head of state of the Azad Hind Government, Netaji Subhas Chandra Bose visited the islands on 29th December, 1943. He stayed at Ross Island in the former Government House of the then Chief Commissioner. Tricolour was hoisted during Netaji's stay for four days.

The Japanese forces had demolished the public buildings at Ross Island, extracted materials for various strategic construction works all over the Islands. In the process of making operational bunkers, they destroyed the settlement. The Ross Island remained to remind the past glory and the citadel of the Indian Penal settlement. When it became uninhabited, nature occupied the dilapidated buildings with huge trees and aerial roots to thrive on the neglected remnants. Ross Island was used as segregation camp during epidemics.

During 1960, a nursery of coconut was developed and rearing of deer and peacocks also started. Now the Ross Island is under the control of Andaman and Nicobar Command. The small island with its treasure of ruins in it became the hot tourists spot in the territory. One can see remnants of an opulent past in the ruins of the Church, the old 'Andamanese Home', Hospital, Bakery, Press, Swimming Pool, Troop Barracks and the Chief Commissioner's residence with its huge gardens and grand ballrooms. There is also a cemetery and a small museum managed by the Indian Navy. The museum has on display a collection of old records.

"Ross glittered with all modem amenities packed with architecturally beautiful buildings and govt. institutions. Though overpopulated the precinct was maintained and kept spotlessly clean. Generators were installed and electricity was made available, so that at night it appeared the massive bed-necked ship underway from neighbouring island. Ross Island thus came to be known as PARIS OF EAST. Its residents enjoyed all comforts of modem living with amenities for their physical and mental wellbeing." This inscription stands even today when one visits Ross Island.

IV

Soon the Andaman penal settlement attracted so much attention that Lord Mayo, the Governor-General, paid a visit and paid for it with his life. Mohd. Sher Ali Khan, a Pathan and a Wahabi Movement activist, stabbed the Viceroy to death at the foot of Mount Harriet, now called Panighat, on February 8, 1872. The murder of Lord Mayo was not the result of any Wahabi plot or in any way related to the Indian Freedom Movement, but a personal revenge of a convict who regarded his punishment of imprisonment for life as an act of injustice perpetrated by the Government. Sher Ali was later executed at the gallows at Viper Island on March 11, 1872. After this unusual incident, the settlement became a hell for other convicts. Every convict was a suspect and had to undergo severe punishment.

Many charismatic personalities belonging to the First War of Independence, Wahabi Movement and later revolutionary activities were deported to the penal settlement to undergo their sentences. They were Musai Singh, Allama Fazal Haq Khiarabadi, Bahadur Singh, Bhima Naik, Moulavi Liaqat Ali, Garbadas Patel, Bhikaji Ganesh Gokhale, Venkat Roa, Syed Alauddin, father and son Himanchal Singh and Kura Singh, Mohd. Ismail Hussain Muneer, Hattee Singh, Maya Ram Jawahar Singh, Ahmedullah, Yahya Ali, Jafar Thaneswari, Maharaja Brij Kishore Singh Deo, among others.

Musai Singh was only 21 years of age at the time of First War of Independence. He was sentenced to transportation for life on the charges of "being a ring leader in the murder of Mr. Moore and arson, dacoity and rebellion." It was decided in May 1907 to conditionally "release him with permission to reside at Rangoon under Police surveillance".

Viceroy Lord Minto sent a Telegram dated 1st May, 1907 to this effect to the Secretary of State which reads as under:

> "Please refer Home Department dispatch dated 11th May on the subject. I have just seen the dispatch, and consider that his conditional release with permission tc reside in Rangoon under Police surveillance should be sanctioned. He is the last survivor of the Mutiny convicts in the Andamans, where his record has been excellent. I strongly recommend his release which could be most appropriate on the 50th anniversary of the Mutiny. Finally, Musai Singh was released from the penal settlement of Andaman at the age of seventy one after 47 years, the longest ever incarceration. He reached Rangoon in July 1907, where he was directed to present himself before the Superintendent of Police on the first day of every month.

Another stalwart of the First War of Independence was Fazal Haq Khairabadi. He was sentenced to transportation for life to *Kala Pani* with confiscation of his property. He, along with other Freedom Fighters of 1857 reached Andamans on 8 October, 1859 aboard the Steam Frigate Fire Queen. During his imprisonment in the penal settlement, Fazal Haq wrote on pieces of cloth with charcoal sticks and sent these clothes to his son Maulana Abdul Haq in the mainland in the year 1860 through Mufti Inayat Ahmed Kakurri, another scholar who took part in the First War of Independence. His works were rendered in Arabic which later came to be known as Al-Surat-ul-Hindia and Al-Fitnat-ul-Hindia. It contained all the incidents of the First War of Independence and his days in *Kala Pani* respectively.

He expressed about the miserable life in the Andaman in his books. In his words, "All huts of the prisoners had temporary roofs which leaks frequently like non-ending tears of my eyes. No sorrow of the world can be compared with the painful life here. When a prisoner dies, he is buried in the sandy shore without performing any last rituals such as bath and coffin. Neither proper grave is dug nor is the last prayer offered. If this would have not been the practice adopted here for burial of dead bodies, death in the Andamans would have been everyone's desire."

Colonel Haughton, the then Superintendent of Port Blair, had recommended to the Government for the release of Fazal Haq. Meanwhile his son Shams-ul-Haq also appealed to the Government for the release of his father. At last he managed to obtain the release order of his father from the Viceroy of India, Lord Curzon. But, on arrival at Port Blair in 1861, he could only join the funeral procession of his father.

Maharaja Bir Kishore Singh Deo, popularly known of Maharaja of Puri, was deported to the Andamans on life imprisonment on charge of involvement in India's First War of Independence. He was treated like the most ordinary criminal convict often in fetters. He was made to do the hardest of works and often put under severe physical torture including whipping with rattan cane. The Maharaja died in 1879-unsung, unmourn and unheard in this remote jail in the Viper Island.

With the freedom movement picking up momentum the number of freedom fighters sentenced to transportation also increased. The need arose for a high security jail that could hold a large number in solitary confinement.

V

Cellular Jail

The penal settlement in the Andamans was not a prison, but a place for the detention of a certain class of prisoners only, viz., transported convicts. The entire Island was like a jail and was converted into a natural Jail after the 1857 Uprising. Indeed the penal settlement in the Andamans had all the administrative appendages including military, post office, electricity and full-fledged system to maintain a colony or settlement. The penal system was primarily to impose strict discipline, secondly to provide for the wants of the settlement so far as these can be supplied locally and thirdly, for establishment of a colony maintained for strategic reasons.

The Lyall and Lethbridge Committee was of the view that "the confinement within the walls of an Indian prison was much more severe form of punishment than transportation and convicts preferred going to the Andamans for undergoing sentence rather than undergoing the same in Indian jails." It specially recommended that the convicts in the Andamans should be confined in separate cells in a limited area to cut off all means of communication between the prisoners-based on the 'Model Prison' or infamous 'Pentonville Prison' in England.

On the recommendation of this Committee, the construction of the massive structure called the Cellular Jail was undertaken in 1896 at the Atlanta Point Hill across the sea passage facing Ross as a 'mailer of great urgency' at considerable cost. The work was completed in 1906. It was only possible because labour force was extracted from the convicts. One of the groups employed for the prison-project was the so-called 'catamite gang', which consisted of 'habitual offenders' who were also the first to be detained in the already completed cells of the new jail by order of the Superintendent even before 1905. Thus sexual deviants were among those who had to build this jail, which later became a national symbol for colonial oppression, and also the first to be imprisoned in it. The unique structure of the jail spreads out like a seven-petal flower. In its centre it had a tower with a turret. Connected to this were the three storied high seven wings with 698 isolated cells. This is why it is called the Cellular Jail.

In almost perennial rainy weather, with heavy bar fetters and shackles on their feet, surrounded by snakes, leeches and scorpions the freedom fighters were to make roads through marshy land. They were punished and faced hard labour if they slowed down. The British authorities were not content with banishment alone. They thought of preventing 'contamination' of ideas and thoughts between these men and large number of hardened criminals by separate confinement for a period of at least 6 months. Accordingly, plans to accommodate 698 convicts in separate cells were drawn. The Cellular Jail system in Andamans had definite impact on the Auborn (silence) system that in essence meant associated work by day and separate cells for sleeping in the night to prevent contamination.

Mr. Mukherji describes: "Standing at the sea coast in the north-eastern part of the Port Blair, the Cellular Jail has a unique architecture. In its original form, it had seven wings, much like the spokes of a bicycle. A three-storied structure, it had 698 cells and no dormitories. The central tower was used by the sentries to keep watch and control the cells. Built with bricks brought from Myanmar, the jail was constructed during 1896-1906 at a cost of Rs. 5,17,352. The purpose of the jail was to condemn the largest number of revolutionary elements to long terms of imprisonment at the minimum cost. It was designed that the front of each wing faced the back of the other. Each cell measuring 13 and a half feet by 7 and a half feet had an iron grill door well secured with sturdy iron bolt and lock on the rectangular groove on the outside of the cell wall and also a few inches away from the entrance door making it impossible to reach it from within."

All the wings, fanning out from the central hub, were three storied structures with long rows of dingy cells measuring 13′5″ × 7′ 5″ having a small iron grilled door in front. A ventilator measuring 3′ × 1′ nearly 10 feet high from the floor was provided in each cell. In order to minimize the conversation between the inmates of the cells and to isolate them from each other the construction was so made that the front portion of each wing was to face the back side of the other wing.

During twelve hours of the night the prisoners would have no occasion to ease themselves. The urine pot was so small that one could hardly urinate even once during the night. The doctor's report on ailment of the prisoners had to go to Barry, the jailor, who was the ultimate authority to take action on it.

Shortly after the completion of the Cellular Jail in 1906, the revolutionary activity in Bengal, Punjab and Maharshtra developed into a pan Indian revolutionary movement the British rule. A few journalists convicted for rebellious writings, were recommended to be confined in the Cellular Jail. But with the conclusion of the trial of the Alipur Bomb Case in Calcutta High Court, the first batch of revolutionaries from Bengal sentenced to transportation for life or for long term imprisonment was sent to the Cellular Jail in 1909. The Andaman Settlement was not to become an issue till the British government decided to deport political prisoners there in 1909. Since then, the history of the Andamans for a period of more than 29 years is practically the history of the revolutionary prisoners from different parts of India who were sent there in successive batches with occasional intervals. The majority of the freedom fighters who were sent to the Cellular Jail in two phases—from 1909 to 1921 and from 1932 to 1938—were from Bengal and the Punjab.

The forbiddingly high walls conjure up fearsome visions where the Indian freedom fighters underwent unspeakable brutalities for many, many years. The alien government used the Cellular Jail to incarcerate anyone who raised his or her voice against the British Empire. It is a symbol of the cruelty of the British imperialism, while in another way it is a symbol of the sacrifices for the cause of independence.

Indubhusan Roy, a young revolutionary from Bengal, of strong robust nature could not bear the humiliation of Barry, tore his shirt and hanged himself. Ullaskar Dutta's was more tragic and pathetic. As a result of hard work, torture and insults, Ullaskar Dutta became seriously ill so much so that he had to spend his life in a lunatic asylum.

Barin Ghosh, younger brother of Rishi Arabindo Ghosh, while describing about the inadequate and insufficient quantity of food said that "next morning we came out and washed our face and then had for the first time of *ganji*, otherwise called '*Kanji*'. It means boiled rice churned in water. We were given each a *dabbu* full of this boiled rice. *Dabbu* is a kind of primitive spoon with a half coconut shell with a cane handle fixed to it. It was saltless and tasteless."

First Hunger Strike

In protest against the British barbarism and tyranny, the freedom fighters resorted to all sorts of defiance and resistance. When the situation went beyond the stage of any reconciliation, hunger strike was declared on 12th May, 1933. About their demands, the British Chief Commissioner said: "I shall not budge an inch. Let their dead bodies be floating in the ocean." The strike lasted for 46 days and took the toll of the precious lives of patriots Mahabir Singh, Mohit Moitra and Mohan Kishore Namdas. The death of three strikers and heroic struggles of others created a widespread excitement throughout the country. Rabindranath Tagore, emotionally upset sent a telegram advising the strikers to call off the strike. "Your Motherland will never forget her full blown flowers", he said.

British Government ultimately conceded some of their demands. The prisoners were allowed to mix freely among themselves. They were provided with study materials like newspapers, books etc. and were allowed to participate in indoor and outdoor games. These concessions made the prisoners' life a bit tolerable and prepared them for a greater and offensive movement.

Second Hunger Strike

After the first hunger strike, political prisoners tried to draw the attention of the British Government to their representations regarding their repatriation and uniform classification. But the British Government did not pay any heed to it. So, on 25th July, 1937 they started a second mass hunger strike. Their political demands now included the demands of movements to other jails and camps. The political prisoners of Alipur, Deoli, and Berhampore jails joined them.

The hunger strike lasted for 35 days and everybody became worried about health of the strikers. Gandhiji, Rabindra Nath Tagore, Jawaharlal Nehru, Fazlul Haque sent telegrams to suspend the strike. The hunger strike was called off on 28th August, 1937. As a result of intervention of national leaders, political prisoners started leaving for their respective states from 22nd September, 1937. By January 1938 when the last batch left the Andaman shores, Cellular Jail, the Indian Bastille was completely denuded of all political prisoners.

The plaques bearing the names of those incarcerated in the Jail reads like a "who's who" of the freedom movement. Prominent among them are the names of Vinayak Damodar Savarkar, Barindra Kumar Ghosh (brother of Shri Aurobindo), Bhai Parmanand of the Ghadr Party, and many more, convicted in various conspiracy cases.

Two wings of the Jail got damaged during the Second World War. Another two wings of the jail were demolished after India achieved independence. However, this led to protests from several former prisoners and political leaders who saw it as a way of erasing the tangible evidence of their persecution. The remaining three wings and the central tower were, therefore, converted into a National Memorial in 1969.

The Govind Ballabh Pant Hospital was set up in the premises of the Cellular Jail in 1963. It is now a 500-bed hospital with about 40 doctors serving the local population. The Cellular Jail is the most prominent landmark of Port Blair, or, for that matter of the Andaman and Nicobar Islands. The first stop for anyone visiting the Islands is the Martyrs Memorial inside the Jail. Those familiar with the history of the freedom struggle are moved to tears at the sight of the flogging stand, oil mill, and the other instruments of torture on display in the Jail museum. A 'must' on the itinerary of all tourists is the 'Sound and Light Show' every evening, which brings to life a dark chapter in the history of the Islands as a penal settlement.

The Jail marked its centenary on March 10, 2006. Many erstwhile prisoners were felicitated on this occasion by the Government of India. It has been a long journey for the Jail—from a torture machine to a National Memorial, from a dreaded prison to a place of pilgrimage, a place where the memories of brave freedom fighters are revived and patriotic fervour surges through the veins of the visitors.

VI

As the settlement grew, "hardened criminals" from undivided India and Burma were also brought in. On frequent intervals ships, namely Semiramis, Dalhousie, Pluto, Roman Emperor, Edward, Sesotris etc. continued to arrive at the penal settlement with prisoners on board from Rangoon, Moulemin, Karachi, Calcutta and so on. The gross number of the convicts sent to the penal settlement up to year 1901 was 49,592, as shown in Table 16.1. The persons transported to Port Blair settlement were murderers, who for some reasons have escaped the death penalty, and the perpetrators of the more heinous offences against person and property. The sentences they had to undergo were chiefly for life, but convicts, with long term sentences were also sent from time to time. Except under special circumstances, convicts were neither under 18 years of age nor over 40 years, and were mentally fit for hard labour. Youths between 18 and 20 were kept in the Boys Gang under special conditions. Girls were occasionally of 16 or thereabouts. They were kept along with women—both married and unmarried—In the 'Female Jail', which was a large enclosure consisting of separate sleeping wards and work shed. There were no special rules for them. The male convicts were held in a jail on Viper island and women convicts in South Point barracks, near the present day hotel Sinclair.

Table 16.1: Year-wise Convict Deportation to Andamans, 1874-1901

Year	*1-16*	*17-40*	*41-60*	*Over 60*
1874	20	4,582	1,991	476
1881	–	8,730	2,180	542
1891	–	8,815	2,421	502
1901	–	7,264	3,945	635

Source: Census Report 1901, Andaman and Nicobar Islands, p. 92.

Table 16.2 shows that persons convicted of the charges of murder, dacoity (gang robbery with murder or preparation for murder) and heinous offences against property made up the bulk of convict population.

The Lyall and Lethbridge Committee (Sir Charles James Lyall, Secretary in the Government of India and Surgeon—Major Sir Alfred Lethbridge, Inspector General of Jails, Bengal) was formed in 1890 to study the Penal Settlement in the Andamans and suggest

Table 16.2: Persons Convicted of Murder, Dacoity and Offences Against Property

Year	Murder	Crime Against Person	Dacoity Against Property	Crime	Others	Total
1874	5,575	107	1,262	325	298	7,567
1881	7,445	158	2,444	1,012	381	11,440
1891	7,946	308	1,711	1,337	416	11,718
1901	7,795	817	2,262	904	196	11,974
1904-05	8,386	752	2,881	1,874	219	14,112
1905-06	8,559	812	3,050	2,038	237	14,696

Source: *Census Report 1901, Andaman and Nicobar Islands*, p. 92.

recommendations. They visited Port Blair in January 1890 and submitted their report on 26 April, 1890. The Committee recommended that the convicts in the Andamans, especially those who were consistent criminals or guilty of extremely grave crimes, must pass through a much harder life at least during the preliminary stages. It was recommended that the prisoners should be confined during the first six months in solitary cells in a jail to be specially built for this purpose. In the next stage, prisoners were to be confined for eighteen months in barracks where they could work in association with other prisoners, but were not to be allowed beyond a compound. Thereafter, in the third stage for a period of four years, the convicts were to be given the liberty to work outdoors during the day and return to the barrack for the night. Then the convicts were to become a second-class convict. During the next five years they were to remain as drudging convicts, and were to be eligible for the petty posts of supervision and easier form of labour. They were also to receive a very petty allowance for little luxuries, or to deposit it in the special saving bank. After completing ten years in deportation, they could receive a "ticket-of-leave" being termed as self-supporter." In this condition he used to earn his own living in a village, he could do farming, keep cattle, and marry or send for his family. But, he was not free from fetters, he had no civil rights and he could not leave the settlement or remain idle. These rules concerning the treatment to the ordinary criminals suggested by the Committee were implemented stringently.

Herbert Hope Risley, influential ethnographer and Home Secretary in Lord Curzon's administration, assessed the reformatory influence of the colonial penal regime in 1906 rather negatively and self-critically: "Finally whatever reformative influence there may be in the Port Blair system it certainly does not commence until the man becomes a self-supporter, that is to say, until he has spent ten years in association with a mixed crew of criminals under the laxest control and in charge of officers who are convicts themselves, and has passed his nights in barracks where unnatural crime is habitually practiced. If he goes through these and eventually turns out a respectable self-supporter the result is assuredly due to himself and not to his surroundings." However, this form of outspoken self-criticism was not the norm among colonial officers.

The geographical factors greatly influenced the pattern of penal settlement in the Andamans. Indeed, the Andaman Penal system has grown up on its own lines and has gradually adapted to the requirements of penal character. There were serious problems with the manner in which the colonial state punished the male and female offenders and few cases highlighted the quality of the system being implemented in this remotest part of India. The penal authorities were under the impression that the voice of these convicts would not travel beyond the islands. But too much of their annoyance the convict prisoners successfully managed to dispatch secretly the news about subhuman living conditions, and tales of sufferings and torture. For the repressive, humiliated, insubordination, homosexuality and general despondency among the convicts because of lack of personal and social ties, the penal system in the Andamans was rightly termed as a 'hellish inferno'.

In the beginning of the twentieth century the press and public in India expressed their resentment over reports of the cruel treatment to convicts in the '*Kala Pani*'. Both public and official aversion towards the Penal Settlement developed gradually. In fact, the idea of closing the Settlement was first suggested as early as in 1904 by W.R.H. Merk, Chief Commissioner, A & N Islands. He pointed out to the Government of India that the prisoners in the Penal Settlement enjoyed far greater amenities and freedom than in the Indian (mainland) jails and therefore it has lost the terror and the deterrent effects on the criminals of the worst type. There was no indication that the system had actually produced any salutary effect on the convicts by way of improvement in their moral character. There was hardly any justification, he argued, for the enormous expenditure incurred by the Government for maintaining such a huge establishment. But the opinion of the State governments went against it: "They were opposed to total abolition of penal settlement as a place for reception of criminals." Moreover, they were worried for the shortage of space in the jails of different provinces for accommodating a large number of prisoners in case the transportation to Andaman ceased altogether.

Demands for the abolition of the settlement were, however, continuously made by political leaders in their writings and speeches. In November 1913, Sir Reginald Craddock, the Home member, visited the Andaman penal settlement to study the situation personally. In a lengthy report he mentioned that the penal system in the Andamans appeared to be perfect in theory. According to him, the terror of crossing the '*Kala Pani*' was now an exploded bogey to Indians who were voluntarily going to distant places like Fiji and Columbia. The existence of immorality among the prisoners on a wide scale on account of shortage of women in the settlement was deplored by him. In this circumstances he suggested following three alternatives:

- To abolish the Andaman penal settlement;
- To remedy only the serious defects of the system in order to make it less harmful; and
- To reform the entire penal system of India including the existing system of the Andamans.

The Cellular Jail started receiving revolutionary Freedom Fighters from the year 1910. Within four years following a strike by the political prisoners in April 1914, the repatriation of the selected Andaman prisoners to particular Indian jails was carried out. The first batch of the ex-Andaman prisoners reached Calcutta before the end of May 1914 and the repatriation was completed by the middle of September 1941. This could be regarded as a definite landmark in the history of the Penal Settlement in the Andamans.

But due to the fresh outbreak of revolutionary activities in India during the First World War, the policy of denuding the Cellular Jail of a large number of political prisoners had to be given up within two years. The policy adopted in 1914 by the Government was thus revised and groups of political prisoners convicted in Bengal and other provinces were transported to the Andamans during the period of 1916-1920.

In 1920 an All-India Jails Committee was appointed by the Government of India to look into the conditions of the colonial penal institutions. The members of the Committee visited the jails, conducted interviews with prison officers, warders, convicts and native experts, collected statistical and other material on the various jails and finally came up with a six-volume report by October 1920. The report generally painted a very unfavourable picture of the colonial jail system, and the Government of India had a heated debate about what impact this negative report would have on the unstable political situation. It feared that the report would feed into the rising nationalist critique of colonial rule and thus decided to publish only the first volume, which contained the Committee's report, but not the five other volumes, which were the appendices with the transcriptions of the interviews.

The All-India Jails Committee made a remarkable statement stating that the existing system in the Andamans was regarded undesirable even if increased staff was provided to the administration of the penal settlement. In their opinion the Andaman penal system had lost its deterrent effect, involved enormous expenditure and exposed prisoners to adverse climatic conditions. The Committee did not regard the self-support system a success, mainly due to paucity of women in the settlement. The Committee recommended that the deportation of prisoners to the Andamans should cease except in regard to such prisoners as the Governor-General in Council may by special or general order direct. In 1921 when Government decided to close the Settlement, the convict population numbered 11,532 and by December 1926 the number had been reduced to 7740 of whom 4377 were self-supporters (2105 living on government wages and 2272 on apicultural income).

Based on the recommendations of Jails Committee, punishment of solitary confinement and chain gang were abolished. Flogging was rare. No convicts outside the jail were kept in fetters. Facilities for outdoor games and library were provided during leisure time. Some more steps were taken to improve the conditions of the penal system in Andamans and few unmarried female convicts were repatriated to their native places.

Considering the conditions in Andaman and Nicobar and press and public criticism in general to the penal system in Andamans, Sir William Vincent, Home Secretary to the Government of India announced (July 1922) the abolition of the penal settlement and arrangement of a speedy return of prisoners to the Indian jails. Further he issued orders that the repatriation of the prisoners from Andaman would be gradual because the local governments were not in a position to accommodate about twelve to fifteen thousand prisoners in a short period. Meanwhile overcrowding due to political agitation in the several provincial jails the local governments expressed their inability to accommodate such large numbers. British authorities thus considered the reopening of the Andaman penal system temporarily. Keeping aside all the criticism, the Deputy Secretary Gwynne laid great stress on the development of the resources of the islands and indeed he observed that there was no alternative but to reopen temporarily the deportation of the prisoners.

Sir Alexander Muddiman, the Home Member visited the islands in November 25, 1925 and recommended the penal settlement to be continued because he felt that:

- There was lack of accommodation in the jails of several provinces of India for prisoners repatriated from the Andamans;
- If the penal settlement of Port Blair is abandoned the whole administration of the island would collapse;
- The closing of the settlement would adversely affect about three thousand self-supporters in the islands who were living in a state of semi-independence; and
- The strategic location of these islands in the Bay of Bengal was another important reason and the immense natural wealth of these islands, which would be developed into valuable assets, prevented the British Government to abandon the settlement.

The Government of India further clarified that the reduction of convict population in the settlement considerably hampered the progress of the development programmes of the islands. On account of shortage of labour in the islands several plans could not be executed. In order to promote self-supporters and free population, the Government of India extended grants of land on lease for fifty years to attract more people from mainland. The Government of India declared plans for the development of forest and agriculture in the islands to make semi-self-sufficient penal system. This policy of developing the islands through the agency of an enlarged population of ex-convicts and their families was followed by the British Government.

The resurgence of the revolutionary activities in the country in the early 30s of the last century compelled a re-thinking of the policy on deportation to the Andamans. In or about 1932 it was decided to renew the system of transporting political prisoners to the Andamans. In accordance with the new policy twenty-five political prisoners, convicted mostly in the Chittagong Armoury Raid case, were transferred to the Andamans on 15th August, 1932. During the period 1932-37 a total of 366 political prisoners were deported to the Andamans of whom 332 were from Bengal alone. By the end of 1934 there were more than two hundred political prisoners in the Cellular Jail. The first batch was sent back in September 1937, and by January 1938 when the last batch left the Andaman shores, Cellular Jail was complexly denuded of all political prisoners.

The Japanese occupied the Islands on 23rd March, 1942. The islands were reoccupied by the British after the Japanese surrender on 18th August, 1945, and indeed they granted general pardon to all the convicts and self-supporters. Finally, the Government of India abolished the penal settlement in 1945.

VII

One of the frequent criticisms voiced with regard to the Andamans concerned the exceptionally high number of alleged cases of 'unnatural vice' among the largely male convict population for which the Andamans had become infamous, even though the Port Blair officials never became tired of stressing that these 'evil habits' existed in every Indian jail and was not unique to the Andaman settlement.

As early as in 1870 a discussion arose among colonial officials about convicts' same-sex behaviour and possible remedies. One of the first Superintendents, Colonel H. Man, wrote in November 1870 to the Secretary of the Government of India, E.C. Bayley, alluding to the danger of an all-male penal settlement and proposing to 'provide' women for the Nicobar settlement.

One year later, his successor General Stewart resumed the discussion on how to put an end to 'unnatural crime' one year later. He stated that the question was 'not restricted to the case of the Nicobars alone', but applied 'in equal force' to the Port Blair Settlement, thus being a pan-penal settlement problem. He proposed 'strict supervision coupled with the encouragement of marriage' in order to fight the 'unnatural crime', while also toying with the idea of arranging for a 'supply of public women' as it was practised in the military cantonments of the British Raj at that time in order to prevent same-sex relations among soldiers.

Ten years later the Lyall-Lethbridge Committee decried again the existence of 'unnatural offences'. The report came up with two different approaches to suppress the crime. Firstly, it argued that separation of offenders could successfully put an end to same-sex behaviour. This separation was to be realized through the visual setting apart of those prisoners 'habitually given to unnatural offences' by them 'having to wear coloured coats' as well as by means of spatial separation.

Spatial segregation was not an easy task to accomplish as there was no cellular jail structure in the penal colony at that time and convicts would work together in large groups during the day anyway. To suppress the vice at least during night hours, the Lyall-Lethbridge report underlined the necessity to isolate 'incorrigible prisoners' from each other at night in cubicles or cells, Due to the financial restraints of the colonial regime, building of cells on a large scale was impossible, and so different officers with engineering talent experimented with a novel, explicitly colonial technology of disciplining deviant convicts—the Indian cubicle. The cubicle was an iron cage that was to be installed in large wards so that the jail wardens could ensure separate confinement at night. Colonial officials hoped that this form of panoptic visibility of the immoral prisoners would serve as a remedy against the sexual vice, but construction and delivery of the cubicles only moved at a slow pace and the Cellular Jail was built before the cubicle-scheme could be implemented. The second and main recommendation of the report was to transport female term-convicts to Port Blair to balance the gender disparity and thus discourage male-male sexual relations.

The large inconsistency in number between male and female population posed serious problem in the settlement, Normally the families of the convicts were not willing to come to the Andamans as they thought that by crossing the sea, they would lose their caste. In 1869 only 35 willing female convicts were sent from Bengal to Port Blair. In 1897, there were only 363 women out of 2447 "self-supporters."

Any convict who was eligible to become a "self-supporter" and who wished to marry and settle down was allowed to choose from amongst the female prisoners as his life-partner. On an appointed day, the female prisoners who were eligible for marriage were paraded in a room and the eligible bachelors were introduced. If any bachelor considered that a particular lady of his choice was likely to be a good wife, he pointed out the lady of his choice and if she was willing they were married shortly thereafter and were settled in one of the "self-supporters" villages. The superintendent registered the marriage and it acquired legality. This practice lasted for a few years only.

After some experience with settling female convicts in the Andaman penal colony, the colonial regime changed its mind and called the system of supplying women in 1914 'morally indefensible' because it 'disregards all marriage laws, caste, religious, social and customary', 'licences prostitution under a cloak', and finally, because children born out of these convict marriages would 'grow up in the worst surroundings with strong hereditary tendencies to crime'. There was also anxiety surrounding the alleged usage of female and male convict children as prostitutes by their parents.

VIII

After the brutal suppression of the First War of Independence of 1857 the great heroes of 1857 were transported to the far distant Island of Andaman. Following the footsteps of the great heroes of the revolt of 1857, there were many anti-British uprisings such as the movements of the Wahabis, the Rumpa revolt, the Mopillas rebellion, the Tharawardy and Manipuri insurgencies, and the rebels of these movements were convicted on the charges of sedition and were either executed or transported to Andaman.

The first to arrive were the Wahabi revolutionaries from the Central and United Provinces who rose against the British rule during 1869-70. But their total number is not known. Dr. R.C. Mazumdar rightly observed: "... large number of Wahabi prisoners were sent there (Andaman), neither the total number (of Wahabis) nor details of individual prisoners are available."

The Mopillas or Moplas of Malabar, a valiant Muslim community revolted against the British in 1921. After suppression, about 1400 Moplas were sent to Andaman from the Madras jail as a special measure. A general amnesty was granted to the Mopla prisoners in 1932 and some 500 women with their children joined their folk in the Andamans. More and more Mopla prisoners opted to settle in Andaman and they numbered as many as 1885 in 1931. By 1989, their population grew to more than six thousands and as their mother tongue is Malayalam, the number of Malayalam speaking people became 26075 according to the 1991 Census.

The Bhantus, commonly called 'Bhatu', were brought to Andaman from the United Provinces, now Uttar Pradesh as convicts from 1922 onwards. Between 1926 and 1928, nearly 300 Bhantus along with their families were transported from different jails and Salvation Army Settlements. In the following years, others came voluntarily to live with their relations who had come to Andaman earlier as convicts.

The peasants of Rampa Chidavaram Agency within Godavari and Visakhapatnam districts of the then Madras Presidency involved in the Rumpa Revolt of 1922-24, were also transported to the Andaman. The descendants of the heroes of the Rumpa peasants' revolt settled down in the Andaman.

During the British period, the Burmese convicts were also brought from Burma by the British who engaged them to clear jungles and to act as forest guards, department or to accompany the British officials in their survey works in the dense forests. On being granted self-supporter status, many of the Burmese convicts settled in Andaman.

Again after the suppression of the Tharawardy rebellion in 1933, a large number of Burmese involved in the said revolt was transported to Andaman as convicts.

The Karens from Burma were also brought to Andaman for clearing jungles. In due course, they were settled and concentrated in Webi village under Mayabandar Tehsil in North Andaman.

Not only the Moplas, the Bhantus, the Rumpa peasants but also the Karens, the Burmese convicts and the Tharawardy rebels were all granted pre-1942 'Local' status to enjoy all sorts of privileges accorded by the government to the local people enjoying the facilities of free-settlers as granted by the British authorities. They were granted lands and other facilities to settle there after the expiry of their specific terms.

Since the inception of the penal settlement, several hundred notorious criminals on being charged with heinous crimes, like murder, dacoity, arson etc., were transported to Andaman, and after spending specific period of penal servitude and on satisfactory completion of terms of rigorous punishments, they were granted the ticket-of-leave or self-supporter status. Then many of them got married to female convicts or brought back their families from the mainland and settled in the villages around Port Blair on being allotted lands by the government.

In "*Penal Settlement in Andamans*", R.C. Majumdar observed that "although the self-supporter convict was entitled to send for his wife from India, he very seldom did so and his wife would also not, as a general rule, choose to join her convict husband across the sea, even apart from the fact that the Hindu wife would thereby lose her caste. So, the 'local born', nearly all of them, were the issues of convict marriages."

Indeed, these 'local born' people irrespective of their caste, creed, colour or culture have formed the foundation of a unique society and their progeny are true champions of nonpareil culture contributing to the emergence of a Mini-India and comprise every kind of personal character.

After the partition of India, a large number of the Bengali-speaking Hindus from East Pakistan crossed over to this side of the border for shelter. Considering the paucity of resources of West Bengal, the then Chief Minister, Dr. B.C. Roy took initiative to settle at least a few thousand East Bengal refugees in the Andamans. But the Communists opposed the settlement of the refugees in Andaman, and instead demanded their settlement only in West Bengal. The Central Government also did not quite relish the idea of the islands developing into an appendage of West Bengal. Consequently, the settlement of the East Bengal refugees in Andaman had been stopped. Later, the Tamil repatriates from Burma and Sri Lanka, as well migrants from Kerala, Andhra Pradesh, Ranchi and other places got settled there.

Andaman, originally a land of autochthones, was made a haven for the descendants of convicts, known as the Andaman Indians. The great variety of the settlers in the Andamans can be classified into two broad groups—colonial settlers and post-colonial settlers. The former includes the Andaman Indians or 'Local Born' consisting of people from all communities including the Moplas, Bhantus, Rumpa peasants, Karens, Bumans etc., and the later one comprises the refugees from East Pakistan, migrants from other States, mainly from South India, and people from the mainland on Government service or in search of jobs and to try their luck in business.

From a natural jail the Andaman Nicobar group of Islands has over the years become one of the important limbs of the great country of ours. It was a long, arduous but fruitful journey from its establishment as a Penal Settlement in the middle of the nineteenth century to its present position as vibrant unit of the Union of India.

17
PVTGs of A & N Islands

Present Status, Policies and Developmental Challenges

Aiman Fatima

The Andaman and Nicobar Islands have originally been the abode of Particularly Vulnerable Tribal Groups (PVTGs) but during the British Raj in the Indian Sub-continent, the British transported convicts, both political and criminal, to these Islands from the mainland India to start a Penal Settlement which commenced from March 1858 (Census 2011). The convicts, both men and women were from a heterogeneous background. Gradually due to British policies, convicts marriages irrespective of caste and religion and environmental harshness, gradually a new society emerged other than tribes. After independence the Government of India used these Islands for rehabilitation of the Bengali refugees, who had come to India after their exodus from East Bengal and the Malayalis, Tamilian, the Telugu from their respective states. This non-tribal society is unique in nature that's why Andaman is also called "Mini India".

The Andaman and Nicobar Islands (Protection of Aboriginal Tribes) Regulation, 1956, promulgated by the President of India, provides for the protection of the interests of aboriginal tribes and declaration of the geographical area which are predominantly inhabited by these tribes as reserved areas (A & N Gazette, 1956). In these Islands, there are six Scheduled Tribes, i.e. the Great Andamanese, Onges, Jarawas, Sentinelese, Nicobarese and the Shompens notified by the President of India under Article 342(1) of

Indian Constitution (Andaman and Nicobar Islands Scheduled Tribe Order, 1959). Five of these six aboriginal tribes of Andaman and Nicobar Islands are PVTGs (Particularly Vulnerable Tribal Groups) which are very less in numbers and are facing threat of extinction viz. the Great Andamanese, Ongese, Jarawas, Sentineleseand the Shompen (AAJVS 2011) while the Nicobari tribe has been mainstreamed and their population is approximately 28,653.

These tribes are found in the following Islands:

Table 17.1: Aboriginai Tribes of Andaman & Nicobar Islands

1.	Great Andamanese	Strait Islands
2.	Onges	Little Andaman
3.	Jarawas	South Andaman and Middle Andaman
4.	Sentinelese	North Sentinal Island
5.	Shompen	Great Nicobar
6.	Nicobarese	Car Nicobar, Chowra, Teressa, Bampuka, Katchal, Kamrota, Nancowry, Trinket, Little Nicobar, Kondul, Pilomilo

Source: Directorate of Tribal Welfare, 2014, Port Blair.

The Archipelago is characterized by two distinct native races and cultures. One is of the Negrito population in the Andamans that is the Andamanese, Onges, Jarawas, and the Sentinelese (living in Andaman group of Islands) and the other is of the Mongoloid population which includes the Nicobarese and the Shompens (living in Nicobar group of Islands). This created two distinct cultural zones-that of the Andamanese Culture and the Nicobari culture, shows a marked difference in the way of life adapted by them over the centuries.

Total population of the Andaman and Nicobar Islands is 3,79,944 (as per 2011 Census) of which, the tribal population is 29,469 (as per 2011 Census). The population of PVTGs is 840 (estimated) (*Ibid.*, 2014).

Table 17.2: Population of the PVTGs of A & N Islands

Sl.No.	*Name of Tribes*	*Total Number of Tribes*
1.	Great Andamanese	61 till date
2.	Ongese	117
3.	Jarawas	406
4.	Sentinelese	50 estimated
5.	Nicobarese	28653 (as per 2011 Census)
6.	Shompen	219 (as per 2011 Census)

Source: Directorate of Tribal Welfare, 2014, Port Blair.

Great Andamanese

The Great Andamanese belonging to the Negrito race, have been settled at Strait Island in Andaman District. They were once 8000 strong tribal population but now they are only 61 in numbers. They were first in the Islands which came in the contact of then British Administration and modern civilization. They professed hostility in the beginning towards outsiders and fought for their territory but defeated by the technologically advanced colonists in the battle of Aberdeen (1859)(Portman M V 1899). Subsequently the "Andaman Home" was founded by the British Administration at Port Blair (Imperial Gazette, 1901). British policy of friendly contact and the hospitality of "Andaman Home" was, however, the cause for the introduction of "civilized vices" including veneral diseases, opium, liquor for which the Great Andamanese became addicted ultimately. Apart from this they were decimated by a series of epidemics. Gradually they lost their identity, cultural traditions, economic activities and their number had dwindled to below 20.

After independence the Andaman and Nicobar Administration decided to rehabilitate the surviving Andamanese in the Strait Island (1969), a Tribal Reserve. Today after significant efforts by the Administration in terms of protection and preservation, the Andamanese population gradually increased to 61. Now, they are settled at the Strait Island.

Onges

Onges are one of the Negrito tribes of Andaman Islands. In the late 19th century, after continuous efforts and attempts to control the Islands, the British established "friendly" relations with the Onges also. Similarly, they have been in contact with outsiders/civilization for more than 100 years (AAJVS, 2014). In 1951 they were 150 in numbers now they are 117. The present-day Onges have no Idea about Britishers as nobody of that period is alive. The Onges are different from Andamanese in term of their indigenous identity because they are still keeping their traditional activities of hunting, fishing and gathering and perform traditional rituals (DTW, 2013).

Initially the Onges were scattered all over Little Andaman Island in different bands and also in nearby islets. After Independence the Government of India passed a resolution under the special area development programme to resettle the refugee population from East Pakistan (now Bangladesh) to Little Andaman. As well as in 1973 the Andaman and Nicobar Forest and Plantation Development Corporation (ANFPDC) established an intensive field station in Little Andaman to expedite the forest based programmes. In 1975, the ANFPDC in Little Andaman launched a regeneration project called Red Oil Palm Plantation in an attempt to restock the cleared forests. So the different Development Schemes in Little Andaman have inadvertently forced the Onges to move away from the outsiders settlements into smaller pockets of Little Andaman. In 1976 the Andaman Administration resettled the Onges at Dugong Creek and South Bay of Little Andaman. After Tsunami, 2004, all the Onges have, on their own choice, shifted to Dugong Creek, Little Andaman (Kar, 2015). Now all the Onges are living in Dugong Creek of Little Andaman and semi-dependent on Administration of Andaman and Nicobar Islands.

Jarawa

The Jarawas are also a Negrito tribe of the Andaman group of Islands. They have been residing at the western coast and forest belt of South and Middle Andaman islands. During British period the British Administration tried to develop friendly contacts towards the Jarawa but the Jarawas had rejected the offer of friendship from alien world. The Jarawas had preferred to live in dense forest instead of accepting slavery in civilized world (DTW, 2013). After independence the penal settlement had been abolished but soon after began a new period of resettlement of displaced persons, millions of whom were sacrificed at the altar of freedom. Thousands of family resettled in Andamans during the period from 1947-1996 till the Jarawas gave up their hostility and entered in to the period of friendliness with the outsiders. Now the Jarawas are friendly with the contact team of Administration (Janjati Sevak) and outsiders but still they are living in forest (reserve area demarcated by the Law and Administration) and doing their traditional hunting and gathering till now. Most of them do not wear clothes (Policy Notified, MHA 2004). They are 406 in numbers (DTW, 2013).

Protection and welfare measures are extended to the Jarawas as per the Jarawa Policy framed in the year 2004. According to the policy an area of about 1028 sq. km. in the landward side and also up to

5 km. in the coastal waters from the high tide line on the western side of the South and Middle Andaman Islands have been declared as the Jarawa Tribal Reserve (16 per cent area of South, North and Middle Andaman District) (*Ibid.,* 2013). In the reserve area the entry of unauthorized person is banned. The land and resources in the reserve area will be at the full and exclusive of the tribal community. Stringent penalties have been provided against violators who may trespass in to the tribal reserve area, to poach and exploit. The Administration through AAJVS, extends health and other calibrated amenities preferably *in situ.*

Sentinelese

The Sentinelese who belong to the Negrito race, inhabit in the North Sentinal Island of the South Andaman District. Their population is 50 (estimated). Sentinelese are still the hunting, gathering self reliant tribe having adequate forest resources in the Sentinal Island. This is only tribe probably in the world which still professed hostility towards outsiders and remain in total isolation.

However, the Administration of Andaman and Nicobar is trying to establish friendly contact with the Sentinelese and some expeditions has been done. But the Administration is not in favour of continuing regular friendly expeditions because it may lead to spread of foreign diseases among Sentinelese. The Administration has adopted an "eyes-on and hands off" policy to ensure that no poachers enter to the Islands.

Shompen

The Shompens are the semi-nomadic, hunting, gathering tribe, belonging to the Mongoloid race. The Shompens live in different bands in thick tropical forest and in coasts of the Great Nicobar Island in the Nicobar District. Their number is approximately 220. The Shompens practice horticulture, hunting, fishing and gathering.

Present Socio-economic and Health Status of the PVTGs

The Andaman and Nicobar Administration, through AAJVS (Andaman Adim Janjati Vikas Samiti) constituted and registered as a Society on 25.03.1976 under Societies Registration Act, 1860, extends all financial support to the tribal students of the Onges and the the

Great Andamanese communities for their education at the primary, middle and higher secondary levels. Exclusively middle level schools have been established in the tribal settlements of the Onges at Dugong Creek, Little Andaman and for the Andamanese at Strait Islands. Informal education system has been introduced among the Jarwa tribes through bilingual-bicultural curriculum developed by ANTRI and AAJVS. Eight HOT SPOTS (Annaholey Chaddha) have been established in the Jarawa Reserve Area by the administration which act as community centre cum health centre and also as informal schools for the Jarawa children.

At present 22 Great Andamanese children are studying. In the first time of their history, two Great Andamane boys have successfully passed 10th standard during 2011-12 session.

At present 38 Onges children are enrolled in Middle School, at Onges settlement, Dugong Creek, Little Andaman. Other two tribes, viz. the Sentinelese and the Shompen are not taking any formal education.

The Andaman and Nicobar Administration, through Andaman Adim Janjati Vikas Samity, extends all financial, infrastructural support to the settlements of the Onges and the Great Andamanese. The Administration has introduced a few economic activities like rearing of poultry, raising and maintenance of the coconut plantation so as to provide them permanent means of subsistence. Administration provides free ration and clothes to them. The water supply, electrification of settlement at free of cost, free medical care, school, Police Wireless, community hall, footpath, jetty etc. have been provided at the settlement. A Great Andamanese Multipurpose Co-operative society is functioning at Strait Island. All the Great Andamanese are the member of this society. The society provides the consumer goods to the Great Andamanese and also helps them in marketing of their agricultural produce. An Onge Multipurpose Co-operative Society at Dugong Creek is also functioning which collect and sale the coconuts and provides consumer goods to all of them. By and large, the Andamanese are fully dependent and the Onges are semi-dependent on Administration for their livelihood and other basic amenities.

Although after much efforts of Administration and with the help of AAJVS, 8 Onges and 22 Great Andamanese are employed in Government service. One Great Andamanese girl has completed the ANM training and a boy completed ITI (Welder) training.

The Shompens are also assisted by the Administration for the different economic activities. The Administration has introduced an exchange system. Under this system the Shompens bring the forest products like nuts, resins, lemon etc. These produce are sold under the supervision of Administration and they got iron tools, rice etc.

As far as the Jarwas are concerned, they are doing their traditional hunting and gathering in the deep forest, although Administration is providing fishing kits, iron tools and implements to them. On the recommendation of the study group a "Kangapo" project started. In this project, the stitched garments are being given to jarwas in exchange of their artifacts.

The Administration of the Andaman and Nicobar Islands have set up health unit and framed policies for the tribal health. Exclusive medical wards in PHCs located near the Jarwa Reserve at Tushnabad, Kadamtala, and G.B. Pant Hospital, Port Blair have been set up for the treatment of the Jarawas. Such wards are also declared as Tribal Reserve under the Protection of Aboriginal Tribes Regulations, 1956.

Medical Sub Centres have been established at Dugong Creek in Little Andaman and Strait Island for providing the health care facility to the Onges and the Great Andamanese Tribes.

The Deputy Director, Tribal Health along with paramedical staff of Directorate of Health services periodically visits the Jarwa/ Shompen/Onges/Andamanese areas to provide *in situ* health care. In case of emergency, the patients are evacuated for specialized treatment to the nearest Hospital at the Port Blair or even to the mainland along with an attendant and the entire expenses are borne by the Administration.

During the year 2014-15, the Jarawas, Onges, and the Great Andamanese have availed medical care on 388, 1123, and 216 occasions respectively. A Health and Nutritional study of the Great Andamanese Tribe of Strait Island and the Onge Tribe of Dugong Creek in Little Andaman was conducted during December 2013 and 2014, shows alarming condition for this primitive tribe.

There is high prevalcnce of obesity and overweight (66%), hypertension, diabetes in Andamanese (19%). Anaemia was found to be widely prevalent (65.5%) among them. The nutritional status of the school going children is poor approximately 70 per cent children are undernourished.

The population of 112 Onges comprising 54 females and 58 males were surveyed by the team. The nutritional disorders, both under and over nutrition were prevalent amongst the Onge community. The school age children and adolescents suffered from both under nutrition and over nutrition while almost all pre-school children had severe degree of under nutrition. The emergence of overweight and obesity was viewed among them which shows that the adult population of the Onges is moving towards a high cardiovascular risk zone. Apart from this there are two registered cases of pulmonary tuberculosis, one case of extra-pulmonary tuberculosis, three cases of heart diseases and three cases of bronchial asthma found.

Probably it is all because of sedentary life style, dependency on Administration and due to discontinue their conventional way of life.

The Deputy Director (Tribal Health) in the Directorate of Health Services, A & N Administration had carried out the health survey of the Shompen and the Jarawa Tribes in 2014. The results are different from the survey of the Onges and the Andamanese.

The health survey of 21 Shompen, Lawful Bay area in Great Nicobar Island, was conducted. There was no obesity or underweight. None of them were found to be suffering from Anaemia, vitamin deficiency, protein energy malnutrition, cardiac or respiratory diseases. Overall fitness of Shompens is good and satisfactory.

As far as the Jarawas are concerned, the Administration has done a specific survey on them regarding vaccine—preventable diseases to check the normality of immune related cells and their ability to induce immune response against known antigens. Now the immunization of the Jarawa children has been started. So far as the health and nutritional status is concerned, it is likely to be completed soon. But it is a well known fact that the overall health and fitness of the Jarawas is good and satisfactory.

The fitness and health status of above two tribes, viz. the Jarawa and the Shompen raise a big question mark on the assimilation and main streaming of the Great Andamanese and the Onges. Both are suffering from so many civilized and modern diseases. While the Jarawa and the Shompen, who are living in their natural habitat, performing their traditional hunting and gathering, taking their own style of food are more healthy and fit. So there is a big question that what should be the policy of Administration about their mainstreaming and assimilation?

As far as the Sentinelese is concerned, they are living in total isolation, so no data are available regarding their health but they appear to be hail and healthy by their physical appearance.

Developmental Challenges

The PVTGs of Andaman are passing through a very crucial time of their history where they find themselves standing at cross roads of their future. Conventionally there have been two schools of thoughts among Anthropologists regarding their development and identity—which are as follows:

1. Keeping these tribals aloof from the outside world and to let them stay as they have been living for thousands of years.

As far as this thought is concerned, it may be looking very fascinating but in reality it is almost impossible in the present world where the so called civilized societies have penetrated in to all corners of the Globe. In the Andaman and Nicobar Islands, non-tribals are living all around tribal reserve areas of various tribes and interaction between them is inevitable in spite of existence of stringent regulations like Protection of Aboriginal Tribe Regulation, 1956. The PVTGs like the Jarawas are coming in constant touch with outside people and naturally they are influenced and fascinated towards the way of life of outside world which is materially and technologically more developed but this is not their informed choice and it is our responsibility to help them in facing these influences.

2. Second school of thought advocates for their complete mainstreaming so that they can also avail the fruits of modern development.

This thought may be looking much convincing but the past experiences of mainstreaming of PVTGs in the Islands and other parts of the globe have put a big question mark on this. As mentioned above in the Andaman and Nicobar Islands, efforts were made to mainstream two Primitive Tribes, namely the Great Andamanese and the Onges. They were settled in settlements outside their natural forest world and provided basic necessities and amenities like food, water, power, education and health etc. The overall results of these experiments have been very disappointing as far as the quality of life is concerned. They have become totally dependent on the Government and lost their self-esteem and pride. They have left their traditional way of life, and are unable to adopt our way of life hence they are sitting idle and their physical and mental health is deteriorating. Actually it is very difficult for any community to adopt to such sudden changes, and we must keep in our mind that our mainstream society has also taken thousands of years in this evolution process from hunting gathering to agriculture to non-agriculture, and how can we expect that we are able to bring them into mainstream in a generation or two.

The feasible solution could be their empowerment rather than their mainstreaming by focusing on following points:

1. To not to disturb their way of life and habitat by protecting and preserving their forest, land and culture from outside forces.
2. To support them preserving their culture and identity by instilling a sense of pride for their culture among them.
3. To empower them by providing them a non-conventional informal education which should be connected to their geography and society.
4. To provide them basic health care facilities with minimum intervention and by including their own medical and health practices.
5. To completely avoid giving them doles, e.g. a Kangeppo project has been initiated among the Jarawa tribe where clothes are being given to them in exchange of their artifacts.
6. To gradually engage them in the activities of plantation and Animal husbendry so that they could be prepared for future changes.
7. Last but not the least giving them choice and seeking their willingness through more and more informed interactions so that they could participate in formulation and implementation of their welfare policies.

BIBLIOGRAPHY

"Background Notes on Scheduled tribes of Andaman and Nicobar Islands-2013", DTW, A & N Administration, A & N Islands, p. 4.

"Background Notes on Scheduled Tribes of Andaman and Nicobar Islands-2013", DTW, A & N Administration, Port Blair, A & N Islands, pp. 12-13.

"Basic Information on Onge Settlement of Dugong Creek—November 2011", Report on Onges Settlement, DTW, A & N Administration, p. 4.

"Presentation to the Honourable Committee on Estimates of Lok Sabha", 2013, D.T.W., A & N Administration, Port Blair, A & N Islands, p. 2.

"Presentation to the Honourable Committee on Estimates of Lok Sabha", 2013, DTW, A & N Administration, Port Blair, A & N Islands, p. 8.

A Report on "Status of Health of Great Andamanese of Strait Island-2014-2015", A Survey conducted by District Health Society—South Andaman in collaboration with the experts from the Regional Medical Research Centre (ICMR), Port Blair, the Directorate of Health Services, and Andaman and Nicobar Adim Janjati Vikas Samiti (AAJVS) of the Department of Tribal Welfare, A & N, p. 7.

A Report on "Status of Health of Onges of Little Andaman-December 2013", pp. 3-5.

Records available with AAJVS (Andaman Adim Janjati Vikas Samiti).

Census of India 2011, *District Census Handbook, Andaman and Nicobar Islands*, pp. 2, 5 & 9.

Imperial Gazetteer, A & N Islands, Calcutta, 1901, p. 25.

Local Gazetteer, A & N Islands, pp. 114-115.

Policy Notified by Ministry of Home Affairs (MHA), Government of India, 2004.

Portman, M.V. 1899, *A History of our Relations with the Andamanese*, Vol. 1, Calcutta, 1899, p. 278.

R.C. Majumdar, 1974. *Penal Settlement in Andaman,* New Delhi: Ministry of Information.

Ratan Chandra Kar, 2015, *The Jarwas of the Andamans*, Anjali Kar, Ghol Ghar, Port Blair, p. 27.

Report on "Inputs for Study Group on the Issue of Social Reforms and Social Indicators, Integrating Tribal Areas with Other Parts of Andaman and Nicobar Islands", Directorate Welfare Department (D.T.W), A & N Administration, Port Blair, pp. 2-5.

Report on "Inputs for Study Group on the Issue of Social Reforms and Social Indicators, Integrating Tribal Areas with Other Parts of A & N Islands", DTW, A & N Administration, Port Blair, p. 3.

The Andaman and Nicobar Gazette, Extraordinary, No. 4, Port Blair, June 30, 1956.

Index